THE ART AND THOUGHT
OF THE *BEOWULF* POET

THE ART AND THOUGHT OF THE *BEOWULF* POET

LEONARD NEIDORF

CORNELL UNIVERSITY PRESS
Ithaca and London

First published 2022 by Cornell University Press

Library of Congress Cataloging-in-Publication Data

Names: Neidorf, Leonard, author.
Title: The art and thought of the Beowulf poet / Leonard Neidorf.
Description: Ithaca [New York] : Cornell University Press, 2022. | Includes bibliographical references and index.
Identifiers: LCCN 2022011094 (print) | LCCN 2022011095 (ebook) | ISBN 9781501766909 (hardcover) | ISBN 9781501766923 (pdf) | ISBN 9781501766916 (epub)
Subjects: LCSH: Beowulf. | Epic poetry, English (Old)—Themes, motives. | Poetry, Medieval—Themes, motives.
Classification: LCC PR1585 .N45 2022 (print) | LCC PR1585 (ebook) | DDC 829/.3—dc23/eng/20220805
LC record available at https://lccn.loc.gov/2022011094
LC ebook record available at https://lccn.loc.gov/2022011095

Contents

PREFACE

The present book attempts to answer one large question: Why is *Beowulf* the unique poem that it is? Though connected to a mountain of heroic and folkloric analogues, *Beowulf* is formally and ethically distinct from all of them. I argue that the poem's peculiarity results from one author's distinct and coherent vision, expressed in the combination and alteration of various source materials. The *Beowulf* poet, having inherited an amoral heroic tradition that focused on acts of kin-slaying and oath-breaking committed under compulsion, sought to lend his creation greater moral clarity than he found in his sources without violating their aesthetic norms or altering the facts, as he understood them, of legendary history. To achieve this, the poet concentrated his narrative not on ill-fated conflicts between kinsmen but on a benevolent hero's struggle against malevolent monsters. He consigned the transgressive heroes of antecedent tradition to his poem's background, while populating its foreground with an unconventional set of courteous monotheists, who could be admired and emulated without reservation. I develop this argument over the course of three chapters, each of which presents a reading of *Beowulf* through a particular lens. The first chapter examines how the poet's refusal to valorize characters known to have killed kinsmen or broken oaths shaped the composition of *Beowulf.* The second chapter argues that the poet modified the heroic and folkloric traditions he inherited by making ideals of courtesy and courtliness central to the matter of his epic poem. The third chapter explores how the poet uses monotheism and monstrosity to endow *Beowulf* with a moral framework absent from its analogues. The introduction contextualizes the three central chapters, while the conclusion synthesizes their findings and answers potential objections.

The three central chapters of this book take the form of long and continuous discourses. As the author of numerous papers on *Beowulf* and related poems, I wanted the writing in this book to differ in form and substance from the rest of my corpus. I viewed each chapter as an opportunity to develop an argument that could not adequately be developed over the course of a single journal article. Criticism is engaged with selectively rather than exhaustively in these chapters, which concentrate less on points of disagreement than my other writings. The book consequently resembles older monographs on *Beowulf*, such as Dorothy Whitelock's *The Audience of Beowulf* or Kenneth Sisam's *The Structure of Beowulf*, in certain respects. The writing of this book was nevertheless animated by the purpose that has animated all of my writing: it aims fundamentally to shed light on problems in the study of *Beowulf* and help modern readers understand this difficult and enigmatic medieval work. It is not animated by a desire to advance any academic trend of the present moment. There are books about *Beowulf* written a century ago that remain inspiring and illuminating to readers today. My ambition has been to produce a book that will remain useful whenever it happens to be read by a person with an earnest desire to understand *Beowulf*. Clarity has been my highest priority. I therefore use no abbreviations and no jargon, and I avoid erecting any artificial barriers that might prevent an educated member of the general public from comprehending the claims of my book.[1]

Clarity, moreover, is the reason why I refer to the *Beowulf* poet in my title and throughout my text. Though some might regard this as a provocative or retrograde gesture, I do not consider it a particularly innovative or distinctive feature of my book. As scholars such as John Farrell have shown, nearly all published criticism is concerned with authorial intention even when it professes to have no interest in the matter.[2] Linguists now consider it more or less impossible to interpret any

---

1. The text of *Beowulf* will be cited throughout by line number from R. D. Fulk, Robert E. Bjork, and John D. Niles, eds., *Klaeber's Beowulf and The Fight at Finnsburg*, 4th ed. (Toronto: University of Toronto Press, 2008). Translations of block quotations from *Beowulf* are provided throughout from R. D. Fulk, ed. and trans., *The Beowulf Manuscript: Complete Texts and The Fight at Finnsburg* (Cambridge, MA: Harvard University Press, 2010), unless otherwise noted. Discussions of individual words and phrases will necessarily involve occasional departures from Fulk's translation.

2. John Farrell, *The Varieties of Authorial Intention: Literary Theory beyond the Intentional Fallacy* (Cham, Switzerland: Palgrave Macmillan, 2017), 1–17. See also E. D. Hirsch Jr., *Validity in Interpretation* (New Haven, CT: Yale University Press, 1967); John R. Searle, "Reiterating the Differences: A Reply to Derrida," *Glyph* 1 (1977): 198–208; P. D. Juhl, *Interpretation: An Essay in the Philosophy of Literary Criticism* (Princeton, NJ: Princeton University Press, 1980); Steven Knapp and Walter Benn Michaels, "Against Theory," *Critical Inquiry* 8, no. 4 (1982): 723–42; John R. Searle, "Literary Theory and Its Discontents," *New Literary History* 25, no. 3 (1994): 637–67; Duncan Salkeld, "Shakespeare and 'the I-word,'" *Style* 44, no. 3 (2010): 328–41.

piece of language without reference to the intentions of the individual who uttered it.[3] Accordingly, I offer no extended defense of my explicit intentionalism and see no need for any such defense in view of the implicit intentionalism of nearly everything that has been published about *Beowulf*. While much of this writing abstains from mentioning an author and uses circumlocutory language to avoid the appearance of intentionalism, logical consideration of the claims involved tends to reveal that the critic is ultimately concerned with an author's intended meaning rather than anything else. When critics debate about the meaning of *lofgeornost*, the final word of the poem, they are not debating about what this word means to them or what this word could mean in the abstract—they are debating about what one human being intended the word to mean, the same human being who created much, if not all, of the surrounding textual matrix.[4] In this case and most others, the interpretation of *Beowulf* is "allocratic" (concerned with another person's meaning) rather than "autocratic" (concerned with one's own

3. See Dan Sperber and Deirdre Wilson, *Relevance: Communication and Cognition*, 2nd ed. (Oxford: Blackwell, 1995); Seana Coulson, *Semantic Leaps: Frame-Shifting and Conceptual Blending in Meaning Construction* (Cambridge: Cambridge University Press, 2001); Robyn Carston, *Thoughts and Utterances: The Pragmatics of Explicit Communication* (Malden, MA: Blackwell, 2002); Donald Davidson, *Truth, Language, and History* (Oxford: Oxford University Press, 2005), 89–108; Deirdre Wilson and Dan Sperber, *Meaning and Relevance* (Cambridge: Cambridge University Press, 2012).

4. For contributions to the debate over *lofgeornost*, see E. G. Stanley, "*Hæþenra Hyht* in Beowulf," in *Studies in Old English Literature in Honor of Arthur G. Brodeur*, ed. Stanley B. Greenfield (Eugene: University of Oregon Books, 1963), 136–51, at 148; Margaret E. Goldsmith, *The Mode and Meaning of Beowulf* (London: Athlone Press, 1970), 224–28; M. P. Richards, "A Reexamination of *Beowulf* ll. 3180–3182," *English Language Notes* 10 (1973): 163–67; T. A. Shippey, *Beowulf* (London: Edward Arnold, 1978), 19; Roberta Frank, "Skaldic Verse and the Date of *Beowulf*," in *The Dating of Beowulf*, ed. Colin Chase (Toronto: University of Toronto Press, 1981), 123–40, at 135; Fred C. Robinson, *Beowulf and the Appositive Style* (Knoxville: University of Tennessee Press, 1985), 81–82; Dennis Cronan, "'*Lofgeorn*': Generosity and Praise," *Neuphilologische Mitteilungen* 92, no. 2 (1991): 187–94; George Clark, "*Beowulf*: The Last Word," in *Old English and New: Studies in Language and Linguistics in Honor of Frederic G. Cassidy*, ed. Joan H. Hall, Nick Doane, and Dick Ringler (New York: Garland, 1992), 15–30; Andy Orchard, *A Critical Companion to Beowulf* (Cambridge: D. S. Brewer, 2003), 54–55; Gale R. Owen-Crocker, *The Four Funerals in Beowulf and the Structure of the Poem* (Manchester: Manchester University Press, 2000), 104–5; Janet Bately, "Bravery and the Vocabulary of Bravery in *Beowulf* and the *Battle of Maldon*," in *Unlocking the Wordhord: Anglo-Saxon Studies in Memory of Edward B. Irving, Jr.*, ed. Mark C. Amodio and Katherine O'Brien O'Keeffe (Toronto: University of Toronto Press, 2003), 274–301, at 280–81. The debate over *lofgeornost* is sometimes framed as if it were about the meaning of a word rather than the intentions of a poet, but since the meaning of *lofgeorn* in *Beowulf* appears to differ from the meaning it possesses in all other attestations, the debate is clearly not about what the word usually means in Old English (there is no disagreement about the word's usual meaning). The debate is about what *lofgeorn* means in *Beowulf*, that is to say, it is about what the creator of *Beowulf* intended the word to mean.

meaning) in orientation.[5] While it is possible in shorter papers to use passive constructions to conceal one's interest in the human being behind *Beowulf*, it would be exceedingly difficult to write a readable book about this person's art and thought without ever referring explicitly to him.[6] Additionally, I believe that certain insights into the poem can be obtained only when it is consciously viewed as the result of one author's engagement with the sources and traditions he inherited.

The possibility that multiple authors contributed to the composition of *Beowulf* might appear to complicate matters, but if it were credited, it would not fundamentally alter the nature of interpretive enterprise: composite authorship merely forces an interpreter to determine what multiple authors, rather than a single author, intended a unit of language to mean. Nevertheless, the possibility that *Beowulf* is a product of multiple authorship appears increasingly improbable in view of the growing evidence for the poem's unitary authorship. Numerous studies have now shown that there are compelling metrical, lexical, and syntactical reasons to believe that *Beowulf* was composed by a single author. There are subtle linguistic regularities that pervade the text of *Beowulf* and distinguish it from all other extant Old English texts; likewise, there are archaic linguistic features found throughout the text of *Beowulf* that are either absent from or infrequent in the rest of the Old English corpus.[7] In my previous monograph, I put together

---

5. On the distinction between allocratic and autocratic interpretation, see E. D. Hirsch Jr., "The Politics of Theories of Interpretation," *Critical Inquiry* 9, no. 1 (1982): 235–47.

6. Considerations of readability likewise prompt the use throughout of masculine singular pronouns in reference to the *Beowulf* poet. Convention and probability support this usage, though it should be acknowledged that the gender of every anonymous Old English poet is unknown.

7. See Klaus R. Grinda, "Pigeonholing Old English Poetry: Some Criteria of Metrical Style," *Anglia* 102, nos. 3–4 (1984): 305–22; Janet Bately, "Linguistic Evidence as a Guide to the Authorship of Old English Verse: A Reappraisal, with Special Reference to *Beowulf*," in *Learning and Literature in Anglo-Saxon England: Studies Presented to Peter Clemoes on the Occasion of His Sixty-Fifth Birthday*, ed. Michael Lapidge and Helmut Gneuss (Cambridge: Cambridge University Press, 1985), 409–31; T. A. Shippey, "Old English Poetry: The Prospects for Literary History," in *Proceedings of the Second International Conference of SELIM (Spanish Society for English Medieval Language and Literature)*, ed. A. León Sendra (Córdoba: SELIM, 1993), 164–79; Daniel Donoghue, "On the Non-Integrity of *Beowulf*," *SELIM* 1 (1991): 29–44; John D. Sundquist, "Relative Clause Variation and the Unity of *Beowulf*," *Journal of Germanic Linguistics* 14, no. 3 (2002): 243–69; R. D. Fulk, "On Argumentation in Old English Philology, with Particular Reference to the Editing and Dating of *Beowulf*," *Anglo-Saxon England* 32 (2003): 1–26, at 16–24; R. D. Fulk, "Archaisms and Neologisms in the Language of *Beowulf*," in *Studies in the History of the English Language III: Managing Chaos; Strategies for Identifying Change in English*, ed. Christopher M. Cain and Geoffrey Russom (Berlin: Mouton de Gruyter, 2007), 267–87; R. D. Fulk, "Old English Þa 'Now That' and the Integrity of *Beowulf*," *English Studies* 88, no. 6 (2007): 623–31;

an extensive case for the claim that the text of *Beowulf* transmitted in its sole extant manuscript (from ca. 1000) is essentially the same text that a single author committed to parchment around the year 700.[8] Scribal errors and alterations naturally crept into the text during the course of its transmission, but changes to the text were largely minor and superficial: the text retained its structural homogeneity and linguistic coherence. Computer-assisted n-gram analysis of the text of *Beowulf* subsequently corroborated my claim and furnished additional evidence consistent with the evidence for unitary authorship accumulated in traditional philological scholarship.[9] At this point, theoretical discussions unmoored from the text might continue to cast doubt on the singular *Beowulf* poet, but empirical analysis of the text itself appears unlikely to do so. The arguments of the present book, which show that there is a single mind at work in the reshaping of inherited material, complement the linguistic evidence for unitary authorship and aim to restore some flesh and spirit to our anonymous author's bones.

Categorizing this book within one of the major schools of thought in *Beowulf* criticism might prove difficult. On the one hand, my view of the *Beowulf* poet as a somewhat censorious author, who was concerned about the moral opacity of his source materials, might appear to align my book with those written by critics who emphasize the spiritual dimension of *Beowulf* and read the poem predominantly in the context of patristic and hagiographical Latin sources. On the other hand, the frequent comparisons in my book between *Beowulf* and other witnesses to early Germanic legend might appear to align it with those written by critics who focus on the secular dimension of *Beowulf* and read it predominantly in the context of medieval Scandinavian and German sources. Readers familiar with my prior work on *Widsith, Hlǫðskviða,* the

Aaron Ecay and Susan Pintzuk, "The Syntax of Old English Poetry and the Dating of *Beowulf,*" in *Old English Philology: Studies in Honour of R. D. Fulk,* ed. Leonard Neidorf, Rafael J. Pascual, and Tom Shippey (Cambridge: D. S. Brewer, 2016), 144–71.

8. Leonard Neidorf, *The Transmission of Beowulf: Language, Culture, and Scribal Behavior* (Ithaca, NY: Cornell University Press, 2017).

9. Leonard Neidorf et al., "Large-Scale Quantitative Profiling of the Old English Verse Tradition," *Nature Human Behaviour* 3, no. 6 (2019): 560–67. Much to my surprise, this paper went on to be covered in the *Guardian,* the *Times* of London, the *Boston Globe,* and other major news outlets. Though such attention is gratifying, it creates an impression that the evidence presented in this paper (and others like it) is dramatically more decisive than the evidence presented in traditional philological scholarship. In my view, the multifaceted arguments propounded in *Transmission of Beowulf* establish an equally strong, if not stronger, probability of unitary authorship.

Nibelungenlied, and the *Finnsburg* fragment, among other poems, might take it for granted that I belong to the Germanicist school of thought and will consequently underemphasize the religious learning and moral seriousness of the *Beowulf* poet. In actuality, it was my immersion in the Germanic sources that convinced me of the poet's earnest religiosity and led me to believe that this poet was one of the most morally serious authors to rehandle material from Germanic legend in the entire medieval period. Only when one recognizes the profound amorality of the other witnesses to migration-period legend, with their concentration on kin-slaying and oath-breaking heroes, can one appreciate how morally distinct *Beowulf* is from other works rooted in the same tradition. The *Beowulf* poet is not the homilist keen to condemn heroism that some critics have made him out to be, but he was deeply concerned about the moral ambiguity of the tradition he inherited, and this concern is registered throughout *Beowulf* in an array of salient and subtle manifestations.

Many of the ideas put forward in this book were developed during a series of courses on *Beowulf* that I taught at Nanjing University. In these courses, I spent the whole semester working through the entire text of *Beowulf*, and only *Beowulf*, with my students. Having occasion to comment on every passage rather than merely the purple ones caused me to realize that courtliness mattered much more to the *Beowulf* poet than it has mattered to the poem's critics. The experience also brought home to me just how different *Beowulf* is from everything with which it might be compared. For the opportunity to teach these courses on *Beowulf*, I express my deepest thanks to He Ning, the dean of the School of Foreign Studies at Nanjing University, who has supported the development of Old English studies in Nanjing and granted me all the time and resources required to write this book. I also thank the four graduate students I supervise at Nanjing University—Wei Zixuan, Xu Na, Zhang Kexin, and Zhu Chenyun—for making my work more meaningful and breathing new life into the study of Old English poetry for me. I especially thank Zhu Chenyun for assisting me with the bibliographical preparation of this manuscript and offering many helpful suggestions for revision. I also thank my collaborator Rafael J. Pascual and the anonymous referees for reading the manuscript thoroughly and improving it in various ways. I thank Paul Cavill, Susan Deskis, Robert D. Fulk, Joseph Harris, John Hines, Carole Hough, Francis Leneghan, Marijane Osborn, Geoffrey Russom, and Tom Shippey for invaluable correspondence. I thank Sam Newton for meeting often with me and my students on Zoom to read Old English and Old Norse poems together. These meetings were a vital source of ideas and inspiration, which alleviated the solitude of writing and provided me with a vital opportunity to test out my arguments. Without the support of my friends, colleagues, and students, this book would not have been written.

THE ART AND THOUGHT
OF THE *BEOWULF* POET

Introduction

The canonicity of *Beowulf* has obscured its peculiarity. As the poem's position in academic and popular culture has become more entrenched, readers throughout the twentieth century have become less inclined to regard *Beowulf* as an entity fundamentally unlike anything with which it might be compared.[1] Few today concern themselves with the question of why the poem is so strange, if they even consider it strange at all. The *Beowulf* poet is not thought of as an artist who radically altered the focal points of the material he inherited, yet that is what he appears to be when his creation is compared with all other extant works rooted in migration-period legend. None of these works is focused on a hero's struggles against three monstrous adversaries. Instead, what we consistently find are stories of conflicting ethical imperatives, where protagonists are driven by circumstances to kill kinsmen, break oaths, and commit other atrocities. The *Beowulf*

---

1. For the history of the reception of *Beowulf* first among antiquarians and then among professional scholars, see T. A. Shippey and Andreas Haarder, eds., *Beowulf: The Critical Heritage* (London: Routledge, 1998). For discussion of the poem's growing influence outside of the academy, see Kathleen Forni, *Beowulf's Popular Afterlife in Literature, Comic Books, and Film* (New York: Routledge, 2018); David Clark, ed., *Beowulf in Contemporary Culture* (Newcastle upon Tyne: Cambridge Scholars, 2020); Nickolas Haydock and E. L. Risden, *Beowulf on Film: Adaptations and Variations* (Jefferson, NC: McFarland, 2013).

poet knew these stories—they were attached to Ingeld, Hengest, Sige-mund, Eormenric, and nearly every major migration-period hero—yet he chose not to make one of them the central narrative of his epic. Such stories and their heroes are relegated to the poem's background, while its foreground is focused on a gentle hero who fights against monsters, kills no kinsmen, breaks no oaths, believes in God, and behaves courte-ously. Compared with the heroes of the *Nibelungenlied* or *Vǫlsunga saga*, Beowulf appears an odd hero in a very odd poem. Reassessing the rela-tionship between *Beowulf* and the tradition that likely existed prior to its composition, I attempt in this book to figure out why the poem is the way it is.

The contemporaneous poem *Widsith*, the most informative witness to the circulation of Germanic legend in early medieval England, provides reason to believe that *Beowulf* seemed odd in its own time.[2] The cata-logues preserved in *Widsith* include the names of dozens of kings and heroes who flourished (or were believed to have flourished) during the migration period, a semi-historical heroic age that extended from the end of the fourth century, when the Gothic king Eormenric died (ca. 375), to the end of the sixth century, when the Langobardic king Ælf-wine died (ca. 572). The legends that were attached to the names listed in *Widsith* cannot always be found in external sources, but when they are preserved, it is fair to say that they do not resemble the legend attached to Beowulf, whose name is not present. As far as we can tell from extant sources, no person mentioned in *Widsith* was known in legendary tra-dition for exterminating monsters, exemplifying courtesy, abstaining from transgression, and dying well in old age. It is possible, of course, that legends of this sort were attached to other migration-period he-roes in Old English sources that have not been preserved. Nevertheless, the impression given by *Widsith*, and corroborated by the digressions in *Beowulf*, is that the legends in circulation prior to the composition of *Beowulf* were predominantly tragic and amoral in character, focused

---

2. For discussion of the dating of *Widsith*, see R. W. Chambers, ed., *Widsith: A Study in Old English Heroic Legend* (Cambridge: Cambridge University Press, 1912), 147–52; Kemp Malone, ed., *Widsith*, 2nd ed. (Copenhagen: Rosenkilde & Bagger, 1962), 116–17; Leonard Neidorf, "The Dating of *Widsið* and the Study of Germanic Antiquity," *Neophilologus* 97, no. 1 (2013): 165–83; Rafael J. Pascual, "Old English Metrical History and the Composition of *Widsið*," *Neophilologus* 100, no. 2 (2016): 289–302. Most of the poem's scholars have considered *Widsith* a product of the seventh or eighth century, contemporary with if not anterior to the composi-tion of *Beowulf*. On the value of *Widsith* as a witness to the circulation of Germanic legend in England, see R. M. Wilson, *The Lost Literature of Medieval England* (London: Methuen, 1952), 1–26, as well as the extensive commentary in the editions of Chambers and Malone.

on conflicting ethical imperatives and spectacular deaths.[3] The *Widsith* poet accords considerable space to the heroes of the battle of Goths and Huns (ll. 109–130): he knows the dramatis personae of the Old Norse *Hlǫðskviða*, discussed below, which tells of a conflict between Gothic brothers that results in reluctant transgressions and innumerable deaths. Like the *Beowulf* poet, the *Widsith* poet knows of the tales of kin-slaying and oath-breaking associated with names such as Finn, Hnæf, Ingeld, and Hrothulf (ll. 27–29, 45–49). The *Widsith* poet also knows of the great kings killed in legend by their spouses or in-laws, such as Ætla, Guðere, Ælfwine, and Eormenric (ll. 5b–9a, 18, 65–67, 70–74, 88–92). What the *Widsith* poet appears not to have known is a migration-period hero comparable to Beowulf.

Critics active a century ago considered the peculiarity of *Beowulf* relative to antecedent legendary tradition one of the central problems emanating from the poem. For some critics, it was a defect to be lamented, while for others, it was a mystery requiring explanation. The cohort of major critics active during the first decades of the twentieth century turned away from the disintegrating practices characteristic of nineteenth-century scholarship. While the prevailing tendency among the previous generation was to explain the ostensible incongruities of *Beowulf* as signs of composite authorship—the by-products of a monkish redactor's inartful combination of older pagan lays with newer Christian texts—the emerging tendency at the beginning of the twentieth century was to read *Beowulf* as a single poem, possibly composed by a single author, that happens to contain certain defective or perplexing features.[4] W. P. Ker, writing at the very end of the nineteenth

---

3. The term "amoral" is used here and throughout in reference to the absence of a comforting or edifying "moral of the story" in migration-period legend. It does not imply that the characters depicted within this tradition have no sense of right and wrong. Hildebrand and Signý know that it is wrong to kill their children, and Hengest knows it is wrong to break his oath and kill his lord, yet circumstances compel them to do what they consider abhorrent. What is absent is not a concern with right and wrong but a concern with good and evil. Hildebrand, Signý, and Hengest (among many others) commit the most profound transgressions conceivable, but they are not conceived of as evil or malevolent characters. Their legends focus not on conflicts between good and evil but on conflicting imperatives and compelled transgressions.

4. For a lucid account of this paradigm shift, see T. A. Shippey, "Structure and Unity," in *A Beowulf Handbook*, ed. Robert E. Bjork and John D. Niles (Lincoln: University of Nebraska Press, 1997), 149–74. For examples of the disintegrating approach, see Karl Müllenhoff, "Die innere Geschichte des *Beovulfs*," *Zeitschrift für deutsches Altertum* 14 (1869): 193–244; Bernhard ten Brink, *Beowulf: Untersuchungen* (Strassburg: K. J. Trübner, 1888); F. A. Blackburn, "The Christian Coloring in the *Beowulf*," *PMLA* 12, no. 2 (1897): 205–25.

century, acknowledges the "theories of agglutination and adulteration" that had developed around *Beowulf* but proposes that it may still be worthwhile to evaluate the poem as a unitary work, since it "continues to possess at least an apparent and external unity." As it stands, the poem constitutes "a single book, considered as such by its transcribers, and making a claim to be so considered."[5] Ker proceeds from here to develop a reading of *Beowulf* as a work that is magnificent in its tone and style but defective in its plot and structure. Seven years later, Ker summarized his position in words that would reverberate in much subsequent criticism:

> The great beauty, the real value, of *Beowulf* is in its dignity of style. In construction it is curiously weak, in a sense preposterous; for while the main story is simplicity itself, the merest commonplace of heroic legend, all about it, in the historic allusions, there are revelations of a whole world of tragedy, plots different in import from that of *Beowulf*, more like the tragic themes of Iceland. Yet with this radical defect, a disproportion that puts the irrelevances in the centre and the serious things on the outer edges, the poem of *Beowulf* is undeniably weighty. The thing itself is cheap; the moral and the spirit of it can only be matched among the noblest authors.[6]

Embedded in Ker's assessment is an argument about the relationship between *Beowulf* and antecedent legendary tradition. In his view, *Beowulf* has retained the dignity and grandeur of earlier heroic tradition but implausibly attached this elevated style to a plot derived from folkloric tradition. The genuinely dignified and grand plots of heroic legend remain present in *Beowulf*, but they are confined to the digressions ("the outer edges"), while the monster fights that might have been digressions in a well-constructed epic (along the lines of the cyclops episode in the *Odyssey*) are here presented as the central narrative. For Ker, writing in an evaluative mode, the prominence accorded monster fights rather than conflicting loyalties in *Beowulf* is both a departure from antecedent tradition and a serious aesthetic defect.

R. W. Chambers concurred with Ker's assessment. In his 1912 edition of *Widsith*, Chambers attempts to reconstruct the legends potentially

---

5. W. P. Ker, *Epic and Romance: Essays on Medieval Literature* (London: Macmillan, 1897), 182, 183.

6. W. P. Ker, *The Dark Ages* (Edinburgh: William Blackwood & Sons, 1904), 253.

known to the *Widsith* poet. In the course of a discussion of the Ingeld legend, Chambers turns to the digression on Ingeld in *Beowulf* and expresses some dismay that the poet did not do more with this material: "Nothing could better show the disproportion of *Beowulf*, which 'puts the irrelevances in the centre and the serious things on the outer edges,' than this passing allusion to the story of Ingeld. For in this conflict between plighted troth and the duty of revenge we have a situation which the old heroic poets loved, and would not have sold for a wilderness of dragons."[7] Quoting Ker and regarding *Beowulf* as a structurally disproportionate work, Chambers shares the view that the poem's concentration on a plot that had nothing to do with conflicting loyalties is both an untraditional feature and an aesthetic defect.[8] A similar view was expressed by Ritchie Girvan in 1935 at the conclusion of his study of the folkloric elements in *Beowulf*. In defense of the theory that Beowulf was a historical (or pseudo-historical) Geatish nobleman to whom folktales had been attached, Girvan writes that an advantage of this theory is that it helps explain why the poet "chose just this [folkloric] subject, when to our modern judgment there were at hand so many greater, charged with the splendour and tragedy of humanity, and in all respects worthier of a genius as astonishing as it was rare in Anglo-Saxon England."[9] A paradoxical assessment of the *Beowulf* poet emerges from the criticism of Ker, Chambers, and Girvan: on the one hand, this poet is a towering genius who imbued his work with a dignified style and a noble spirit; on the other hand, he erred in his selection of subject matter and would have composed a better poem if he had chosen to focus on a traditional plot of heroic legend, such as we find in the tale of Ingeld, rather than on the monster fights of a benevolent hero.

The passages from Ker, Chambers, and Girvan quoted above have become infamous in *Beowulf* criticism on account of their inclusion in

---

7. Chambers, *Widsith*, 79–80.

8. In a separate essay on *Beowulf* first published in 1925, Chambers went on to write: "The inferiority of *Beowulf* is manifest first of all in the plot. The main story of *Beowulf* is a wild folk-tale. There are things equally wild in Homer: Odysseus blinds the Cyclops, and Achilles struggled with a river-god: but in Homer these things are kept in their right places and proportions. The folk-tale is a good servant but a bad master: it has been allowed in *Beowulf* to usurp the place of honour, and to drive into episodes and digressions the things which should be the main stuff of a well-conducted epic." See R. W. Chambers, "*Beowulf* and the 'Heroic Age' in England," in *Man's Unconquerable Mind: Studies of English Writers, from Bede to A. E. Housman and W. P. Ker* (London: Jonathan Cape, 1939), 64–65.

9. Ritchie Girvan, *Beowulf and the Seventh Century: Language and Content*, 2nd ed. (London: Methuen, 1971), 84.

J. R. R. Tolkien's seminal 1936 lecture to the British Academy on "*Beowulf*: The Monsters and the Critics." These three authors, addressed with reverence by Tolkien, were the principal critics taken to task for failing to appreciate the monsters. Tolkien wonders "if something has not gone wrong with 'our modern judgement'" insofar as it assumes that a heroic story "on a strictly human plane" must be superior to a story that involves the supernatural. He observes the contradiction present in criticism that simultaneously praises and disparages *Beowulf*: "Correct and sober taste may refuse to admit that there can be an interest for *us* . . . in ogres and dragons; we then perceive its puzzlement in face of the odd fact that it has derived great pleasure from a poem that is actually about these unfashionable creatures."[10] Tolkien queries the assumption that the epic of Ingeld desired by modern critics would be superior to *Beowulf*; he doubts that it would possess the same noble spirit and moral gravity. He contends, ultimately, that the untraditional character of the poem is the source of its aesthetic strength rather than a fundamental weakness: "Beowulf is not, then, the hero of an heroic lay, precisely. He has no enmeshed loyalties, nor hapless love. *He is a man, and that for him and many is sufficient tragedy*. It is not an irritating accident that the tone of the poem is so high and its theme so low. It is the theme in its deadly seriousness that begets the dignity of tone: *lif is læne: eal scæceð leoht and lif somod*."[11] The *Beowulf* poet, in Tolkien's view, is "a learned man writing of old times, who looking back on the heroism and sorrow feels in them something permanent and something symbolical." The poet knows that his heroes lived before the Christian revelation, and he finds poignancy in the defiant heroism and virtuous conduct of characters who were "heathen, noble, and hopeless." As a symbolic meditation on the transitory nature of life that is both fantastical and historical, a cosmic struggle between good and evil set in "the named lands of the North," *Beowulf* is manifestly not one of the traditional poems but is rather "a measure and interpretation of them all."[12]

Tolkien's rebuttal to Ker, Chambers, and Girvan was wildly successful. Redirecting the study of *Beowulf* and putting to rest the notion

---

10. J. R. R. Tolkien, "*Beowulf*: The Monsters and the Critics," *Proceedings of the British Academy* 22 (1936): 245–95, at 254, 256, 257.

11. J. R. R. Tolkien, "*Beowulf*: The Monsters and the Critics," 260. The Old English text can be translated as "life is transitory: everything dissipates, light and life together."

12. J. R. R. Tolkien, "*Beowulf*: The Monsters and the Critics," 269, 264, 259.

that the poem is an artistic failure, Tolkien's lecture has become "the single most influential article ever written on *Beowulf* in the poem's 200-year critical history."[13] There are good reasons for it to have been as influential as it has been. Read nearly a century later, Tolkien's lecture remains a brilliant and persuasive piece of writing, peppered with insightful assertions that could form the subject of book-length studies. My purpose in reviewing the debate between Tolkien and his predecessors is not to suggest that Tolkien was wrong—indeed, I consider the majority of his claims to remain valid—but to make the observation that this debate centered on the relationship between *Beowulf* and antecedent legendary tradition. What made *Beowulf* a disappointment to Ker, Chambers, and Girvan was that it did not focus on a legend comparable to those known to have been attached to the heroes catalogued in *Widsith*. What made *Beowulf* a masterpiece, in Tolkien's view, was precisely that it did not focus on one traditional legend but instead offered "a measure and interpretation of them all." Tolkien called for *Beowulf* criticism that is "directed to the understanding of the poem as a poem," and subsequent critics have enthusiastically followed his exhortation, construing it to mean that matter extraneous to the poem is unnecessary for a critical appreciation and potentially a pedantic distraction.[14] Few critics active in the past half century would think that a prerequisite for the study of *Beowulf* should be familiarity with the compendium of legends associated with the names in *Widsith*—legends that must often be reconstructed from fragments, allusions, and prose summaries. Yet it is difficult to see how a reader could meaningfully concur with Tolkien and regard *Beowulf* as "a measure and interpretation" of all that came before it if limited effort is made to understand the antecedent legendary tradition and perceive how the poem is in dialogue with it.

The present book explores the relationship between *Beowulf* and the legendary tradition that existed prior to its composition. This relationship has been probed in some profound and suggestive essays—most notably by Bertha S. Phillpotts prior to Tolkien and Thomas D. Hill after him (two essays to be discussed below)—but there exists no book-length study about how exactly *Beowulf* represents an author's reaction to the corpus of legends concerning the heroes of the migration period.

---

13. Michael D. C. Drout, "'*Beowulf*: The Monsters and the Critics' Seventy-Five Years Later," *Mythlore* 30, no. 1 (2011): 5–22, at 6.

14. J. R. R. Tolkien, "*Beowulf*: The Monsters and the Critics," 245.

A sense of what the poetry relating these legends might have been like is not easily obtained, but it can be acquired from the patient iden-tification of features that reoccur in dozens of disconnected sources preserved in multiple languages (Old English, Old Norse, Old and Mid-dle High German, Latin, etc.) in multiple countries (England, Iceland, Germany, France, Denmark, etc.) over the course of multiple centuries (from the sixth to the fifteenth).[15] While the systematic comparison of all of this material clearly falls beyond the scope of the present study, the following discussion aims to provide the reader with a deepened understanding of the tradition of migration-period legend that the *Be-owulf* poet inherited and radically altered.

If one extant poem needed to be used to introduce this tradi-tion and exemplify its features, I would argue that the Old Norse *Hlǫðskviða* makes the strongest claim to be that poem. Although it is preserved in late manuscripts of *Saga Heiðreks konungs ins vitra* (*The Saga of King Heidrek the Wise*), *Hlǫðskviða* has widely been considered "one of the oldest, if not the very oldest, pieces of poetry in the Norse language," and with good reason: it contains an array of place-names and tribal names relevant to the earliest dealings of the Goths that are not preserved in any other vernacular source from the Middle Ages.[16] The date of the poem's composition is unknown, but *Hlǫðskviða* is possibly the most thematically conservative, if not actually the most archaic, extant poem concerned with migration-period legend. The poem contains no sign of Christian influence in either its language or its sentiment, a trait it shares with other archaic Eddic poems such as *Atlakviða* and *Hamðismál*, yet *Hlǫðskviða* possesses two other advan-tages that facilitate comparison with *Beowulf* and encourage its use as a potential illustrator of antecedent legendary tradition: it is a sub-stantial narrative poem, preserved in twenty-nine strophes or strophic

---

15. For an overview of the relevant witnesses, see Theodore M. Andersson, *A Preface to the Nibelungenlied* (Stanford, CA: Stanford University Press, 1987), 3–16; Edward Haymes and Susann T. Samples, *Heroic Legends of the North: An Introduction to the Nibelung and Dietrich Cycles* (New York: Garland, 1996); Carolyne Larrington, "Eddic Poetry and Heroic Legend," in *A Handbook to Eddic Poetry: Myths and Legends of Early Scandinavia*, ed. Carolyne Larrington, Judy Quinn, and Brittany Schorn (Cambridge: Cambridge University Press, 2016), 147–72. See also Chambers, *Widsith*, 12–126.

16. Christopher Tolkien, "The Battle of the Goths and the Huns," *Saga-Book* 14 (1955–56): 141–63, at 141. For similar views on the poem's antiquity, see Andreas Heusler and William Ranisch, eds., *Eddica minora: Dichtungen eddischer Art aus den Fornaldarsögur und anderen Pro-sawerken* (Dortmund: W. Ruhfus, 1903), xiii–xiv; Nora K. Chadwick, ed. and trans., *Anglo-Saxon and Norse Poems* (Cambridge: Cambridge University Press, 1922), 142–44; Larrington, "Eddic Poetry and Heroic Legend," 155.

fragments embedded in a prose saga that supplies the legendary background and clarifies the sequence of events, and it concerns legendary heroes who were certainly known in early medieval England. The collocation of the names of four characters central to the narrative of *Hlǫðskviða* (Heiðrekr, Sifka, Hlǫðr, and Angantýr) in a single line of *Widsith* ("Heaþorīc ond Sifecan, Hlīþe ond Incgenþēow," l. 116) suggests that poems dealing with similar subject matter once existed in Old English.[17] Such poems might well have been known to the author of *Beowulf*, who happens to display knowledge of Gothic legend in his casual allusions to Eormenric, Hama, the Gepids, and possibly the Herulians.[18]

Hlǫðskviða depicts the aftermath of a dispute over inheritance between the two sons of the Gothic king Heiðrekr. Angantýr, the king's legitimate heir, succeeds to the Gothic throne, but his rule is challenged by the arrival from Hunland of his half brother, Hlǫðr, whom Heiðrekr conceived with Sifka, a daughter of the Hunnish king Humli, after she was taken captive and enslaved in an earlier war between Goths and Huns. Hlǫðr demands that Angantýr grant him rule over half of the Gothic kingdom and control of half of its wealth; Angantýr counters by offering him a third of the kingdom along with ample wealth in the form of slaves and treasures. Before Hlǫðr can respond to this offer, an old counselor named Gizurr, who had been the foster father of Heiðrekr, objects that such an offer is being made to "a bondmaid's child" (*þýjar barni*) and a "bastard" (*hornungr*).[19] Enraged by the insult, Hlǫðr returns to Hunland and tells Humli, his grandfather, what transpired. Humli, angry that his nobly born daughter should be called a bondmaid, provides Hlǫðr with an army consisting of all of the able-bodied men in the Hunnish kingdom. Hlǫðr leads this army into Gothic territory and kills his half sister, Hervǫr, in an initial skirmish. When word of Hervǫr's death reaches Angantýr, the king who initially wished to avoid conflict with his half brother is compelled to take action and

---

17. On the relationship between *Hlǫðskviða* and *Widsith*, see Kemp Malone, "*Widsith* and the *Hervararsaga*," PMLA 40, no. 4 (1925): 769–813; Christopher Tolkien, "Battle of the Goths and the Huns"; Chadwick, *Anglo-Saxon and Norse Poems*, 144–45.

18. For analysis of the relevant passages, see R. E. Kaske, "The Sigemund-Heremod and Hama-Hygelac Passages in *Beowulf*," PMLA 74, no. 5 (1959): 489–94; Michael D. C. Drout and Nelson Goering, "The Emendation *Eorle* (Heruli) in *Beowulf*, Line 6a: Setting the Poem in 'The Named Lands of the North,'" *Modern Philology* 117, no. 3 (2020): 285–300; Leonard Neidorf, "The Gepids in *Beowulf*," ANQ 34, no. 1 (2021): 3–6.

19. The text and translation of *Hlǫðskviða* are cited from Christopher Tolkien, ed. and trans., *The Saga of King Heidrek the Wise* (London: Thomas Nelson & Sons, 1960), 51.

lead a massive army of Goths into battle against the Huns. After eight days of combat, Angantýr kills Hlǫðr and the Goths massacre the Huns, with the result that rivers are clogged and valleys are filled with their corpses. The poem ends with Angantýr delivering a lament over the body of his dead brother.

Reading *Hlǫðskviða*, one is forced to wonder what moral significance, if any, was attached to the events the poem describes. Was Angantýr wrong to avenge his sister by killing his brother? Was Hlǫðr wrong to feel insulted and demand retribution? Was Gizurr wrong to defend tradition and object to the division of the kingdom? Would Hlǫðr have been a coward if he ignored Gizurr's insult and thereby obviated the need for a war in which thousands of people perished? Would it have been shameful for Angantýr to give a third of his father's kingdom to the grandson of Humli, who had been his father's enemy? The poem itself provides no straightforward answers to these questions. An answer is suggested, however, in Angantýr's lament, a crucial passage that sheds considerable light on the moral significance that this legend was understood to possess. Standing over his brother's corpse, Angantýr speaks sorrowful words:

> Bauð ek þér, bróðir,   basmir óskerðar,
> fé ok fjǫlð meiðma,   sem þik fremst tíddi;
> nú hefir þú hvárki   hildar at gjǫldum,
> ljósa bauga,   né land ekki.
> Bölvat es okkr, bróðir,   bani em ek þinn orðinn;
> þat mun æ uppi,   illr er dómr Norna.

(Treasures uncounted, kinsman, I offered you, wealth and cattle well to content you; but for war's reward you have won neither realm more spacious nor rings glittering. We are cursed, kinsman, your killer am I! It will never be forgotten; the Norns' doom is evil.)[20]

Angantýr's lament suggests that no character in the poem was to blame for what transpired. By railing against the cruelty of the Norns, goddesses believed to weave a person's destiny at the moment of his or her birth, Angantýr attributes the tragic outcome not to the willfulness of

---

20. Christopher Tolkien, *Saga of King Heidrek*, 58.

his brother but to an overwhelming and inexorable fate.[21] What generated the tragedy in *Hlǫðskviða* was not the evil behavior of a malevolent individual but the ill-fated collision of ethical imperatives. The poem reflects a fundamentally amoral perspective: no character in it is decidedly good or bad; each person acts in a justifiable manner. Caught between Hlǫðr's sense of personal honor and Gizurr's devotion to the memory of Heiðrekr, Angantýr is compelled to abandon his desire for peace and become the slayer of his kinsman. This story is not a morality tale but an illustration of the potency of heroic ideals and the sublimity of sacrificing everything in service of them. There is beauty and pathos in the figure of Hlǫðr, the young and promising nobleman, who could have lived out a pleasurable aristocratic life but chose to sacrifice it in response to an insult.

Lest it be thought that *Hlǫðskviða* is atypical, we should note that the conventional and antique character of its legend, if not of the poem itself, is established by the distinct resemblance it bears to other legends of migration-period heroes that were certainly known to the *Beowulf* poet. For example, the legend of Ingeld also focuses on a situation wherein a peaceful but arguably shameful arrangement is shattered through the intervention of an old man, who speaks up for the honor of the deceased.[22] Ingeld, son of Froda, is betrothed to a daughter of a man responsible for the death of his father in order to settle a multigenerational feud. In *Beowulf*, the peace is undermined by an anonymous "old ash-fighter who remembers all" ("eald æscwiga sē ðe eall geman," l. 2042), a veteran of the earlier wars, who incites a young man to break the peace by pointing out that his father's sword is borne by a member of the foreign queen's retinue. In the version of the story told in Saxo Grammaticus's *Gesta Danorum*, the role of the "old ash-fighter" is played by the preternaturally old Starkaðr, who is explicitly said to

---

21. On the Norns, see Paul C. Bauschatz, *The Well and the Tree: World and Time in Early Germanic Culture* (Amherst: University of Massachusetts Press, 1982), 1–30; John Lindow, *Handbook of Norse Mythology* (Oxford: ABC-CLIO, 2001), 243–46. On the concept of fate in early Germanic literature, there is a vast critical corpus. For examples of some distinct perspectives that have developed, see Prisca S. Augustyn, "The Semiotics of *Fate, Death*, and the *Soul* in Germanic Culture: The Christianization of Old Saxon" (PhD diss., University of California, Berkeley, 2000); Hans Naumann, *Germanischer Schicksalsglaube* (Jena: Eugen Diederichs, 1934); Walter Gehl, *Der Germanische Schicksalsglaube* (Berlin: Junker & Dünnhaupt, 1939); Gerd Wolfgang Weber, *Wyrd: Studien zum Schicksalsbegriff der altenglischen und altnordischen Literatur* (Bad Homburg: Gehlen, 1969).

22. For a reconstruction of the Ingeld legend and overview of the relevant witnesses, see Kemp Malone, "The Tale of Ingeld," in *Studies in Heroic Legend and Current Speech*, ed. Stefán Einarsson and Norman E. Eliason (Copenhagen: Rosenkilde & Bagger, 1959), 1–62.

have been a retainer of Froda and a foster father of Ingeld.[23] In both accounts, then, there is a figure comparable to Gizurr, the foster father of Heiðrekr, who will not allow the dead to be dishonored by their descendants. In the version of the legend known to the *Beowulf* poet, Ingeld is compelled by circumstances to break his oath to Freawaru and wage war against Hrothgar, his father-in-law. Ingeld will burn down Heorot, but he will lose his life in the battle, and the Heathobardic army will be massacred.[24] In the end, Ingeld resembles Angantýr, insofar as circumstances compel him to abandon his peaceful inclinations and break a sacred oath (oath-breaking being a moral transgression comparable in gravity to kin-slaying).[25] At the same time, Ingeld also resembles Hlǫðr, in that his renewed commitment to the heroic ideal of filial piety will prompt him both to throw away his promising young life and to wage a disastrous war that probably results in the subjugation of his people.

Beyond the resemblances between characters, the essential connection between the legends of Ingeld, Angantýr, and Hlǫðr is that each of these men is forced to choose between two hateful alternatives: to escape from a dishonorable situation, one is forced to do something dishonorable; to preserve life, one is forced to commit transgressions that are difficult to live with. In assessing the peculiarity of *Beowulf* relative to antecedent legendary tradition, it must be noted that this traditional plot was attached to women as well as men. In Paul the Deacon's *Historia Langobardorum* (ca. 790), there is a prose summary of a legend centered on Rosimund, a Gepid princess married to Alboin, king of the Langobards.[26] Alboin had killed Rosimund's father in earlier warfare between the Gepids and the Langobards, but the pair was successfully married until one evening when an inebriated Alboin offered Rosimund wine in a cup fashioned from her father's skull and exhorted her to

---

23. See Karsten Friis-Jensen, ed., *Saxo Grammaticus: Gesta Danorum: The History of the Danes*, trans. Peter Fisher, vol. 1 (Oxford: Clarendon Press, 2015), 414–46. The significant figure of Starkaðr will be discussed in later chapters.

24. This reconstruction reflects triangulation between *Beowulf* (ll. 81b–85) and *Widsith* (ll. 45–49). See Malone, "Tale of Ingeld," 25; Chambers, *Widsith*, 80–81.

25. See Gregory L. Laing, "Bound by Words: Oath-taking and Oath-breaking in Medieval Iceland and Anglo-Saxon England" (PhD diss., Western Michigan University, 2014); Anne Irene Riisoy, "Performing Oaths in Eddic Poetry: Viking Age Fact or Medieval Fiction?," *Journal of the North Atlantic* 8 (2015): 141–56.

26. See Ludwig Bethmann and Georg Waitz, eds., *Pauli Historia Langobardorum* (Hannover: Hahnsche Buchhandlung, 1878), 104–7. On the probable derivation of this prose account from a heroic poem, see Otto Gschwantler, "Die Heldensage von Alboin und Rosimund," in *Festgabe für Otto Höfler zum 75. Geburtstag*, ed. Helmut Birkhan (Vienna: W. Braunmüller, 1976), 214–54; Andersson, *Preface to the Nibelungenlied*, 7–8.

share a drink with her father. Incensed by this insult to the memory of her parent (rather like Hlǫðr), Rosimund brings about the murder of Alboin through an elaborate scheme that eventually results in her own death as well. A comparable figure to Rosimund is Signý in *Vǫlsunga saga*, who also arranges the murder of her husband, Siggeirr, in order to avenge her kinsmen.[27] Because Siggeirr had killed her father and all of her brothers except Sigmundr, Signý commits incest with her one surviving brother in order to produce an offspring, Sinfjǫtli, to aid in the vengeance against her husband. In the end, after bringing about the deaths of her husband and the children she bore him, Signý deems herself unworthy to live and voluntarily perishes in her husband's hall, which had been set on fire by Sigmundr and Sinfjǫtli. Although Rosimund and Signý are not mentioned by name in Old English sources, it is not unlikely that their legends were known in early medieval England: Rosimund's husband, Alboin (OE Ælfwine), is the subject of a vignette in *Widsith* (ll. 70–74), and Signý's brother and child, Sigmundr (OE Sigemund) and Sinfjǫtli (OE Fitela), are the subject of a digression in *Beowulf* (ll. 874b–902a) that alludes to "feuds and crimes" ("fæhðe ond fyrena," l. 879a) in which they were involved.[28]

Beowulf's major deeds, in contrast, bear little resemblance to those of the aforementioned heroes and heroines. Fate treats him well: though he has an unpromising youth, he lives a rather charmed life thereafter, and he is never put into a position wherein honor requires him to harm a brother, a child, a friend, a spouse, or an in-law. Aspects of Beowulf's biography—his unpromising youth, his preternatural strength, his swimming contest, and his combat with various monsters (*eotenas, nicoras*, Grendel, Grendel's mother, and the dragon)—establish the derivation of his character not from migration-period legend but from folkloric traditions that tell of heroes with similar attributes performing similar deeds.[29] In particular, the life of Beowulf betrays the

---

27. See R. G. Finch, ed. and trans., *The Saga of the Volsungs* (London: Nelson, 1965), 4–14. For discussion of Signý and related figures, see Jenny Jochens, *Old Norse Images of Women* (Philadelphia: University of Pennsylvania Press, 1996), 132–61.

28. On the connections between these passages and legendary tradition, see, respectively, Chambers, *Widsith*, 123–26, and M. S. Griffith, "Some Difficulties in *Beowulf*, Lines 874–902: Sigemund Reconsidered," *Anglo-Saxon England* 24 (1995): 11–41.

29. See T. A. Shippey, "The Fairy-Tale Structure of *Beowulf*," *Notes and Queries* 16, no. 1 (1969): 2–11; Daniel R. Barnes, "Folktale Morphology and the Structure of *Beowulf*," *Speculum* 45, no. 3 (1970): 416–34; Bruce A. Rosenberg, "Folktale Morphology and the Structure of *Beowulf*: A Counterproposal," *Journal of the Folklore Institute* 11, no. 3 (1975): 199–209; Kent Gould, "*Beowulf* and Folktale Morphology: God as Magical Donor," *Folklore* 96, no. 1 (1985):

influence of the folktale known as "the Bear's Son" (type 301 in Antti
Aarne and Stith Thompson's classification), some of the manifesta-
tions of which relate a narrative bearing uncanny resemblances to the
story of Beowulf's fight with Grendel and Grendel's mother.[30] While
the heroic-legendary tradition attaches a more or less fixed set of major
deeds to a particular figure from the migration period, the folkloric
traditions behind *Beowulf* feature mobile collections of variable motifs
that could be attached (in whole or in part) to heroes from any time or
place. Inheritors of this folkloric material had considerable freedom as
to the moral and aesthetic purposes to which they might direct it. As
J. Michael Stitt observes of the relationship between *Beowulf* and the
"Bear's Son" tradition:

> It is impossible to determine the meaning of the tradition and
> then project it onto *Beowulf* or a particular saga. The tradition, as
> defined here, is simply a sequence of motifs related in structur-
> ally constant patterns. The tradition *per se* is essentially mean-
> ingless. Ultimately, meaning is created (or recreated) anew each
> time the tradition is realized in some specific narrative and social
> context.[31]

The folktale narratives and the associated motifs that the *Beowulf* poet
inherited, foregrounded, and made central to the life of his exemplary
protagonist were morally malleable. They could be made consistent
with the characterization of a hero who is more courteous and pious

98–103. On Beowulf himself as a hero in antecedent folkloric tradition, see Larry D. Benson,
"The Originality of Beowulf," in *The Interpretation of Narrative: Theory and Practice*, ed. Morton
W. Bloomfield (Cambridge, MA: Harvard University Press, 1970), 1–43; Leonard Neidorf, "Be-
owulf before *Beowulf*: Anglo-Saxon Anthroponymy and Heroic Legend," *Review of English Stud-
ies* 64, no. 266 (2013): 553–73; Francis Leneghan, *The Dynastic Drama of Beowulf* (Cambridge:
D. S. Brewer, 2020), 104–52.

    30. See Antti Aarne and Stith Thompson, *The Types of the Folktale: A Classification and Bib-
liography* (Helsinki: Academia Scientiarum Fennica, 1961), 90–92; Friedrich Panzer, *Studien
zur germanischen Sagengeschichte*, I: *Beowulf* (Munich: C. H. Beck, 1910); J. Michael Stitt, *Beowulf
and the Bear's Son: Epic, Saga, and Fairytale in Northern Germanic Tradition* (New York: Garland,
1992). For further discussion, see Peter A. Jorgensen, "The Two-Troll Variant of the Bear's Son
Folktale in *Hálfdanar saga Brönufóstra* and *Gríms saga loðinkinna*," *Arv: Journal of Scandinavian
Folklore* 31 (1975): 35–43; Peter A. Jorgensen, "Additional Icelandic Analogues to *Beowulf*,"
in *Sagnaskemmtun: Studies in Honour of Hermann Pálsson on His 65th Birthday, 26th May 1986*,
ed. Rudolf Simek, Jónas Kristjánsson, and Hans Bekker-Nielsen (Vienna: Hermann Böhlaus,
1986), 201–8; R. Mark Scowcroft, "The Irish Analogues to *Beowulf*," *Speculum* 74, no. 1 (1999):
22–64; Magnús Fjalldal, "*Beowulf* and the Old Norse Two-Troll Analogues," *Neophilologus* 97,
no. 3 (2013): 541–53.

    31. Stitt, *Beowulf and the Bear's Son*, 208.

than any of his predecessors. Far less malleable was the tradition of migration-period legend that the poet inherited. Within this tradition, narratives were fundamentally tragic and amoral; they were also less alterable, as they were attached to specific individuals and rooted in particular historical contexts. While details could change over time, the narratives do not readily lend themselves to retellings that stress God's benevolent providence or champion a novel ethical system.

From the foregoing accounts of migration-period legend, we can perceive that the predominant type of traditional plot, in which a character must choose between two hateful alternatives, is often intertwined with an interest in the sensational deaths of kings and the consequent ruination of their peoples. It is significant that whenever a character in these legends is a verifiably historical migration-period king, whose exploits were recorded in Latin historiography, the legends concentrate on moments of defeat rather than victory. Comparable to Alboin are figures like Attila and Ermanaric, both of whom are known in legendary poetry less for conquering peoples and winning territory than for being killed by a spouse (as happens to Attila in *Atlakviða*) or her kinsmen (as happens to Ermanaric in *Hamðismál*).[32] Furthermore, if the Hengest of the Finnsburg legend is the same Hengest involved in the Anglo-Saxon conquest of Britain, it is remarkable that he was celebrated in legendary poetry not for the land he obtained but for the anguish he experienced when circumstances compelled him to kill his new lord in order to avenge his previous lord. A related expression of the poets' interest in disaster inheres in the fact that legends formed around Gundaharius, the king who presided over the Burgundians at the time of their annihilation in 436, but not around Alaric, the leader of the Goths associated with their greatest triumph, the sacking of Rome in 410. Just as legends of Gundaharius are connected to the demise of the Burgundians, the legends of Hlǫðr and Ingeld contain within them mythical explanations for the disappearance from post-migration-period history of the Huns and the Heathobards. By situating personal encounters in the context of national tragedies, poets amplified the gravity of the circumstances that compelled protagonists to choose between hateful alternatives.

---

32. For overviews of the legends pertaining to these two figures, see Caroline Brady, *The Legends of Ermanaric* (Berkeley: University of California Press, 1943); Michael A. Babcock, *The Stories of Attila the Hun's Death: Narrative, Myth, and Meaning* (Lewiston, ME: Edwin Mellen Press, 2001).

Why did the poets responsible for the creation of migration-period legendry decide to make protagonists out of kin-slayers, oath-breakers, vengeful wives, and vanquished kings? Why did they not tell stories of conquest or stories in which a hero struggles valiantly against the odds and actually wins? Why does the earliest recorded fragment of legendary poetry in a Germanic language, the *Hildebrandslied*, tell an amoral tale about a father compelled to kill his son rather than a morally comforting story? The best answer to these questions, which are addressed with surprising infrequency in the critical literature, remains the answer offered by Phillpotts in 1928. She argues that these legends, which are rooted in the events of the fifth and sixth centuries, retain a "pagan attitude to life" and articulate a kind of "pagan philosophy" through their concentration on heroes caught in unbearable circumstances. Fundamental to the traditional plot is a conviction that the world is governed by a cruel and arbitrary fate, "which can put men and women into positions whence it seems impossible for them to emerge with honor." Indeed, the plots are designed to illustrate the cruelness and arbitrariness of fate. Yet by focusing on the choices made by heroes in disastrous situations, the legends express a conviction that although mankind cannot overcome fate, "man's will was free and, therefore, in some way superior to the Fate that crushes him."[33] Furthermore, poets redressed the balance of power between mankind and fate through their conception of fame:

> Fame is for the man who has the courage to choose: whether he chooses resistance to the uttermost against hopeless physical odds, knowing that his death is ordained, or whether he chooses one course rather than another of two that are hateful to him, and makes something magnificent of it by a single-minded pursuit of it. . . . [Fame] is an assertion that there is something greater than Fate: the strength of will and the courage of human beings, and the memory which could preserve their deeds. Fame and human character: these were two things against which Fate could not prevail.[34]

In Phillpotts's reading, heroes such as Angantýr and Hlǫðr merited the fame that comes with inclusion in the legendary tradition not because

---

33. Bertha S. Phillpotts, "Wyrd and Providence in Anglo-Saxon Thought," *Essays and Studies* 13 (1928): 7–27, at 7, 13, 14.

34. Phillpotts, "Wyrd and Providence," 14–15.

it was considered admirable to kill kinsmen but because it was considered admirable to maintain one's character and one's commitment to heroic ideals under trying circumstances. Forced to choose between hateful alternatives, each man commits to a course of action and can be celebrated for his commitment, even if it causes one to die prematurely and the other to bear the stain of kin-slaying for the rest of his life. Likewise, even though it was not considered admirable for a wife to orchestrate the killing of her husband and her children, Signý "is a heroine, worthy of men's admiration, because having chosen her path she never looks back until her purpose is accomplished."[35] Heroes in legendary tradition were not celebrated for doing the right thing—in the traditional plot, there is no right thing—but for doing *something* under circumstances that might have crushed the spirits of lesser mortals and caused them to do nothing.

Naturally, some Christian authors, but certainly not all of them, felt uncomfortable handling a story in which circumstances drive an apparently good-natured hero to kill a kinsman, break an oath, or commit other atrocities. Phillpotts observes that later authors occasionally bowdlerized the traditional plot: the clearest case is found in the fifteenth-century *Jüngeres Hildebrandslied*, where father and son are reconciled after a brief skirmish and then enjoy a family dinner together.[36] Happy endings, she notes, also replace tragic outcomes in *Waltharius* and *Kudrun*, where situations that had conventionally led to the killing of a kinsman or a sworn friend lead instead to mere wounding and reconciliation.[37] Like the authors of these works, the *Beowulf* poet clearly had reservations about the sustained depiction of amoral tales from legendary tradition. Yet for the *Beowulf* poet, who composed for an

---

35. Phillpotts, "Wyrd and Providence," 14.
36. Phillpotts, "Wyrd and Providence," 17–18. For further discussion, see George T. Gillespie, "Heroic Lays: Survival and Transformation in Ballad," *Oxford German Studies* 9, no. 1 (1978): 1–18, at 8, who remarks: "In the one poem [*Hildebrandslied*] fate proceeds relentlessly, albeit under God, while in the later ballad [*Jüngeres Hildebrandslied*] a benevolent deity has brought the meeting between father and son to a fortunate outcome." For the text of *Jüngeres Hildebrandslied*, see John Meier, ed., *Deutsche Volkslied: Balladen I* (Berlin: Reclam, 1935), 1–21; for a translation, see Francis G. Gentry and James K. Walter, eds., *German Epic Poetry: The Nibelungenlied, The Older Lay of Hildebrand, and Other Works* (New York: Continuum, 1995), 295–302.
37. For a text and translation of *Waltharius*, see Dennis M. Kratz, ed. and trans., *Waltharius and Ruodlieb* (New York: Garland, 1984); for related sources, see H. M. Smyser and Francis P. Magoun Jr., eds. and trans., *Walther of Aquitaine: Materials for the Study of His Legend* (New London: Connecticut College, 1950). For the text of *Kudrun*, see Karl Bartsch, ed., *Kudrun*, 5th ed., rev. Karl Stackmann (Tübingen: Max Niemeyer, 2000); for a translation, see Brian Murdoch, trans., *Kudrun* (London: Dent, 1987).

audience in possession of extensive knowledge of the legendary tradi-
tion (to judge from the terseness of the poem's allusions), drastic altera-
tion of the stories themselves was not an option. It was this dilemma,
in Phillpotts's view, that caused *Beowulf* to be the peculiar work that it
is. She offers the following assessment of the poet's predicament and
its aesthetic consequences:

> He and his audience are still so near to pagan times that no one
> will expect him to celebrate the past with no references to pagan-
> ism, but on the other hand, he must have a respectable hero and
> plot. He must not take one of the old traditional plots which turn
> on an evil choice being offered to man or woman; because in a
> world governed by justice, and leading to Heaven or Hell, it is ob-
> viously impossible that a human being should be forced to do one
> wrong in order to avoid another. Yet our poet wants to keep the
> heroic atmosphere, and to use all the knowledge of the kings and
> peoples of the pagan past, which is his stock in trade. In this di-
> lemma he chooses a dragon-slayer as his hero: but a dragon-slayer
> who can be placed in the environment of which he has always
> sung—the dynasties of Southern Sweden and Denmark. He loses
> the close-knit structure of a story of the old type, and the Wyrd of
> the old religion becomes a mere body-snatcher. But at least he can
> have fighting, and ceremonial, and loyal and disloyal retainers,
> and he can put fine speeches into the mouths of his characters,
> and he can allude constantly to the web of ancient stories which
> is still present in the minds of his audience.[38]

Contained within these words is a theory concerning the genesis of
Beowulf that accounts exceptionally well for its idiosyncratic structure
and its retention or rejection of elements from antecedent legendary
tradition. The *Beowulf* poet retains what he considered admirable or
unobjectionable, but his discomfort with the traditional plot results
in "the loss of a certain spirit, a sort of grim satisfaction in recount-
ing the actions of men driven into a corner by adverse circumstances,"
which is replaced instead "by a wholly alien spirit, one of melancholy
resignation."[39] The veracity of this judgment can be perceived by

---

38. Phillpotts, "Wyrd and Providence," 21.
39. Phillpotts, "Wyrd and Providence," 22. For an extended discussion of this spirit of
"grim satisfaction," see T. A. Shippey, *Laughing Shall I Die: Lives and Deaths of the Great Vikings*
(London: Reaktion Books, 2018).

comparing the final third of *Beowulf* with the final third of the *Nibelun-genlied*, both of which concentrate on a hero fighting a battle in which he knows he will perish. The *Nibelungenlied* poet takes grim satisfaction in the depiction of Hagen's unyielding resistance: his slaughter of countless opponents before finally succumbing is recounted with enthusiasm and admiration. We find there an extended and moving depiction of the triumph of the human spirit over a cruel fate, which could kill the man but not destroy his character. The note of triumph is muted, however, in the final third of *Beowulf*, where melancholy pervades the text, as elegiac passages both precede and follow the hero's fight with the dragon. By killing the dragon that has mortally wounded him, Beowulf obtains a form of victory in defeat, but the poet emphasizes defeat rather than victory, suggesting that there is no earthly compensation sufficient to offset the loss of this stainless and irreplaceable king.

If Tolkien deserves to be known as the first great champion of the poet's *art*, Phillpotts deserves to be known as the first great explicator of the poet's *thought*. Tolkien provided a compelling account of *what* the poet did, but Phillpotts provided, in my view, the more compelling account of *why* the poet did it—*why* the poet eschewed the traditional plot and decided to concentrate on a monster-fighting hero. While a tradition of scholarship has formed around Tolkien's lecture, no such tradition has formed around Phillpotts's study. It was reprinted in one collection of essays on *Beowulf*, but it has not exerted much influence on the direction of subsequent scholarship.[40] There are many conceivable reasons for this disparity of influence, but one salient reason must be that it is easier to follow Tolkien than to follow Phillpotts. One finishes Tolkien's lecture with a sense that *Beowulf* rises so far above the antecedent legendary tradition that it exists in a world of its own and can be admired in isolation—that it is a work of world literature, comparable only to the *Aeneid* or *Gilgamesh*, which would be belittled through pedantic comparisons with the dull and fragmentary witnesses to Germanic legend. Phillpotts, in contrast, begins her essay by using these witnesses to reconstruct the plots of all of the legends that might have been known to the *Beowulf* poet. Whereas Tolkien briefly discusses the legend of Ingeld in order to depreciate the putative Ingeld epic desired by Ker and Chambers, Phillpotts surveys nearly all of the major witnesses to

---

40. Her essay is reprinted in R. D. Fulk, ed., *Interpretations of Beowulf: A Critical Anthology* (Bloomington: Indiana University Press, 1991).

migration-period legend. Tolkien knew and loved this material—his er-
udition in it is prominently displayed in *Finn and Hengest*—but he wore
this learning lightly in his seminal lecture on *Beowulf*, which created the
impression that the poem could be brilliantly explicated without refer-
ence to the scattered debris of the legendary tradition.[41] It set a power-
ful example that subsequent scholars cannot be faulted for emulating.

One essay appearing after the paradigm shift effected by Tolkien
that could be considered a continuator of the line of thought inaugu-
rated by Phillpotts is Thomas D. Hill's comparative study of *Beowulf*
and *Vǫlsunga saga*. What distinguishes this study from most others is
not that it is comparative but that it undertakes comparison in order
to highlight and explore the extent to which *Beowulf* differs from other
works rooted in legendary tradition. Hill begins his essay by quoting
Klaeber's remark on the atypical characterization of the protagonist:
"Those readers who, impressed by Beowulf's martial appearance at
the beginning of the action, expect to find an aggressive warrior hero
of the Achilles or Sigfrit type, will be disappointed to find him some-
what tame, sentimental, and fond of talking."[42] Hill notes that one re-
action to the phenomenon observed by Klaeber has been "to assume
that the contrast between Beowulf and other great figures of Germanic
heroic epic is deliberate and meaningful—that the *Beowulf*-poet knew
Germanic heroic literature well and intended to present a quite dif-
ferent type of hero." Significantly, he then remarks: "This view is cur-
rent in the critical literature on *Beowulf*, but it has never received much
elaboration."[43] Indeed, in the four decades that have elapsed since Hill's
meticulous excavation of the intertextual resonances of the hero's dy-
ing words, the view that *Beowulf* is in a continuous, contrastive dialogue
with antecedent legendary tradition has still not received much elabo-
ration. One aim of the present book is to follow the example of Hill's
study and demonstrate the explanatory power of Phillpotts's theory in
relation to aspects of *Beowulf* that Phillpotts naturally could not ad-
dress in the course of a single essay. Although Hill does not cite Phill-
potts, his essay substantiates her central insight: namely, that *Beowulf*

---

41. See J. R. R. Tolkien, *Finn and Hengest: The Fragment and the Episode*, ed. A. J. Bliss (Lon-
don: George Allen & Unwin, 1982).

42. Fr. Klaeber, ed., *Beowulf and The Fight at Finnsburg*, 3rd ed. (Boston: Heath, 1950), 1.

43. Thomas D. Hill, "The Confession of Beowulf and the Structure of *Volsunga Saga*,"
in *The Vikings: Papers from the Cornell Lecture Series Held to Coincide with the Viking Exhibition
1980–1981*, ed. Robert T. Farrell (London: Phillimore, 1982), 165–79, at 165.

is an untraditional poem, with various departures from tradition motivated by its author's aspiration to morally renovate an amoral legendary tradition.

Another essay that displays intellectual kinship with Phillpotts and Hill is James W. Earl's "The Forbidden *Beowulf*," which compares the poem with numerous analogues in order to argue that the poet suppressed the theme of incest whenever it appeared in the tradition he inherited.[44] One place where such tampering with tradition has long seemed likely is in the digression concerning Sigemund and Fitela, who are described in *Beowulf* as uncle and nephew, though they are elsewhere known as father and son, with Fitela being the product of incest between Signý and an unwitting Sigemund. Earl notes that he is not the first to suspect a departure from tradition at this point in the poem; he cites Klaeber's supposition that if the story has been changed, the alteration "may be attributed to the Christian author's desire to suppress that morally revolting motive."[45] Following Klaeber, Earl also identifies Christianity as an explanation for the poem's departures from tradition. He writes: "Compared with the analogues, *Beowulf* is hardly the consummate Germanic poem; it is a poem struggling to subdue its Germanic nature, to bring it into rough harmony with Christianity."[46] Although I concur with Klaeber and Earl in recognizing that *Beowulf* is untraditional, I would resist the tendency to explain the poem's uniqueness as a sign of tension between impersonal forces such as Christianity and paganism or Mediterranean learning and Germanic tradition. This tendency is widespread and by no means restricted to Earl and Klaeber: in Phillpotts as well, there is a sense that *Beowulf* represents a Christian reaction to a pagan tradition. While there is truth to such generalizations, a central argument of the present book is that the untraditional features of *Beowulf* are best understood to stem not from impersonal forces but from one idiosyncratic poet, who possessed a peculiar set of aesthetic and intellectual priorities. Other medieval Christian authors, such as Saxo Grammaticus and the author of the *Nibelungenlied*, handled the same kind of material the *Beowulf* poet inherited, but their works display a very different attitude to this material and exhibit far fewer moral reservations than *Beowulf*.

---

44. See James W. Earl, "The Forbidden *Beowulf*: Haunted by Incest," *PMLA* 125, no. 2 (2010): 289–305.
45. Klaeber, *Beowulf*, 159.
46. Earl, "Forbidden *Beowulf*," 291.

There are, of course, many reasons why scholars might be inclined to efface the author of *Beowulf* and discuss the poem as if it generated itself or were the offspring of clashing historical forces. In the nineteenth century, as noted above, it was fashionable to regard *Beowulf* as a product of multiple authorship and analyze its dissonant elements as Christian, pagan, Mediterranean, or Germanic in origin. Although that fashion rightly faded, a tendency to interpret *Beowulf* as an impersonally generated object persisted throughout the twentieth century on account of two other developments: post-structural theorists established a critical taboo against open discussion of authorial intention in professional criticism, and oral-formulaic theorists created the impression that the individual behind *Beowulf* might have been a kind of tradition-bearing automaton.[47] Compounding these developments was a lingering uncertainty as to whether a single human being is genuinely responsible for the entirety of *Beowulf*, with several prominent arguments for multiple authorship or scribal recomposition emerging throughout the twentieth century.[48] At the same time, however, philological research into the authorship of *Beowulf* has been generating a formidable mass of evidence consistent with the conclusion that the poem was composed by a single author in an Anglian kingdom during the first half of the eighth century.[49] Research into the written transmission of *Beowulf*, meanwhile, suggests that the sole extant manuscript of the poem, written out around the year 1000, essentially preserves the text that this one

---

47. For a critical account of the development of the taboo against authorial intention, see Farrell, *Varieties of Authorial Intention*, 1–17. The trend had previously been documented and critiqued by Hirsch, *Validity in Interpretation*. Oral-formulaic theory emerged with Francis P. Magoun Jr., "Oral-Formulaic Character of Anglo-Saxon Narrative Poetry," *Speculum* 28, no. 3 (1953): 446–67; for its most sophisticated articulation, see John Miles Foley, *Traditional Oral Epic: The Odyssey, Beowulf, and the Serbo-Croatian Return Song* (Berkeley: University of California Press, 1990); John Miles Foley, *Immanent Art: From Structure to Meaning in Traditional Oral Epic* (Bloomington: Indiana University Press, 1991).

48. See Francis P. Magoun Jr., "*Béowulf A*: A Folk-Variant," *Arv: Journal of Scandinavian Folklore* 14 (1958): 95–101; Francis P. Magoun Jr., "*Béowulf B*: A Folk-Poem on Beowulf's Death," in *Early English and Norse Studies Presented to Hugh Smith in Honour of His Sixtieth Birthday*, ed. Arthur Brown and Peter Foote (London: Methuen, 1963), 127–40; Kevin S. Kiernan, *Beowulf and the Beowulf Manuscript* (New Brunswick, NJ: Rutgers University Press, 1981); Roy Michael Liuzza, "On the Dating of *Beowulf*," in *Beowulf: Basic Readings*, ed. Peter S. Baker (New York: Garland, 1995).

49. See Grinda, "Pigeonholing Old English Poetry"; Bately, "Linguistic Evidence"; Shippey, "Prospects for Literary History"; Donoghue, "Non-Integrity of *Beowulf*"; Sundquist, "Relative Clause Variation"; Fulk, "On Argumentation," 16–24; Fulk, "Archaisms and Neologisms"; Fulk, "Old English *Þa*"; Ecay and Pintzuk, "Syntax of Old English Poetry"; Neidorf et al., "Large-Scale Quantitative Profiling."

poet committed to parchment three centuries earlier.[50] The linguistic homogeneity of the transmitted text, which exhibits archaic features from beginning to end, constitutes strong counterevidence to the supposition that scribes might have substantially altered the poem while reproducing it. The present book augments the evidence for unitary authorship by demonstrating that there is a coherent, if idiosyncratic, perspective to be discerned throughout the entirety of *Beowulf*, a single mind at work in the reshaping of inherited material.

Along with Ker, Chambers, Tolkien, and Phillpotts, I view *Beowulf* as a fundamentally atypical poem and regard its concentration on a monster-fighting hero, rather than a hero caught in a conflict of loyalties, as a sign that its poet has chosen to depart radically from the tradition he inherited. Yet I would extend this perspective beyond the most salient structural feature and argue that the departures from tradition in *Beowulf* are far more pervasive and profound than has hitherto been recognized. The most prominent characters in *Beowulf* are not merely not the kin-slayers, oath-breakers, and vengeful wives of antecedent tradition (who are relegated to digressions)—they are also represented as courteous monotheists who spend much of the poem giving pious and courtly speeches. Beowulf is clearly represented in an untraditional manner, but a similar case can be made for the representation of Hrothgar, Wealhtheow, and others. The kings and queens in the foreground of *Beowulf* contrast with characters in antecedent tradition by markedly abstaining from the kinds of behavior that had conventionally earned characters their position in Germanic legend. In my reading, the *Beowulf* poet focuses on these untraditional characters not to disparage the earlier tradition but to recover and repurpose it for a new kind of narrative poem with different moral and ethical emphases. Retaining the heroes and the setting but not the amoral perspective, the poet creates an epic that is rooted in the legendary world of the migration period yet serves as a vehicle for the expression of ideas and values that were alien to the antecedent tradition. This reading of *Beowulf* as an untraditional poem is developed over the course of the following three chapters. The first chapter focuses on what was omitted and minimized, while the second and third chapters focus on what was added and augmented.

---

50. See Neidorf, *Transmission of Beowulf.* See also Michael Lapidge, "The Archetype of *Beowulf*," *Anglo-Saxon England* 29 (2000): 5–41; Leonard Neidorf, "The Archetype of *Beowulf*," *English Studies* 99, no. 3 (2018): 229–42.

Chapter 1 argues that kin-slaying and oath-breaking shaped the composition of *Beowulf*. Such a claim might appear counterintuitive in view of the omission of these acts from the life of the monster-slaying protagonist. Indeed, in his dying words, Beowulf takes satisfaction in the fact that God need not blame him for killing kinsmen and breaking oaths once he is dead. Though these words have not conventionally been thought to offer a key to the poem, I contend that they reflect a set of ideas about kin-slaying and oath-breaking that pervade *Beowulf* and guide the poet in his handling of inherited material. The hypothesis that the poet wished to avoid valorizing characters known to have committed one of the two standard heroic transgressions is shown here to possess considerable explanatory power. In addition to explaining the poem's focus on a folkloric protagonist, it also explains the distribution of material into the poem's background and the selection of the other foregrounded characters. The poet's moral concerns are reflected in his treatment of various characters, but most saliently so in his elevation of Hrothgar and denigration of Unferth. Hrothgar, known elsewhere for staying at home and abstaining from transgression, is made into the poem's second most prominent character and depicted as an exemplar of courtesy and piety. In contrast, Unferth appears to have been a conventional transgressive hero of the sort depicted sympathetically in other sources, yet the poet consistently expresses hostility toward him. I conclude that the poet articulates a distinctly untraditional perspective on the kin-slaying and oath-breaking heroes he found in his sources and that this perspective distinguishes *Beowulf* from other witnesses to migration-period legend.

Chapter 2 argues that the poet modified the heroic and folkloric traditions he inherited by making ideals of courtesy and courtliness central to the matter of his epic poem. *Beowulf* is not generally regarded as a courtly poem: it is routinely excluded from discussions of courtly literature, which normally associate the phenomenon of courtliness with Francophone literature of the later Middle Ages. In view, however, of a growing tendency among historians to predate the origins of courtliness, I contend that *Beowulf* should be considered a courtly poem and demonstrate that insights into many of its passages can be obtained by viewing it as such. Instead of focusing on the extreme and unyielding behavior typically displayed by migration-period heroes, the poet focuses on the ceremonial and restrained behavior of his foregrounded characters. Details of court life assume central importance in *Beowulf*, where much of the narrative is concerned with the protagonist's gradual transition from courtier to king. Displaying greater interest in his courtly behavior than his martial conduct, the poet depicts Beowulf as an ideal courtier who knows how to conduct himself in an aristocratic environment. The hero exhibits the sophisticated self-restraint associated with courtliness, as he displays exaggerated deference toward his superiors and pronounced magnanimity toward his inferiors. *Beowulf*, in addition to its monster fights, tells the story of a lesser nobleman's rise to kingship, as it shows the hero advance from needing to earn an audience with the Danish king to becoming one of the king's intimates and finally a king himself. The poet, evidently dissatisfied with a folkloric inheritance where narratives possess an ahistorical and dreamlike quality, makes a concerted effort to endow his epic poem with a quality of courtly realism. His protagonist is a human being (rather than a bear) whose exemplary life is situated at plausible courts of the semi-historical migration period.

Chapter 3 argues that the poet uses monotheism and monstrosity to bring greater moral clarity to the traditions he inherited. Like Alcuin, the *Beowulf* poet evidently accepted that the traditional poetry on the cruelty of fate and compelled transgressions had little to do with Christ—that it was fundamentally amoral and unsuitable for sustained narration before a Christian audience. Yet the poet managed to preserve as much as he could from this cherished tradition by having it form an allusive background to three foregrounded fights between a pious protagonist and his monstrous adversaries. This chapter aims to establish the precise nature and function of the monotheistic vision expressed by the characters and the narrator, while also exploring the relationship of the monsters to the poem's insistent monotheism. The characters in the foreground are consistently represented as pious monotheists who have apparently intuited the existence of the singular deity of Judeo-Christian tradition without the benefit of Mosaic law or Christian revelation. These intuitive monotheists are viewed by the narrator not as hopeless heathens destined to an eternity in hell but as determined adherents to natural law who can achieve salvation if they follow their better intuitions. There is, moreover, a general doctrinal alignment between the foregrounded characters and the narrator, who stresses God's providence in apparent reaction to a tradition that had stressed the cruelty of a blind fate. Opposed to the poem's monotheistic champion are malevolent monsters, whom the poet renders far more sinister and threatening than the vaguely bad and occasionally comical monsters of folkloric tradition. To rectify the amorality of his inheritance, the poet models his monster fights on those he encountered in hagiographical narratives, which presented a form of moral clarity that was unavailable in native tradition. By pitting a pious protagonist, who receives God's support and is an unwitting agent of God's will, against heinous monsters, the poet endows *Beowulf* with a moral framework that is not paralleled elsewhere in heroic or folkloric tradition.

The concluding chapter synthesizes the findings of the previous chapters. It answers potential objections to their claims by propounding a theory of constrained innovation, arguing that the poet's plan for moral renovation was constrained by respect for the facts and the forms of antecedent tradition. In *Beowulf*, we can discern the presence of a single mind, with a singular sense of decorum, at work in the combination and modification of heroic, folkloric, hagiographical, and historical materials. Rather than perceive *Beowulf* as a disorderly hodgepodge of aspects of early medieval life and literature, I conclude that it should be read as the considered result of one poet's ambition to produce a morally edifying, theologically palatable, and historically plausible epic out of material that could not independently constitute such a poem.

CHAPTER 1

Kin-Slaying and Oath-Breaking

As noted in the previous chapter, the legends that formed around the heroes of the migration period tended to center on a moment in which a protagonist is compelled to kill a kinsman or break an oath. There was more to the legendary tradition than this: there were boasts and insults that preceded the climactic moment, and there were elegies that followed it. Nevertheless, the narrative kernel of each legend was a scene of kin-slaying or oath-breaking brought about by circumstances beyond the protagonist's control. *Beowulf* is an unusual poem for not climaxing in such a scene, and Beowulf is an unusual hero for living a life in which neither kin-slaying nor oath-breaking constituted central themes. Indeed, a critic can reasonably feel surprised when these two themes are mentioned, ostensibly without reason, in the speech that the hero delivers after he is mortally wounded by the dragon. Recognizing that his death is imminent, Beowulf reflects on the life he led during his fifty years on the Geatish throne:

> Ic on earde bād
> mǣlgesceafta,   hēold mīn tela,
> ne sōhte searonīðas,   nē mē swōr fela
> āða on unriht.   Ic ðæs ealles mæg
> feorhbennum sēoc   gefēan habban;

forðām mē wītan ne ðearf   waldend fīra
morðorbealo māga,   þonne mīn sceaceð
līf of līce. (ll. 2736b–2743a)

(I lived out at home my allotment of time, managed well what
was mine, did not go looking for unwarranted aggression, did not
swear multitudes of oaths in injustice. Sickened as I am by mortal
wounds, I can take satisfaction in all that; on that account the
ruler of men need not accuse me of the murder of kinsmen when
the life departs from my body.)

In the course of a magisterial demonstration that Beowulf's last words
belong to a "death song" genre that found widespread expression in
early Germanic literature, Joseph Harris suggests that the hero's men-
tion of kin-slaying and oath-breaking here might be an "incompletely
assimilated element" from poetic tradition.[1] Noting that these two
deeds "seem rather removed from the sterling Beowulf himself," Har-
ris observes that kin-slaying and oath-breaking are also collocated in
a stanza of *Sigurðarkviða in skamma* and suggests that their presence in
Beowulf's speech might be "a carryover from the underlying genre" not
entirely relevant to the poem as a whole.[2] In doing so, Harris registers
disagreement with Thomas D. Hill's argument that the hero's allusion
to kin-slaying and oath-breaking is a deeply meaningful moment that
makes explicit the poet's broader intention to characterize Beowulf as
an unconventional hero. Proposing an intertextual relationship be-
tween *Beowulf* and the legends recorded in *Vǫlsunga saga*, Hill argues
that Beowulf's "asseverations are not pointless banalities, but rather
implicitly contrast this hero with the heroes of the most famous cycle
of heroic legend of the Germanic world, the Volsungs."[3] While concur-
ring with Harris's claim that the death song is the "generic subtext"

---

1. Joseph Harris, "Beowulf's Last Words," *Speculum* 67, no. 1 (1992): 1–32, at 18. For addi-
tional insights into the poetry that Harris characterizes as death songs, see Nora K. Chadwick,
"Norse Ghosts II," *Folklore* 57, no. 3 (1946): 106–27; John C. Pope, "Beowulf's Old Age," in
*Philological Essays: Studies in Old and Middle English Language and Literature in Honour of Herbert
Dean Meritt*, ed. James L. Rosier (The Hague: Mouton, 1970), 55–64; Lars Lönnroth, "Hjál-
mar's Death-Song and the Delivery of Eddic Poetry," *Speculum* 46, no. 1 (1971): 1–20; Peter
Buchholz, "Death Traditions as an Oral Nucleus of Scandinavian Heroic Literature," *Mankind
Quarterly* 28, no. 2 (1987): 151–60. In a response to Harris's paper, Susan E. Deskis suggests
that the book of Proverbs might have influenced the arrangement of material in Beowulf's
final speech. See Deskis, "An Addendum to Beowulf's Last Words," *Medium Ævum* 63, no. 2
(1994): 301–5.

2. Harris, "Beowulf's Last Words," 18.

3. Thomas D. Hill, "Confession of Beowulf," 177.

behind Beowulf's speech,[4] the present chapter champions Hill's position on the speech's import and develops it further. I argue that the hero's dying words, far from being undigested elements of tradition, reflect a set of ideas about kin-slaying and oath-breaking that pervade *Beowulf* and fundamentally shaped its composition.

A significant feature of Beowulf's speech, which did not figure prominently in the arguments of Harris or Hill, is the connection that the hero makes between kin-slaying, oath-breaking, and posthumous judgment. Beowulf rejoices in his abstention from these moral transgressions because he believes that "the ruler of men" (*waldend fīra*) would look unfavorably on them when life leaves his body. It is remarkable, of course, that a non-Christian hero should be endowed with such a thought. Beowulf, although denied the Christian revelation, has evidently intuited the existence of the singular deity of Judeo-Christian tradition; additionally, he has intuited that this deity passes judgment on the dead, and he has intuitions about the kinds of behavior the deity would find displeasing.[5] This is an extraordinary aspect of the protagonist's thinking, which finds expression elsewhere in *Beowulf* and renders his allusion to kin-slaying and oath-breaking rather distinct from the analogous collocation that Harris identified in *Sigurðarkviða in skamma*. In that passage, in which the mortally wounded Sigurðr addresses a weeping Guðrún, the hero exonerates himself and blames Brynhildr for causing his death:

> Mér unni mær   fyr mann hvern—
> en við Gunnar   grand ekki vannk;
> þyrmða ek sifiom,   svǫrnom eiðom,
> síðr værak heitinn   hans kvánar vinr. (28)

(The girl loves me above all other men, but to Gunnar I did no harm; I violated neither kinship nor oaths, so I should not be called his wife's lover.)[6]

While the collocation of oaths and kinship here might indeed suggest that a hero's dying moments were an opportune time to reflect on these

---

4. Harris, "Beowulf's Last Words," 23.

5. For extensive discussion of the intuitive monotheism expressed by Beowulf and the other foregrounded characters, see chapter 3 of the present book.

6. The text is cited from Gustav Neckel, ed., *Edda: Die Lieder des Codex Regius nebst verwandten Denkmälern*, vol. 1, *Text*, rev. Hans Kuhn, 5th ed. (Heidelberg: Winter, 1983), 211. The translation provided is that of Carolyne Larrington, trans., *The Poetic Edda*, 2nd ed. (Oxford: Oxford University Press, 2014), 181.

two themes, there is a world of difference between the last words of
Beowulf and Sigurðr. Whereas Beowulf has unambiguously refrained
from violating oaths and kinship, Sigurðr's situation is rather ambigu-
ous: he has actually committed moral transgressions, but he commit-
ted them either unwittingly or under compulsion, depending on the
particular tradition.[7] Sigurðr's last words thus call attention to his es-
sential similarity to most heroes in legendary tradition, nearly all of
whom were placed into morally ambiguous and ultimately disastrous
conflicts with people to whom they were connected by ties of kinship
or sworn oaths. Beowulf's self-delivered epitaph, on the other hand,
indicates how different his life has actually been from that of the con-
ventional legendary hero, and it is one of several significant passages in
the poem to have such an effect.

Furthermore, while the connection that Beowulf makes between moral
transgression and posthumous judgment is absent from the analogue in
Sigurðarkviða in skamma, it happens to be paralleled within Beowulf over
two thousand lines earlier when the hero condemns Unferth to hell for
killing his own brothers. Unferth, believing that Beowulf lost a swim-
ming contest to Breca, doubts that the newcomer will be able to defeat
Grendel. In response to Unferth's impugning speech, the hero explains
that he did not really lose: the two swimmers were separated, and Be-
owulf killed various sea monsters before returning to land, which shows
that he has experience in the domain of monster-slaying. In the course of
his rebuttal, Beowulf says that neither Unferth nor Breca has committed
comparable deeds, though Unferth has killed his own brothers:

> Breca næfre gīt
> æt heaðolāce,   nē gehwæþer incer,
> swā dēorlice   dǣd gefremede
> fāgum sweordum   —nō ic þæs [fela] gylpe—
> þēah ðū þīnum brōðrum   tō banan wurde,
> hēafodmǣgum;   þæs þū in helle scealt
> werhðo drēogan,   þēah þīn wit duge. (ll. 583b–589)

(Breca has never yet at swordplay, nor either of you, accom-
plished so daring a deed with chased swords—I boast little about

<hr/>

7. For an overview of the numerous sources that relate legends of Sigurðr, see Finch, *Saga
of the Volsungs*, ix–xxxii. See also Theodore M. Andersson, *The Legend of Brynhild* (Ithaca, NY:
Cornell University Press, 1980).

it—though you turned out to be your brothers' killer, your closest kinsmen's, for which you will suffer damnation in hell, clever as you are.)

The alignment in thought between these words and the hero's last words is significant. It demonstrates, first, that even if it is conventional for a hero to consider matters of oaths and kinship in his final moments, this convention has been thoroughly assimilated into its new context in *Beowulf*, where it is now linked to a concern for posthumous judgment. Second, the connection between these two passages, one appearing at the beginning of the hero's career and the other at its end, demonstrates that neither can be dismissed as a case of careless slippage, in which a Christian poet thoughtlessly placed Christian sentiment into a pagan character's mouth. Beowulf is consistently characterized as being in possession of intuitions about posthumous judgment, which are also expressed in his remark about the mortally wounded Grendel:

> nō þȳ leng leofað   lāðgetēona
> synnum geswenced,   ac hyne sār hafað
> in nīðgripe   nearwe befongen,
> balwon bendum;   ðǣr ābīdan sceal
> maga māne fāh   miclan dōmes,
> hū him scīr metod   scrīfan wille. (ll. 974–979)

(the hostile attacker is living no longer afflicted by his crimes, but pain has wrapped him tight in its insidious grasp, in deadly restraints; there the young man stained with guilt shall await the great judgment, how radiant Providence will prescribe for him.)

Beowulf's intuitive monotheism does not make him unique within the world of the poem, since most characters in the foreground use expressions reflective of belief in a single deity: all of the poem's exemplary figures, who abstain from kin-slaying and oath-breaking, are represented as intuitive monotheists. Yet the hero's monotheistic vision, asserted throughout the poem and integrated into his death song, certainly sets him apart from Sigurd and other legendary heroes, who die believing that their deeds are overseen by a cruel fate rather than a benevolent deity.

The contrast between Beowulf and the traditional hero of migration-period legend—a contrast not limited to the heroes of the Vǫlsung cycle—becomes more apparent when his death song is contrasted with that of Hildebrand, preserved in the fragmentary *Hildibrands Sterbelied* in *Ásmundar saga kappabana* and in a fuller Latin version in Saxo Grammaticus's *Gesta Danorum*. Hildebrand, mortally wounded by his half brother Ásmundr, begins his death song by reflecting on how fate has pitted two brothers against each other and caused one of them to become the other's killer. Hildebrand then calls attention to his sword, which signals his kinship with Ásmundr, and to his shield, on which markings have been carved for all of the men he has killed in the course of his life. At the head of the shield, he notes, there is a mark for his own son:

> Liggr þar enn svási   sonr at hǫfði,
> eptirerfingi,   er ek eiga gat, ·
> . . .
> óviliandi   aldrs syniaðak

(There lies my own dear son at my head, the heir that I begot to be my own. Against my will I took his life.)[8]

Though this terse allusion is not elaborated in the death song, it plainly refers to the incident recounted in the Old High German *Hildebrandslied*, where Hildebrand is forced to do battle with Hadubrand, the son from whom he was separated during thirty years in exile. Encountering each other as the champions of clashing armies, Hildebrand indicates to Hadubrand that they are kinsmen, but the son considers it a ruse and insists on combat, compelling his father to commit filicide. Hildebrand's rueful reflection on his lack of an "after-heir" (*eptirerfingi*) is paralleled in Beowulf's final speech, which begins with the hero regretting that he has no son, no "heir" (*yrfeweard*, l. 2731a), to receive his war gear.[9] But whereas Beowulf has simply failed to produce an offspring for reasons that are never made clear, Hildebrand lacks his son and heir because he happens to have killed him. Hildebrand, unlike Beowulf, cannot take satisfaction in his final hour that God need not blame him for kin-slaying. Hildebrand dies only with thoughts of the cruelty and intransigence of

---

8. The text is cited from Heusler and Ranisch, *Eddica minora*, 54. The translation is cited from J. Knight Bostock, "The Lay of Hildebrand," in *A Handbook on Old High German Literature*, rev. K. C. King and D. R. McLintock, 2nd ed. (Oxford: Clarendon Press, 1976), 43–82, at 70.

9. See Harris, "Beowulf's Last Words," 16.

fate, which has caused him to kill his son and be killed by his brother. In the fuller version of the death song preserved by Saxo, his final words are the following:

> Sed quecunque ligat Parcarum prescius ordo,
> Quecunque arcanum supere rationis adumbrat
> Seu que fatorum serie preuisa tenentur,
> Nulla caducarum rerum conuersio tollet.

(Whatever foreknown links are fastened by the Fates,
whatever the mysteries of divine reason sketch out,
whatever events are foreseen and held in the sequence
of destiny, no change in our transitory world will cancel.)[10]

Hildebrand's perspective on his life resembles that of Angantýr, as expressed in the lament at the conclusion of *Hlǫðskviða*, discussed in the previous chapter. Compelled to become the killer of his brother, Angantýr garners our sympathy by decrying, in the poem's final line, the cruelty of his fate: "the Norns' doom is evil" ("illr er dómr Norna"). The presence of the Parcae at the end of the Latin rendering of Hildebrand's death song almost certainly indicates that Saxo was translating a vernacular poem that concluded, like *Hlǫðskviða*, with the protagonist referring to the Norns and the outrageous fate they wove for him.[11] The perspectives of Hildebrand and Angantýr, as they look back on the moral transgressions that fate prompted them to commit, differ considerably from the perspective of Beowulf, who dies believing that a single, benevolent deity sits in judgment over the life he led.

The sympathetic character of the speeches delivered by Hildebrand and Angantýr suggests, moreover, that the traditional heroes of migration-period legend were viewed in the aftermath of their moral transgressions not with condemnation but with a combination of sympathy and admiration. These kin-slaying heroes were, in the words of R. W. Chambers, "rather to be pitied than blamed."[12] Accordingly, it would appear that when Beowulf condemns Unferth to hell for having killed his own brothers, we are witnessing a salient departure from the ethical norms

---

10. The text and translation are cited from Friis-Jensen, *Saxo Grammaticus*, 1:508–9.

11. On the connection between the Norns and the Parcae, see Bauschatz, *The Well and the Tree*, 8–11; Jochens, *Old Norse Images of Women*, 39–41.

12. R. W. Chambers, *Beowulf: An Introduction to the Study of the Poem with a Discussion of the Stories of Offa and Finn*, rev. C. L. Wrenn, 3rd ed. (Cambridge: Cambridge University Press, 1959), 29.

of antecedent legendary tradition. The legend of Unferth is not re-
corded in any extant source, but there are at least two reasons to doubt
that he was known to have killed his brothers in an entirely sinister or
underhanded manner. First, Unferth occupies a position of importance
at the Danish court: he is a confidant of the king, an official counselor
or spokesperson, seated near the royal family. If Unferth had acquired
a reputation for treachery on account of shameful deeds that were
known throughout Scandinavia, it is doubtful that he would be able
to hold this respected position. Second, a legend that told of Unferth
killing his brothers in an unambiguously evil manner would be at odds
with the generic conventions of Germanic legend, where moral ambigu-
ity prevails and kin-slaying normally results from a conflict of ethical
imperatives. In view of these two considerations, the likeliest backstory
for Unferth is one in which loyalty to his lord prevailed over loyalty
to his kinsmen: in a conflict that pitted his lord against his brothers,
Unferth decided that the oath he swore to Hrothgar took precedence
over the ties of kinship; he chose to become a kin-slayer rather than an
oath-breaker. Unferth would emerge from such a backstory meriting
not condemnation but admiration for having, in Phillpotts's words,
"the courage to choose" under circumstances that would have crushed
a lesser individual.[13]

What appears novel about the *Beowulf* poet's perspective on kin-slaying
and oath-breaking is not his disapproval of these two deeds but his
conviction that such disapproval should guide the composition of a
heroic-legendary epic. *Beowulf* exhibits a kind of moral absolutism that
is absent from the other witnesses to migration-period legend, where
circumstances justify and arguably exonerate a hero driven to commit
one moral transgression in order to avoid committing another. There is
no sense in the aforementioned witnesses that Angantýr or Hildebrand

---

13. Phillpotts, "Wyrd and Providence," 14. For reconstructions of Unferth's backstory
comparable to the one adumbrated here, see George Clark, *Beowulf* (Boston: Twayne, 1990),
65; Gernot R. Wieland, "The Unferth Enigma: The *Þyle* between the Hero and the Poet," in
*Fact and Fiction from the Middle Ages to Modern Times: Essays Presented to Hans Sauer on the Occa-
sion of His 65th Birthday—Part II*, ed. Renate Bauer and Ulrike Krischke (Frankfurt am Main:
Peter Lang, 2011), 35–46. For other assessments of Unferth consistent with this reconstruc-
tion, see J. D. A. Ogilvy, "Unferth: Foil to Beowulf?," *PMLA* 79, no. 4 (1964): 370–75; Geoffrey
Hughes, "Beowulf, Unferth and Hrunting: An Interpretation," *English Studies* 58, no. 5 (1977):
385–95; John C. Pope, "*Beowulf* 505, 'Gehedde,' and the Pretensions of Unferth," in *Modes of
Interpretation in Old English Literature: Essays in Honour of Stanley B. Greenfield*, ed. Phyllis Rugg
Brown, Georgia Ronan Crampton, and Fred C. Robinson (Toronto: University of Toronto
Press, 1986), 173–87.

are terrible people deserving of an eternity in hell; they are wretches, who warrant some amount of sympathy for their misfortune. It is not a coincidence that Old English *wrecca*, the ancestor of Modern English "wretch," happened to be a standard word for "hero."[14] There is a sense in *Beowulf*, however, that Unferth is a morally defective character who deserves an eternity in hell regardless of the circumstances that might have led him to kill his kinsmen. Indeed, the poet's untraditional absolutism—the unconditional nature of his disapproval of kin-slaying and oath-breaking—seems to have informed the selection of the peculiar protagonist of *Beowulf*, as it evidently drove the poet to create a moral exemplar out of a folkloric hero, who was known in antecedent tradition only for swimming contests and monster fights, not for killing kinsmen or breaking oaths.[15] Beyond the selection of the protagonist, and the persistent contrast between this protagonist and the traditional heroes of migration-period legend, there are several other respects in which the composition of *Beowulf* appears to have been shaped by the poet's discomfort with the moral ambiguity of antecedent tradition, that is to say, by his refusal to valorize a character known to have killed kinsmen or broken oaths.

It is significant that after the protagonist, the character accorded the greatest prominence in *Beowulf* is Hrothgar, another migration-period king who appears to have lived a life unstained by kin-slaying or oath-breaking. Within *Beowulf*, Hrothgar is depicted as a courteous, wise, pious, and generous king; there is no hint that he committed either of the two major moral transgressions. The poem's allusions to the rivalry between the Danes and the Heathobards suggest that the poet knew a tradition in which Hrothgar and Halga avenged Healfdene by killing Froda, but the poet probably viewed this as a positive accomplishment rather than a moral defect: the protagonist expresses a positive view of vengeance (ll. 1384–1385), and as Dorothy Whitelock observes, "killing for the sake of vengeance was not felt to be incompatible with Christian

---

14. For discussion of *wrecca*, see Michael D. Cherniss, *Ingeld and Christ: Heroic Concepts and Values in Old English Christian Poetry* (The Hague: Mouton, 1972), 102–19; J. R. R. Tolkien, *Finn and Hengest*, 64–66; Griffith, "Some Difficulties in *Beowulf*," 37–40; Scott Gwara, *Heroic Identity in the World of Beowulf* (Leiden: Brill, 2008), 12–25. See also the discussion of this word later in the present chapter.

15. On the probable presence of the figure of Beowulf in narrative traditions prior to the composition of *Beowulf*, see Benson, "Originality of Beowulf"; Neidorf, "Beowulf before *Beowulf*"; Leneghan, *Dynastic Drama of Beowulf*, 104–52. On the derivation of Beowulf ultimately from folkloric traditions, see especially Stitt, *Beowulf and the Bear's Son*.

ethics at any period in Anglo-Saxon times."[16] Outside of *Beowulf*, the sources that mention Hrothgar (Old Norse *Róarr* or *Ró*) consistently convey the impression that he was a minor figure in legendary tradition, less remarkable than his brothers, known for the uneventful character of his reign. The *Chronicon Lethrense* (ca. 1170) records that he established the town of Roskilde and then did nothing further: "King Ro lived in such peace that no man drew a sword against him, nor did he himself lead any expedition abroad." The *Skjǫldunga saga* (ca. 1200) similarly records that after Hrothgar and Halga avenged Healfdene and inherited the kingdom, "Roas indeed lived quietly at home, while Helgo lived the life of a sea-raider." The contrast between Hrothgar and Halga was plainly conventional: Saxo Grammaticus adds in the *Gesta Danorum* (ca. 1200) that "Roe was short and spare, while Helgo was rather tall of stature" and confirms that Roe stayed at home while Helgo lived an adventurous life of piracy and lechery.[17]

The account of Hrothgar's life in *Hrólfs saga kraka* (ca. 1400), the fullest account attested outside of *Beowulf*, corroborates the impression that Hrothgar was known in legendary tradition as an unimpressive and unwarlike king. It records that when Hrothgar and Halga avenged their father by killing Froda, the difference between the brothers was already apparent: "At this time Hróarr was twelve years old and Helgi ten, and yet the latter was the bigger and bolder of them." After they perform their one great deed together, the author reiterates the contrast between the sons of Healfdene: "These brothers were by nature different in character. Hróarr was a cheerful and easy-going man, but Helgi a very warlike man, and he was more highly thought of." The saga then has Hróarr settle in England, where he marries the daughter of the king of Northumbria. Hróarr thereafter relinquishes his right to rule over the kingdom that he obtained with Helgi, saying to him: "You are certainly the better man of us two, and because of the fact that I have settled myself in Northumberland, I am very willing to grant you this kingdom which we both held in common, if you are willing to share some precious possession with me."[18] Hróarr then asks for and receives one splendid ring, which

---

16. Dorothy Whitelock, *The Audience of Beowulf* (Oxford: Clarendon Press, 1951), 13. On the feud between the Danes and the Heathobards, see Fulk et al., *Klaeber's Beowulf*, lv–lvii.

17. G. N. Garmonsway and Jacqueline Simpson, eds. and trans., *Beowulf and Its Analogues* (New York: Dutton, 1971), 128, 129.

18. Garmonsway and Simpson, *Beowulf and Its Analogues*, 133, 139.

will eventually bring about his demise by earning him the enmity of Hrókr. While the story of the ring appears to be a late development unknown to the *Beowulf* poet, the speech that Hróarr delivers to Helgi, in which he calls him the better man, seems to draw on a traditional characterization of the humble king that existed prior to *Beowulf*. This tradition is perhaps reflected in Hrothgar's view of his older brother, Heorogar, whom he briefly eulogizes with the remark: "he was better than I" ("sē wæs betera ðonne ic," l. 469b). Furthermore, the tradition that Halga was more impressive than Hrothgar might be registered in the genealogical line that lists the three sons of Healfdene: "Heorogar and Hrothgar and Halga the good" ("Heorogār ond Hrōðgār ond Hālga til," l. 61). The epithet attached to Halga's name might imply that although he was the youngest, he was the most renowned of the three sons.

The sources external to *Beowulf* consistently suggest that Hrothgar, like the poem's protagonist, was not celebrated in antecedent legendary tradition for committing moral transgressions or displaying an inflexible devotion to heroic ideals. It seems that he was known for being a small, humble, and retiring king who performed one admirable deed under the leadership of his younger brother, then spent the rest of his life at home, where he would eventually meet his end. As M. G. Clarke observes, "in no Scandinavian authority does Ro play an important part: his personality is, on the other hand, distinctly colourless."[19] The sources differ as to how Hrothgar dies, but they agree on him dying in his own hall.[20] Within *Beowulf*, there is a passage that might be construed to mean that Hrothgar died peacefully of old age. As the hero departs from Denmark, the narrator offers a final assessment of Hrothgar before he steps out of the poem's foreground:

> þæt wæs ān cyning
> æghwæs orleahtre,   oþ þæt hine yldo benam
> mægenes wynnum,   sē þe oft manegum scōd. (ll. 1885b–1887)

---

19. M. G. Clarke, *Sidelights on Teutonic History during the Migration Period, Being Studies from Beowulf and Other Old English Poems* (Cambridge: Cambridge University Press, 1911), 91.

20. Sifting through the material, William Cooke observes that the sources present "clear traces of a tradition that Hróar (= Hrothgar) died in a fight corresponding to the repulse of Ingeld's host from Heorot." See Cooke, "Hrothulf: A Richard III, or an Alfred the Great?," *Studies in Philology* 104, no. 2 (2007): 175-98, at 186. A particularly clear trace of this tradition inheres in Saxo's statement that Roe was killed by Hothbrodus, a figure whose name derives from the Heathobard ethnonym.

(that was a unique king in all respects without fault, until old age, which has often robbed many, deprived him of the satisfactions of strength.)

If this passage does not indicate that the peerless king died of natural causes, then it might be taken to mean that Hrothgar was killed during Ingeld's attack on Heorot because he was old and weakened at the time of this battle. The *Beowulf* poet clearly knew a tradition in which Hrothgar's plan to foster peace between the Danes and Heathobards following the deaths of Healfdene and Froda would fail and culminate in Ingeld burning down Heorot (see ll. 81b–85, ll. 2024a–2069b). Since the allusion to this legend in *Widsith* (ll. 45–49) indicates that the Danes were ultimately victorious on this occasion, it might be the case that Ingeld killed Hrothgar and burned down Heorot, but Hrothulf then killed Ingeld and oversaw the destruction of the entire Heathobardic force. Regardless of how the web of allusions is untangled, Hrothgar emerges from them as a rather innocent figure who committed one justified act of violence alongside his brother, then sought peace by marrying his daughter to the son of his slain opponent, and then was perhaps killed when his diplomatic efforts failed. Instead of being an oath-breaker, Hrothgar appears to have died as the victim of a broken oath, if he did not merely die of old age.

By all appearances, then, if there were a traditional death song attributed to Hrothgar, it could contain the epitaph that Beowulf constructed for himself, the passage with which this chapter began. Especially clear is that Hrothgar could boast, as he reflects on his fifty-year (or longer) reign, that he was a sedentary and unadventurous king. Hrothgar, like Beowulf, could assert in his final moments: "I lived out at home my allotment of time, managed well what was mine, did not go looking for unwarranted aggression" ("Ic on earde bād / mǣlgesceafta, hēold mīn tela, / ne sōhte searonīðas," ll. 2736b–2738a). The ease with which Beowulf's words could be placed into Hrothgar's mouth suggests, once again, that Beowulf's epitaph reflects ideas that shaped the poem's composition. Far from being an undigested vestige of tradition, Beowulf's statement that he stayed at home, broke no oaths, and killed no kinsmen appears to reveal the set of criteria that the poet used to select the two characters who would dominate the poem's foreground and receive the largest speaking roles. Although the poet knew traditions pertaining to dozens of migration-period heroes, he chose these two characters— a folkloric monster-slayer and a sedentary, pacifistic king—to present before his audience as the central moral exemplars, whom he uses to illustrate courteous behavior and dispense monotheistic wisdom. As we shall see throughout the present chapter, the poet's preference for these two blank slates reflects a more pervasive reluctance to valorize characters who were known in legendary tradition to have killed kinsmen or broken oaths. The poet evidently could not bring himself to depict such characters as courteous monotheists worthy of his audience's admiration and emulation. This reservation appears to have guided the poet in his determination of what material from antecedent tradition was suitable for sustained and favorable representation in the poem's foreground.

The foregoing considerations provide an explanation for the poet's curious treatment of Hrothulf, the son of Halga, who is depicted in *Beowulf* as a shadowy and enigmatic figure. To judge from the references in both *Beowulf* and *Widsith*, Hrothulf appears to have been known in Old English tradition as Hrothgar's *subregulus* or subordinate coruler, a position he might have assumed when his father died (Halga having previously been the coruler of Denmark with Hrothgar).[21] Yet despite the prominent position he occupies at the Danish court, Hrothulf is never given the opportunity to speak in *Beowulf*. His presence at Heorot is acknowledged on only three occasions in the poem, and every time he is mentioned, there is a hint that strife between kinsmen will eventually afflict the Danish royal family. On the first occasion, Hrothgar and Hrothulf are seen drinking together, and then the narrator comments:

> Heorot innan wæs
> frēondum āfylled;   nalles fācenstafas
> Þēod-Scyldingas   þenden fremedon. (ll. 1017b–1019)

(Heorot's interior was filled with friends; at that time the Nation-Scyldings did not at all practice treachery.)

The hint of future strife is reiterated in the second reference to Hrothulf, where he is depicted sitting beside Hrothgar at the great banquet following Beowulf's victory over Grendel:

---

21. See Cooke, "Hrothulf," 179; Bruce Mitchell, "Literary Lapses: Six Notes on *Beowulf* and Its Critics," *Review of English Studies* 43, no. 169 (1992): 1–17, at 13; Gerald Morgan, "The Treachery of Hrothulf," *English Studies* 53, no. 1 (1972): 23–39, at 29; Clarke, *Sidelights on Teutonic History*, 92. On the custom of joint kingship, see Frederick M. Biggs, "The Politics of Succession in *Beowulf* and Anglo-Saxon England," *Speculum* 80, no. 3 (2005): 709–41.

> Þā cwōm Wealhþēo forð
> gān under gyldnum bēage,   þǣr þā gōdan twēgen
> sǣton suhtergefæderan;   þā gyt wæs hiera sib ætgædere,
> ǣghwylc ōðrum trȳwe. (ll. 1162b–1165a)

(Then Wealhtheow came forward walking under a golden collar where the two good men sat, nephew and paternal uncle; they were still joined in friendship, each true to the other.)

The third reference to Hrothulf suggests the scenario that would engender the eventual turmoil between Scylding kinsmen. Wealhtheow, concerned that Hrothgar intends to make Beowulf an eligible heir to the throne, encourages her husband to leave the throne to his kinsmen and expresses a belief that Hrothulf will be kind to his predecessor's offspring:

> Mē man sægde   þæt þū ðē for sunu wolde
> hereri[n]c habban.   Heorot is gefǣlsod,
> bēahsele beorhta;   brūc þenden þū mōte
> maniġra mēdo,   ond þīnum māgum lǣf
> folc ond rīċe   þonne ðū forð scyle,
> metodsceaft sēōn.   Iċ mīnne can
> glædne Hrōþulf,   þæt hē þā geogoðe wile
> ārum healdan   gyf þū ǣr þonne hē,
> wine Scildinga,   worold oflǣtest;
> wēne ic þæt hē mid gōde   gyldan wille
> uncran eaferan   gif hē þæt eal gemon,
> hwæt wit tō willan   ond tō wyrðmyndum
> umborwesendum ǣr   ārna gefremedon. (ll. 1175–1187)

(I have been informed that you wished to take the warrior [i.e., Beowulf] as your son. Heorot is purged, the bright ring-hall; make use, while you are permitted, of your many blessings, and leave to your family the nation and the rule when you shall go forth to witness the decree of Providence. I know my gracious Hrothulf, that he will treat the young warriors honorably if you, friend of Scyldings, depart the world before he; I expect he will repay our sons with good if he remembers everything, what favors we did to his contentment and to his dignity before, when he was a child.)

A substantial critical literature has developed around this series of passages. A consensus formed among the major critics of the first half of the twentieth century holding that these passages implied treachery on the part of Hrothulf, whose possible crimes include usurpation of the throne, murder of his cousins, and perhaps even murder of his uncle.[22] A reaction to this consensus eventually set in, however, with many critics seeking to exonerate Hrothulf of any wrongdoing and arguing that the text does not necessarily incriminate him.[23] Proponents of the latter view sometimes hold that there is actually no turmoil looming in Heorot and that the throne will pass peacefully to Hrothulf, who will behave in the manner that Wealhtheow has envisioned. Under this interpretation, the passages cited above can be construed as allusions to acts of kin-slaying perpetuated not by Hrothulf but by his cousin Heoroweard, the son of Heorogar, a claimant to the throne who was slighted when it passed to Hrothgar.[24] This reconstruction receives strong support from the poem's analogues, which consistently identify Heoroweard (Old Norse Hjǫrvarðr) as the killer of Hrothulf and do not generally depict Hrothulf as the killer of his cousins.[25] Yet while the

---

22. See Kemp Malone, "Hrethric," *PMLA* 42, no. 2 (1927): 268–313; William Witherle Lawrence, *Beowulf and Epic Tradition* (Cambridge, MA: Harvard University Press, 1928), at 73–79; Adrien Bonjour, *The Digressions in Beowulf* (Oxford: Basil Blackwell, 1950), 31, 60; Klaeber, *Beowulf*, 169; Arthur Gilchrist Brodeur, *The Art of Beowulf* (Berkeley: University of California Press, 1959), 156; Chambers, *Beowulf*, 447–50. Though criticized, the original consensus position has continued to receive credence from the mid-twentieth century to the present. See Rolf H. Bremmer Jr., "The Importance of Kinship: Uncle and Nephew in *Beowulf*," *Amsterdamer Beiträge zur älteren Germanistik* 15, no. 1 (1980): 21–38, at 38; Fred C. Robinson, "History, Religion, Culture: The Background Necessary for Teaching *Beowulf*," in *Approaches to Teaching Masterpieces of World Literature*, ed. Jess B. Bessinger Jr. and Robert F. Yeager (New York: Modern Language Association of America, 1984), 107–22, at 109; Sam Newton, *The Origins of Beowulf and the Pre-Viking Kingdom of East Anglia* (Cambridge: D. S. Brewer, 1993), 83–91; Biggs, "Politics of Succession," 710; Richard North, "Hrothulf's Childhood and Beowulf's: A Comparison," in *Childhood and Adolescence in Anglo-Saxon Literary Culture*, ed. Susan Irvine and Winfried Rudolf (Toronto: University of Toronto Press, 2018), 222–43, at 243.

23. The pivotal publication here is Kenneth Sisam, *The Structure of Beowulf* (Oxford: Clarendon Press, 1965), 34–39, 80–82, though the consensus had previously been queried in Clarke, *Sidelights on Teutonic History*, 91–101. See also Morgan, "Treachery of Hrothulf"; John D. Niles, *Beowulf: The Poem and Its Tradition* (Cambridge, MA: Harvard University Press, 1983), 174–75; Helen Damico, *Beowulf's Wealhtheow and the Valkyrie Tradition* (Madison: University of Wisconsin Press, 1984), 20; Mitchell, "Literary Lapses," 10–14; John M. Hill, *The Anglo-Saxon Warrior Ethic: Reconstructing Lordship in Early English Literature* (Gainesville: University Press of Florida, 2000), 71–73; Michael D. C. Drout, "Blood and Deeds: The Inheritance Systems in *Beowulf*," *Studies in Philology* 104, no. 2 (2007): 199–226, at 219–24; Marijane Osborn, "The Alleged Murder of Hrethric in *Beowulf*," *Traditio* 74 (2019): 153–77.

24. See Cooke, "Hrothulf," 184; Osborn, "Alleged Murder of Hrethric," 174–77.

25. Heoroweard is recorded as the killer of Hrothulf in *Chronicon Lethrense*, *Skjǫldunga saga*, *Gesta Danorum*, *Annales Ryenses*, and *Hrólfs saga kraka*. Hrothulf is said to be the killer of a figure apparently corresponding to Hrethric only in *Bjarkamál*, which is preserved in Saxo's Latin

effort to exonerate Hrothulf is supported by the analogues, it has forced its proponents to produce rather unnatural readings of the text of *Beowulf* itself, which hints at strife between kinsmen whenever Hrothulf is mentioned. Such ominous treatment of this character suggests that the poet knew a tradition about him that was lost prior to the recording of the analogues. In view of the unique preservation in *Beowulf* of the names of both of Hrothgar's children (Hrothmund and Hrethric) as well as the names of his wife (Wealhtheow), counselor (Unferth), and older brother (Heorogar), it is reasonable to suppose that the poet knew stories that fell out of circulation before later authors recorded what they knew about the Scylding dynasty.

The conjectural reconstruction of the legendary tradition known to the *Beowulf* poet that might make the greatest sense of the internal and external evidence is one that combines and modifies the positions outlined above: a dispute over patrimony between Hrothulf and the sons of Hrothgar will result in bad outcomes for the children of Hrothgar, per-haps death for Hrothmund (who is forgotten in later sources)[26] and exile for Hrethric; after Hrothulf assumes the throne, he will be killed by his cousin Heoroweard; and after Heoroweard is killed by one of Hrothulf's retainers, Hrethric will return from exile and become the king of Denmark. This reconstruction would explain why the *Beowulf* poet hints at strife between kinsmen whenever Hrothulf is mentioned, while also explaining why the analogues maintain that Hrothulf was killed by Heoroweard and succeeded by Hrethric.[27] The supposition that Hrethric assumes the throne after a period in exile explains, moreover, why Beowulf extends him an invitation to spend time at the Geatish court (ll. 1836–1839). Furthermore, in this reconstructed

---

rendering in the *Gesta Danorum*. Many scholars have reasonably construed this reference as an indicator that Hrothulf killed Hrethric, but there are cogent reasons to refrain from identifying Hrothulf's victim with the son of Hrothgar in *Beowulf*. See Cooke, "Hrothulf," 187–89; Osborn, "Alleged Murder of Hrethric," 163–65.

26. On Hrothmund and his possible presence in the East Anglian Royal Genealogy, see Newton, *Origins of Beowulf*, 77–104.

27. Hrethric is listed as a king of Denmark after Hrothulf in *Skjǫldunga saga*, *Langfeðgatal*, *Gesta Danorum*, and the *Codex Runicus*. See Osborn, "Alleged Murder of Hrethric," 171–73; Cooke, "Hrothulf," 191–92. A particularly clear indicator that the Hrethric who ruled after Hrothulf should be identified with the son of Hrothgar materializes in *Skjǫldunga saga*, which records that Heoroweard "was succeeded by Rolfo's kinsman Rærecus, who was a paternal cousin to Rolfo's father Helgo" ("successit Rolfonis consanguineus Rærecus, qui Helgoni Rolfonis patri fuit patruelis"). The text and translation are cited from Fulk et al., *Klaeber's Beowulf*, 305. On the exceptional value of *Skjǫldunga saga* as a witness to Scylding tradition, see Jakob Benediktsson, "Icelandic Traditions of the Scyldings," *Saga-Book* 15 (1957–59): 48–66.

scenario, it is unlikely that Hrothulf is a sinister figure who treacherously murders his cousins or his uncle, as some proponents of the original consensus had imagined. Such behavior would be out of place in migration-period legend, which tends not to present characters as purely evil or purely good. To judge from the dispute over patrimony represented in *Hlǫðskviða*, the falling-out between Hrothulf and his cousins likely occurred when one party felt insulted or denied their proper place: perhaps Hrothulf was willing to make the young Hrethric a subordinate king with control of a part of the country, but Hrethric refused to settle for less than equal rulership, and warfare became inevitable. If Hrothulf is a reluctant kin-slayer comparable to Angantýr, the trust that Wealhtheow places in him also makes greater sense. Hrothulf would not then be an evil character, like Richard III, who killed children to usurp a throne; rather, he would be a good-natured hero compelled by circumstances to fight against, and perhaps kill, his own kinsmen. In his dying moments, Hrothulf might have resembled Hildebrand, a hero who was fated to kill one kinsman and be killed by another.

Even if the conjectural reconstruction propounded above were incorrect and the traditions about Hrothulf known to the *Beowulf* poet were identical to those recorded in later sources, a poet concerned about the moral ambiguity of his inherited material would have good reason to prefer Hrothgar over Hrothulf and make the former a central figure while consigning the latter to a shadowy periphery. Even if Hrothulf were not known to have killed his own kinsmen, the other traditions concerning this character make him less suitable than Hrothgar for development into an exemplar compatible with the poet's moral aims. For one, the analogues record with remarkable consistency that Hrothulf was the spawn of an incestuous union between Halga and Yrse, who were both unaware of their kinship at the time (Yrse being the daughter of a woman whom Halga raped).[28] The analogues also indicate that Hrothulf was a less sedentary king than Hrothgar, as they consistently relate stories of Hrothulf's adventures in Sweden, where he fought against his father-in-law, Eadgils, who married Yrse after Halga died.[29] Finally, it is clear from the analogues that Hrothulf

---

28. Hrothulf's incestuous origin is referenced in *Grottasǫngr*, *Chronicon Lethrense*, *Gesta Danorum*, *Ynglinga saga*, *Skjǫldunga saga*, and *Hrólfs saga kraka*. For discussion, see Earl, "Forbidden *Beowulf*," 295–96; North, "Hrothulf's Childhood and Beowulf's," 224–28.

29. Hrothulf's conflict with Eadgils is referenced in *Gesta Danorum*, *Ynglinga saga*, *Skáldskaparmál*, *Skjǫldunga saga*, and *Hrólfs saga kraka*. For discussion, see T. A. Shippey, "*Hrólfs saga kraka* and the Legend of Lejre," in *Making History: Essays on the Fornaldarsögur*, ed. Martin

did not live to see an old age, as they never convey the impression that he was elderly at the time when Heoroweard invaded his hall and killed him. In view of the differences between Hrothgar and Hrothulf (differences conventionally stressed in comparisons between Hrothgar and Halga), one must wonder if the *Beowulf* poet has not modified inherited tradition by situating his monster fights during the reign of Hrothgar. In *Hrólfs saga kraka*, monsters haunt the Danish royal hall and are exterminated by an ursine hero during Hrothulf's reign. It is impossible to know which king suffered from monstrous incursions in the tradition that antedated *Beowulf*—perhaps multiple Scylding rulers were plagued by monsters—but it is clear, in any event, that such a modification would be consistent with the poet's broader aim to minimize Hrothulf and focus attention on Hrothgar. While Hrothulf says nothing, Hrothgar is developed into an altogether faultless (*æghwæs orleahtre*) king to be pitied for his suffering and admired for his wisdom and magnanimity.[30]

In addition to Beowulf and Hrothgar, there are six other named characters who play a role in the poem's foreground: Unferth, Wealhtheow, Hygelac, Hygd, Wiglaf, and Wulfgar. What sets these named characters apart from all the others mentioned in *Beowulf* is that they are depicted speaking or acting in the poem's present, not in digressions that pertain to past or future events. Of these six characters, only one of them, Unferth, is said to have committed the standard heroic transgression of kin-slaying. The poem offers no hints that the other five characters either committed or possessed any reason to commit such deeds. Sources external to the poem provide no further information about the deeds of Wealhtheow, Hygd, Wiglaf, and Wulfgar, but Frankish historians confirm what is said in *Beowulf* about the death of Hygelac, namely, that he perished during a failed raid in Frankish territory. The narrator affirms that the raid was undertaken on account of "pride" (*wlenco*, l. 1206a), which might mean that Hygelac was guilty of seeking the kind of "unwarranted aggression" (*searoníðas*, l. 2738a) that

---

Arnold and Alison Finlay (London: Viking Society for Northern Research, 2010), 17–32, at 27–29.

30. It is perhaps significant in this regard that the *Widsith* poet places Hrothulf before Hrothgar in the verse containing both of their names ("Hrōþwulf ond Hrōðgār," l. 45a), whereas the *Beowulf* poet has the order reversed ("Hrōðgār ond Hrōþulf," l. 1017a). The priority accorded Hrothulf in *Widsith* strengthens the likelihood that Hrothgar was the less significant figure in legendary tradition even before *Beowulf* was composed and that the *Beowulf* poet elevated Hrothgar on account of the less colorful life that he led.

the protagonist, in his final words, rejoices in having avoided.[31] Yet even if Hygelac receives some criticism for his proud miscalculation, there is no suggestion that his possible possession of the conventional heroic flaw of *ofermōd* (excessive self-confidence) makes him a malevolent figure worthy of condemnation. Indeed, the one speech that Hygelac delivers in the poem's foreground conveys a decidedly positive impression of him. He greets a returning Beowulf with the following words:

> Hū lomp ēow on lāde,   lēofa Bīowulf,
> þā ðū fǣringa   feorr gehogodest
> sæcce sēcean   ofer sealt wæter,
> hilde tō Hiorote?   Ac ðū Hrōðgāre
> wīdcūðne wēan   wihte gebēttest,
> mǣrum ðēodne?   Ic ðæs mōdceare
> sorhwylmum sēað,   sīðe ne truwode
> lēofes mannes;   ic ðē lange bæd
> þæt ðū þone wælgǣst   wihte ne grētte,
> lēte Sūð-Dene   sylfe geweorðan
> gūðe wið Grendel.   Gode ic þanc secge
> þæs ðe ic ðē gesundne   gesēon mōste. (ll. 1987–1988)

(How did things turn out for you on your trip, dear Beowulf, after you suddenly determined to go look for action far over the salt water, combat at Heorot? Did you at all ease the celebrated suffering of that renowned lord Hrothgar? I seethed with heavy waves of apprehension over that, did not feel assured about the valued man's undertaking; I repeatedly asked you not to approach the butchering spirit at all, let the South-Danes themselves settle

---

31. There is considerable divergence in critical assessments of Hygelac. For readings of Hygelac as a reckless and unwise king, see Kaske, "Sigemund-Heremod and Hama-Hygelac Passages," 490; R. E. Kaske, "Hygelac and Hygd," in *Studies in Old English Literature in Honor of Arthur G. Brodeur*, ed. Stanley B. Greenfield (Eugene: University of Oregon Press, 1963), 200–206; Fred C. Robinson, "The Significance of Names in Old English Literature," *Anglia* 86 (1968), 14–58, at 57; Stephen C. Bandy, "Cain, Grendel, and the Giants of *Beowulf*," *Papers on Language and Literature* 9, no. 3 (1973): 235–49, at 245; Edward B. Irving Jr., "Heroic Role-Models: Beowulf and Others," in *Heroic Poetry in the Anglo-Saxon Period: Studies in Honor of Jess B. Bessinger, Jr.*, ed. Helen Damico and John Leyerle (Kalamazoo: Western Michigan University Press, 1993), 347–72, at 361; Alaric Hall, "Hygelac's Only Daughter: A Present, a Potentate and a Peaceweaver in *Beowulf*," *Studia Neophilologica* 78, no. 1 (2006): 81–87. For a more positive assessment of Hygelac and his *wlenco*, see Brodeur, *Art of Beowulf*, 78–87; Lawrence Fast, "Hygelac: A Centripetal Force in *Beowulf*," *Annuale Mediaevale* 12 (1971): 90–98, at 97; T. A. Shippey, *Old English Verse* (London: Hutchison, 1972), 38–39; Dennis Cronan, "Poetic Meanings in the Old English Poetic Vocabulary," *English Studies* 84, no. 5 (2003): 397–425, at 400–401.

their war with Grendel. I give thanks to God that I have been per-
mitted to see you again safe and sound.)

In the course of these eleven lines, the poet establishes that Hygelac
is a pious monotheist and an affectionate kinsman who thanks the
singular deity for the safe return of his beloved nephew. If the poet
wished to denigrate the character of Hygelac and suggest that there was
something fundamentally wrong with him on account of his *wlenco*, it
is doubtful that the king would be depicted as one of the poem's en-
lightened monotheists. Likewise, if Hygelac were to be understood as an
especially foolish or immoral figure, it is doubtful that he would receive
the lifelong affection of a protagonist who is explicitly praised for his
wisdom and virtue (ll. 1840–1845a, 2177–2183a). The significance of
these considerations in the present context is that the poet's refusal
to valorize morally ambiguous heroes plainly did not extend to those
guilty of *wlenco*, a quality attributed to Beowulf himself on two occa-
sions (ll. 338a, 508a). Excessive self-confidence, while perhaps being a
regrettable trait, was not considered by the poet to be objectionable
enough to cast a character out of his poem's foreground. He saw noth-
ing wrong with casting the same positive light on Hygelac that is cast
on the other seven named characters who are represented in the poem's
foreground, with the notable exception of Unferth.

Indeed, the poet's treatment of Unferth differs markedly from his
treatment of all other human characters in the poem. In the fore-
ground, the other characters, unstained by kin-slaying or oath-breaking,
are represented as courteous, noble, pious, heroic figures; in the back-
ground, where kin-slayers and oath-breakers do appear, characters are
represented in a terse and impartial manner. At the end of the digres-
sions on Ingeld and Hengest, for instance, it is not clear what exactly
the poet thinks about these two characters, who were compelled by
circumstances to commit the standard heroic transgressions. The pas-
sages concerning Unferth, however, make it entirely clear that the poet
regards this character negatively and does not want his audience to
perceive Unferth as a character deserving of emulation, admiration, or
sympathy. It is notable that in the twenty-three lines of direct speech
placed into the mouth of Unferth (ll. 506–528), there are no expres-
sions that establish him as a pious monotheist. This absence marks his
speech off from that of Beowulf, Hrothgar, Wealhtheow, Wiglaf, Hy-
gelac, and even the anonymous Danish coastguard, each of whom man-
ages to fit monotheistic language into his or her speech. Furthermore,

when other characters speak, the poet feels little need to identify the psychological motive behind their speech, but when Unferth challenges Beowulf's credibility, the poet announces that his challenge was motivated by feelings of jealousy and insecurity:

> Wæs him Bēowulfes sīð,
> mōdges merefaran,   micel æfþunca,
> forþon þe hē ne ūþe   þæt ænig ōðer man
> æfre mærða þon mā   middangeardes
> gehēdde under heofenum   þonne hē sylfa. (ll. 501b–505)

(The mission of Beowulf, that brave sailor, was to him a severe irritation, since he would not allow that any other man of middle-earth should attend more to glory under the heavens than he himself.)

This momentary glimpse into the mind of Unferth establishes that his behavior toward the newcomer cannot be excused as the perfunctory fulfillment of a traditional role. Carol Clover, in the course of a compelling demonstration that the exchange between Unferth and Beowulf constitutes a traditional Germanic flyting, observes that a challenger like Unferth can function as a "delegate" who speaks not from genuine hostility but from professional obligation.[32] The *Beowulf* poet, perhaps recognizing that his audience might construe Unferth as an innocent delegate who is merely doing his job, explicitly attributes his speech to a characterological flaw in order to circumvent that interpretation and encourage his audience to view Unferth as a sincerely ignoble figure whose vanity causes him to feel vexation at the arrival of a philanthropic monster-slayer for fear that the newcomer's reputation could eclipse his own.

There is a notable discrepancy in *Beowulf* between the respect Unferth receives from the Danes and the contempt he receives from the poet. The divergence is made clear in the following passage, which registers that Unferth was seated at the banquet in close proximity to Hrothgar and Hrothulf:

> Swylce þær Ūnferþ þyle
> æt fōtum sæt frēan Scyldinga;   gehwylc hiora his ferhþe trēowde,

---

32. Carol J. Clover, "The Germanic Context of the Unferþ Episode," *Speculum* 55, no. 3 (1980): 444–68, at 460. See also Joseph Harris, "The *Senna*: From Description to Literary Theory," *Michigan Germanic Studies* 5, no. 1 (1979): 65–74; Michael J. Enright, "The Warband Context of the Unferth Episode," *Speculum* 73, no. 2 (1998): 297–337.

þæt hē hæfde mōd micel,   þēah þe hē his māgum nǣre
ārfæst æt ecga gelācum. (ll. 1165b–1168a)

(Likewise the spokesman Unferth sat at the feet of the lord of the
Scyldings; each of them trusted his soul, that he had great cour-
age, though he had not been honorable to his kin at the sport of
swords.)

In this passage, the poet confirms that Beowulf was not making a false
accusation when he consigned Unferth to hell for killing his own broth-
ers. Rather, Beowulf must have been displaying knowledge of a widely
known legend of Unferth, which poets had trafficked from Denmark
to Geatland. The crucial word in the second allusion to this legend is
"honorable" (ārfæst): if Unferth showed himself to be truly dishonor-
able when he killed his kinsmen, why would the Danish royal family
trust his soul and believe that he has "great courage" (mōd micel)? The
answer must be that neither the Danes nor the poets involved in the de-
velopment of antecedent legendary tradition considered Unferth's kin-
slaying to be dishonorable. The passage confirms that Unferth killed
his brothers in a public battle, "at the sport of swords" (ecga gelācum),
not in a clandestine domestic context. If Unferth killed his brothers in
a conventional scenario pitting his lord against his kinsmen, as con-
jectured above, then this deed would have established him among the
Danes as a man so committed to honoring his oath to Hrothgar that he
would perform even the gravest moral transgression in order to avoid
breaking that oath. In considering Unferth to be courageous and trust-
worthy, the Danes merely maintain the interpretation of this character
that earlier poets had probably put forward. In considering Unferth to
be dishonorable, the Beowulf poet evidently departs from antecedent
tradition, offering a new interpretation of this character that is con-
sistent with his programmatic refusal to depict kin-slayers and oath-
breakers in a positive or sympathetic light.

During the flyting, Beowulf compares his killing of monsters with
Unferth's killing of kinsmen and asserts that he performed the more
heroic deed. In doing so, he trivializes the deed that likely established
Unferth as a great hero. Through the protagonist there, the poet sub-
tly contrasts the monster-slaying heroes of folkloric tradition with the
morally transgressive heroes of migration-period legend. The contrast
between the two types of heroes is reiterated in a later passage, which
occurs after Unferth lends Hrunting, his sword and family heirloom,
to Beowulf while the hero prepares to engage in subterranean conflict

with Grendel's mother. Lest the audience should perceive Unferth as a magnanimous figure here, the poet immediately follows the loan with a passage that explicitly and unfavorably compares him to Beowulf:

> Hūru ne gemunde   mago Ecglāfes,
> eafoþes cræftig,   þæt hē ær gespræc
> wīne druncen,   þā hē þæs wæpnes onlāh
> sēlran sweordfrecan;   selfa ne dorste
> under ȳða gewin   aldre genēþan,
> drihtscype drēogan;   þær hē dōme forlēas,
> ellenmǣrðum.   Ne wæs þǣm ōðrum swā,
> syðþan hē hine tō gūðe   gegyred hæfde. (ll. 1465–1472)

(Certainly, the son of Ecglaf, skillful in his strength, did not recall what he had said, intoxicated with wine, when he lent that weapon to the better swordsman; for his own part, he did not dare to venture his life under the tumult of waves, engage in bravery; there he gave up glory, fame from valor. It was not so for the other after he had readied himself for battle.)

This passage suggests that Unferth is the most comparable figure to Beowulf at the Danish court, perhaps its champion warrior; he is not the fool or jester or magician that some critics have interpreted him to be. That Unferth holds the office of *þyle* (ll. 1165b, 1456b), a word associated with speech, need not imply that he is a cowardly or unwarlike figure: in Old Norse legendary sources, the cognate *þulr* is applied to Reginn and Starkaðr, two formidable men of questionable morality, each responsible for the killing of a kinsman.[33] Unferth also resembles the figure of Hagen in the *Nibelungenlied*, who functions there as both the king's champion and his counselor, and whose loyalty

---

33. On the connection between Unferth, Reginn, and Starkaðr, see Adelaide Hardy, "The Christian Hero Beowulf and Unferð Þyle," *Neophilologus* 53, no. 1 (1969): 55–69, at 63–64; Russell Poole, "Some Southern Perspectives on Starcatherus," *Viking and Medieval Scandinavia* 2 (1996): 141–66, at 146. On Unferth's status as *þyle*, see D. E. Martin Clarke, "The Office of *Thyle* in *Beowulf*," *Review of English Studies* 12, no. 45 (1936): 61–66; Norman E. Eliason, "The Þyle and Scop in *Beowulf*," *Speculum* 38, no. 2 (1963): 267–84; Joseph L. Baird, "Unferth the Þyle," *Medium Ævum* 39, no. 1 (1970): 1–12; Ida Masters Hollowell, "Unferð the Þyle in *Beowulf*," *Studies in Philology* 73, no. 3 (1976): 239–65; Leslie A. Donovan, "Þyle as Fool: Revisiting *Beowulf*'s Hunferth," in *Poetry, Place, and Gender: Studies in Medieval Culture in Honor of Helen Damico*, ed. Catherine E. Karkov (Kalamazoo: Medieval Institute Publications, 2009), 75–97. Of the various views put forward, those that interpret the *þyle* as a formidable and respected counselor (rather than a fool or jester) appear most plausible in view of the comparative Germanic evidence.

to his king prompts him to commit the pivotal moral transgression in the poem.[34] If Unferth is the conventional transgressive hero that he appears to be, then an additional layer of significance is attached to his failure to do what the folkloric hero Beowulf does. The comparison of the two men makes a statement about heroism, namely, that it is more heroic to fight against monsters for the sake of communal protection than to commit moral transgressions for the sake of personal honor. The *Beowulf* poet appears here to be introducing a novel point of view into his material, one that is not expressed in other legendary poems focusing on the dilemmas of migration-period heroes. In these poems, Unferth might have been admired for having "the courage to choose" or pitied for being a wretched hero compelled to kill his kinsmen. In the view of the *Beowulf* poet, however, Unferth made the wrong choice and consequently deserves no sympathy. As Arthur G. Brodeur observes, the poet "never fails to show his distaste for Unferth."[35] The poet displays a degree of hostility toward this character that is not displayed in connection with any other human character in the poem.

Two considerations might explain the special treatment of Unferth. First, he appears to be the antithesis of the protagonist: he is the kind of traditional hero in contrast to which the poet crafted his non-transgressive, untraditional hero. Second, Unferth is included in the poem's foreground, where the poet generally focuses attention on sanitized characters suitable for his audience to admire. Had Unferth appeared in the poem's background, the treatment of this character might have been different. The background is full of the morally ambiguous heroes of antecedent legendary tradition who were known to have committed the conventional heroic transgressions: Hengest and Ingeld were oath-breakers; Eormenric killed his son and his wife; Sigemund committed incest; Fitela killed his brothers; Heremod killed his retainers; various Danish and Swedish princes killed their kinsmen. From this cast of minor characters, only Heremod is clearly depicted in a negative light; the others are presented in an impartial light as important and famous heroes whose moral rectitude need not be dwelt on. One might wonder why a poet concerned about the valorization of kin-slayers and

---

34. See Leonard Neidorf, "On *Beowulf* and the *Nibelungenlied*: Counselors, Queens, and Characterization," *Neohelicon* 47, no. 2 (2020): 655–72, at 657–65.

35. Brodeur, *Art of Beowulf*, 149. See also Baird, "Unferth the *Pyle*," 4; Wieland, "Unferth Enigma," 35.

oath-breakers would even mention in passing the names of men guilty of these deeds. The answer, of course, is that the poet had no choice but to mention the names of morally ambiguous heroes if he intended to situate his central narrative within the semi-historical world of migration-period legend. Nearly every significant hero from this legendary world was known to have committed moral transgressions that were hateful to him. This is presumably why the word *wrecca*, which can mean "exile" or "wretch," was also a standard word for "hero": it acknowledges that heroes in Germanic legend are both adventurers and sufferers who might merit exile for performing the transgressive deeds in which they took no pleasure. In this tradition, few became great heroes without acquiring the stain of kin-slaying or oath-breaking.

There are, however, two cases of fratricide in the background in which the poet, while maintaining an impartial tone, articulates the same moralistic perspective on the traditional plot of antecedent legend that he articulates in connection with Unferth: namely, that the hero who had "the courage to choose" between hateful alternatives would have been more admirable if he refused to make the choice and did nothing. The first fratricide mentioned is Cain's killing of Abel; the second is Hæthcyn's killing of Herebeald. One is deliberate, the other accidental, but in both accounts the poet expresses ideas about divine justice righting earthly wrongs: in the first case, God punishes Cain for committing a standard heroic transgression; in the second case, God rewards Hrethel for refusing to commit such a transgression. Cain's killing of Abel is mentioned first in the passage introducing Grendel's name and pedigree:

wæs se grimma gǣst Grendel hāten,
mǣre mearcstapa, sē þe mōras hēold,
fen ond fæsten; fīfelcynnes eard
wonsǣlī wer weardode hwīle,
siþðan him scyppen forscrifen hæfde
in Cāines cynne— þone cwealm gewræc
ēce drihten, þæs þe hē Ābel slōg;
ne gefeah hē þǣre fǣhðe, ac hē hine feor forwræc,
metod for þȳ māne mancynne fram.
Þanon untȳdras ealle onwōcon,
eotenas ond ylfe ond orcnēas,
swylce gī(ga)ntas, þā wið Gode wunnon
lange þrāge; hē him ðæs lēan forgeald. (ll. 102–114)

(the unyielding demon was named Grendel, a well-known wanderer in the wastes, who ruled the heath, fen, and fastnesses; the ill-starred man had occupied for some time the habitat of monstrosities, after the Creator had cursed him among the race of Cain—the eternal Lord was avenging the murder after he killed Abel; he derived no satisfaction from that feud, but Providence banished him far away from humankind on account of that crime. Thence awoke all deformed races, ogres and elves and lumbering brutes, likewise giants, who struggled against God for a long while; he gave them their deserts for that.)

In this passage, we are told that the eternal lord (*ēce drihten*) took vengeance for the killing of Abel by exiling Cain and engaging in warfare against Cain's monstrous descendants. The same essential outline of this cosmic feud is conveyed in the passage introducing Grendel's mother, which reiterates the idea that Cain's primordial kin-slaying led him to become an exile who inhabited desolate terrain and engendered monstrous offspring there:

> Grendles mōdor,
> ides āglǣcwīf   yrmþe gemunde,
> sē þe wæteregesan   wunian scolde,
> cealde strēamas,   siþðan Cāin wearð
> tō ecgbanan   āngan brēþer,
> fæderenmǣge;   hē þā fāg gewāt,
> morþre gemearcod   mandrēam flēon,
> wēsten warode.   Þanon wōc fela
> geōsceaftgāsta;   wæs þǣra Grendel sum,
> heorowearh hetelic   sē æt Heorote fand
> wæċċendne wer   wīġes bīdan. (ll. 1258b–1268)

(Grendel's mother, lady, female troublemaker, kept in mind her misery, who was accustomed to inhabiting dreadful waters, cold currents, after Cain turned out to be the murderer of his only brother, his father's son. He departed outlawed, then, marked by murder, fleeing human society, occupied the wastes. From that arose many fated spirits; one of them was Grendel, hateful war-outlaw, who found at Heorot a waking man waiting for combat.)

In the two passages concerning Cain's killing of Abel, the poet naturally maintains his refusal to depict kin-slayers or oath-breakers in a favorable light, as he associates Cain with the sinister, monstrous forces that imperil human civilization and fight against God. Yet it is conceivable that a poet immersed in Germanic legendary tradition could have depicted Cain in a more sympathetic manner. The story of Cain and Abel, the only two personages from the Bible mentioned by name in *Beowulf*, bears some striking resemblances to the kinds of stories that Germanic poets attached to migration-period heroes; recall the dispute over inheritance that motivates the matter of *Hlǫðskviða*. Were the biblical story adapted into a heroic lay, Cain could be depicted as an honor-bound warrior who feels that the inexplicable favor shown to Abel constitutes a severe injustice and an insult to his sense of personal honor; to rectify the matter, he commits an outrageous deed, merits exile, and establishes kingdoms in new lands. In this hypothetical lay, Cain would be a conventional wretched hero, compelled by one outrage to commit another one, and God would be an equally wretched victim, a father forced to punish one of his creations in order to avenge the killing of another. Consistent with his approach to native tradition, the *Beowulf* poet resists the temptation to adapt biblical tradition in this manner. In his account, though, Cain is never said to be evil himself, which is perhaps a vestige of the amorality of the narrative tradition that the *Beowulf* poet inherited. Yet there is also no sympathy for Cain, whose kin-slaying plainly had evil consequences, as it ultimately resulted in the creation of malevolent, monstrous progeny such as Grendel and Grendel's mother. Cain, forced to choose between suffering an outrage and committing one, made the wrong choice and was punished accordingly.

The *Beowulf* poet found in the story of Cain and Abel a central episode in the mythology of Judeo-Christian religion that resonated with the thematic concerns of migration-period legend. It is perhaps not coincidental that the other account of fratricide in the poem's background, the story of Hæthcyn's accidental killing of Herebeald, is modeled after a central episode in Germanic mythology that also featured kin-slaying and conflicting imperatives. Critics have long recognized that the myth of the death of Baldr, the favored son of Óðinn, at the hands of his blind brother Hǫðr appears to lie behind the story of Herebeald and Hæthcyn, whose names contain elements (-*beald*, *hæð*-) related to those of the deities involved.[36] Beowulf recounts the tragic story in the long

---

36. See Sophus Bugge, *Studien über die Entstehung der nordischen Götter- und Heldensagen* (Munich: Christian Kaiser, 1889), 262; Ursula Dronke, "*Beowulf* and Ragnarǫk," *Saga-Book* 17 (1969): 302–25, at 322–23; Frank, "Skaldic Verse," 132; Joseph Harris, "A Nativist Approach

speech prior to his fight with the dragon. Anticipating his own death in the imminent conflict, the protagonist reflects on the deaths of other members of the Geatish royal family, beginning with that of Herebeald, the eldest son of Hrethel:

> Wæs þām yldestan   ungedēfelīce
> mǣges dǣdum   morþorbed strêd,
> syðð an hyne Hæðcyn   of hornbogan,
> his frēawine   flāne geswencte,
> miste mercelses   ond his mǣg ofscēt,
> brōðor ōðerne   blōdigan gāre.
> Þæt wæs feohlēas gefeoht,   fyrenum gesyngad,
> hreðre hygemēðe;   sceolde hwæðre swā þēah
> æðeling unwrecen   ealdres linnan. (ll. 2435–2443)

(For the eldest a bed of murder was spread unfittingly by the actions of his kinsman, when Hæthcyn struck down his lord and friend with an arrow from a horn-bow, missed the mark and shot his kinsman, one brother the other, with a bloody dart. That was an inexpiable killing, a wrong cruelly done, wearying to contemplate at heart; the prince nonetheless had to lose his life unavenged.)

It is unclear whether the *Beowulf* poet invented this story and modeled it after the death of Baldr or whether the tradition of Geatish dynastic legend that he inherited had already been shaped to fit the mythological pattern. Since the story puts the dynastic founder Hrethel in the position equivalent to that of Óðinn, inheritance is likelier than invention, as the extant genealogies indicate that dynasties were inclined to claim descent from Óðinn or related figures.[37] What is clear in

---

to *Beowulf:* The Case of Germanic Elegy," in *Companion to Old English Poetry*, ed. Henk Aertsen and Rolf H. Bremmer Jr. (Amsterdam: VU University Press, 1994), 45–62; Richard North, *The Origins of Beowulf: From Vergil to Wiglaf* (Oxford: Oxford University Press, 2006), 198–202; Orchard, *Critical Companion to Beowulf*, 116–19; Heather O'Donoghue, "What Has Baldr to Do with Lamech? The Lethal Shot of a Blind Man in Old Norse Myth and Jewish Exegetical Traditions," *Medium Ævum* 72, no. 1 (2003): 82–107. For a skeptical view, see E. O. G. Turville-Petre, *Myth and Religion of the North: The Religion of Ancient Scandinavia* (New York: Holt, Rinehart & Winston, 1964), 121.

37. On the presence of Woden (Óðinn) in Anglo-Saxon royal genealogies, see Kenneth Sisam, "Anglo-Saxon Royal Genealogies," *Proceedings of the British Academy* 39 (1953): 287–348, at 326; J. S. Ryan, "Othin in England: Evidence from the Poetry for a Cult of Woden in Anglo-Saxon England," *Folklore* 74, no. 3 (1963): 460–80, at 464; David N. Dumville, "The Anglian Collection of Royal Genealogies and Regnal Lists," *Anglo-Saxon England* 5 (1976): 23–50; Newton, *Origins of Beowulf*, 54–76. Bede, in his Kentish genealogy, writes of "Woden, from whose stock the royal families of many kingdoms claimed their descent" ("Uoden, de cuius stirpe

Beowulf's account is that although the death was accidental, a desire for vengeance was still felt. Losing any royal son would bring sadness to Hrethel, but having that son become in death an unavenged prince (*æðeling unwrecen*) adds a sense of shame and cosmic injustice to the tragedy. Hrethel's refusal to exact vengeance for one son by punishing the other one throws the world out of order for him and causes him ultimately to die from grief. Beowulf compares this grief to that of a father of an executed criminal, who also cannot take vengeance for his dead son, and then returns to Hrethel:

Swā Wedra helm

æfter Herebealde   heortan sorge
weallinde wæg;   wihte ne meahte
on ðām feorhbonan   fæghðe gebētan;
nō ðȳ ǣr hē þone heaðorinc   hatian ne meahte
āðum dædum,   þēah him lēof ne wæs.
Hē ðā mid þǣre sorhge,   þē him sīo sār belamp,
gumdrēam ofgeaf,   Godes lēoht gecēas;
eaferum læfde,   swā dēð ēadig mon,
lond ond lēodbyrig,   þā hē of līfe gewāt. (ll. 2462b–2471)

(Similarly, the helm of the Weders felt surging, heartfelt sorrow after Herebeald; he could by no means take satisfaction for the offense on the killer, any more than he could hate the warrior for the hated deed, though he was not dear to him. Then with that grief he whom the pain had encompassed gave up human joys, chose God's light; to his sons he left, as a prosperous man does, land and stronghold, when he departed from life.)

This account indicates that Hrethel found himself in the standard position of a migration-period protagonist, who is forced to choose between two hateful alternatives: he needs vengeance for his dead son, but he would have to kill his other son in order to obtain it. Hæthcyn is no longer "dear to him" ("him lēof ne wæs"), but Hrethel cannot bring himself to kill his own son. That Hrethel could desire and be expected to take his son's life is suggested by the fact that Óðinn sires a new son, Váli, so that this son, on the day of his birth, can avenge Baldr by killing Hǫðr. Hrethel, caught in the same dilemma, does not follow the

---

multarum prouinciarum regium genus originem duxit"). See Bertram Colgrave and R. A. B. Mynors, eds. and trans., *Bede's Ecclesiastical History of the English People*, rev. ed. (Oxford: Clarendon Press, 1991), 50–51.

example of Óðinn or other migration-period heroes, who killed kins-
men to rectify an injustice. Forced to choose, Hrethel chooses to do
nothing. Instead, we are told that he "chose God's light" ("Godes lēoht
gecēas"), an expression that strongly implies the salvation of his soul.[38]
Hrethel's forbearance leads to suffering and death in this world, but it
will be rewarded in the next. As in the story of Cain and Abel, an earthly
wrong is set right by God rather than by the reciprocal transgression
of a hero.

The poet's sympathetic treatment of Hrethel conforms to a pat-
tern that has been observed throughout the present chapter. We are
told nothing objectionable about Hrethel, only that he was a loving
foster father to Beowulf, that he suffered grievously when his son was
killed, and that he abstained from committing one of the standard he-
roic transgressions. Hrethel's life is defined by this abstention: whereas
other heroes, such as Hlǫð or Ingeld, die in catastrophic wars waged
against kinsmen or in-laws, Hrethel dies from refusing to take any ac-
tion that could bring him satisfaction and palliate his terminal grief.
Beowulf's statement that Hrethel chose God's light (instead of choosing
between hateful alternatives) asserts that Hrethel's abstention earned
him a favorable outcome in the afterlife. In doing so, this assertion
constitutes another remark from the protagonist about posthumous
judgment that is consistent with the two others discussed above: first,
Beowulf predicted that Unferth will suffer damnation in hell for killing
his brothers; then, over two thousand lines later, Beowulf rejoiced that
God need not blame him, once he is dead, for killing his kinsmen. In
all three cases, the protagonist expresses a conviction that the crucial
deed on which posthumous judgment turns is kin-slaying. His uncon-
ditional disapproval of this deed mirrors that of the poet, whose ab-
horrence at the prospect of celebrating kin-slayers and oath-breakers is
reflected in the design of *Beowulf*, where characters who abstained from
these deeds are accorded prominence and characters who committed
them are minimized. Situating a folkloric protagonist at the court of a

---

38. See Charles Donahue, "*Beowulf* and Christian Tradition: A Reconsideration from a
Celtic Stance," *Traditio* 21 (1965): 55–116, at 103; Thomas D. Hill, "The 'Variegated Obit'
as an Historiographic Motif in Old English Poetry and Anglo-Latin Historical Literature,"
Traditio 44 (1988): 101–24, at 119–20; Thomas D. Hill, "The Christian Language and Theme
of *Beowulf*," in *Companion to Old English Poetry*, ed. Henk Aertsen and Rolf H. Bremmer Jr. (Am-
sterdam: VU University Press, 1994), 63–77, at 70–71; Paul Cavill, "Christianity and Theology
in *Beowulf*," in *The Christian Tradition in Anglo-Saxon England: Approaches to Current Scholarship
and Teaching*, ed. Paul Cavill (Woodbridge, UK: D. S. Brewer, 2004), 15–40, at 38.

stay-at-home king, the poet populates his epic's foreground with sanitized monotheists, whose courteous behavior can be contemplated at length, while consigning the morally ambiguous heroes to terse treatment in the poem's background. The one exception to this rule is Unferth, and the exceptionally negative treatment of this character only reinforces the poet's moral vision.

Beowulf, to be clear, is not a homily against kin-slaying and oath-breaking. No member of any early medieval society needed to be convinced that these deeds should not be performed. There are abundant indications, in sources ranging from sermons to law codes to *Vǫluspá*, that kin-slaying and oath-breaking were widely considered two of the most heinous transgressions that could be conceived.[39] The *Beowulf* poet's abhorrence is not a particularly clerical or pious reaction, but a reaction likely shared with every reputable member of his world. He was not uniquely averse to these two transgressions, and if he were on a campaign to suppress them, he would surely not seek to achieve this outcome by composing a poem in which neither deed is depicted at length in the central narrative. The only reason that kin-slaying and oath-breaking were fundamentally important to the composition of *Beowulf* is that they were fundamentally important to the tradition of migration-period legend that the poet inherited. This tradition focused on protagonists who committed one of the two major transgressions not because they were evil but because they found themselves in a position where it became necessary to choose between evil alternatives. The traditional plot expressed a fascination with the cruelty and arbitrariness of fate, and it celebrated heroes for displaying resistance in the face of this fate, whether by fighting a hopeless battle to the death or by committing resolutely to one of two hateful courses of action. The *Beowulf* poet's refusal to valorize the kin-slaying and oath-breaking heroes of the tradition he inherited was probably motivated less by an aversion to these two deeds than by a conviction that the amoral vision of the antecedent legendary tradition was incompatible with the teachings of Christianity, at least as he understood them.

Whether the amoral vision expressed in migration-period legend is genuinely incompatible with Christianity is a complex theological

---

39. On the presence of these themes in *Vǫluspá*, see Ursula Dronke, ed. and trans., *The Poetic Edda*: vol. 2, *Mythological Poems* (Oxford: Clarendon Press, 1997), 19, 57, 144. See also David Clark, "Kin-Slaying in the *Poetic Edda*: The End of the World?," *Viking and Medieval Scandinavia* 3 (2007): 21–41.

question that need not be considered here. What has been explored in the present chapter is not the doctrinal rectitude of *Beowulf* but the peculiar aesthetic reaction of one Christian artist who attempted to reconcile an originally pagan tradition of storytelling with his understanding of Christianity's teachings and taboos. Certainly not every medieval Christian author shared the *Beowulf* poet's sense that it would be impious to celebrate heroes who committed transgressions that were more or less circumstantially justified. The Christian author of the *Nibelungenlied* makes Hagen a protagonist of his epic and expresses admiration for him despite his numerous transgressions. Saxo Grammaticus was a Christian and probably a canon, yet he saw nothing wrong with making the kin-slaying and oath-breaking Starkaðr a central hero in his *Gesta Danorum*. Late as it is, Saxo's treatment of Starkaðr preserves the combination of admiration and sympathy that poets had attached to the transgressive heroes of migration-period legend centuries earlier.[40] Because Saxo and the *Nibelungenlied* poet were writing around the year 1200, when Christianity possessed an impregnable foothold in their respective societies, they might have worried less about the theological impropriety of originally pagan narratives than the *Beowulf* poet did. If our poet flourished around the year 700, as the linguistic evidence suggests, then he composed his epic poem for a society that might have been Christian for less than a century. Given his proximity to the conversion of his people, the *Beowulf* poet might reasonably feel greater anxiety about the morality (or lack thereof) of migration-period legend than authors operating centuries later.

The other extant monuments in Old English concerned with migration-period legend—*Widsith, Deor, Waldere,* the *Finnsburg* fragment, and *Wulf and Eadwacer*—allude to many morally questionable heroes and legends in a manner comparable to the digressions in *Beowulf,* but none of them preserves a sustained depiction of a kin-slaying or oath-breaking committed under duress. This raises the possibility that the *Beowulf* poet's refusal to depict transgressive heroes in a positive or sympathetic light was shared by his contemporaries and perhaps reflective of an Old

---

40. See Marlene Ciklamini, "The Problem of Starkaðr," *Scandinavian Studies* 43, no. 2 (1971): 169–88, at 179–80. In *Gautreks saga*, Starkaðr delivers a moving elegiac poem known as *Víkarsbálkr* after he is compelled by Óðinn to kill Víkarr, who had been both lord and foster brother to Starkaðr. For the text of *Víkarsbálkr*, see Heusler and Ranisch, *Eddica minora*, 38–43. For a translation with commentary, see Lee M. Hollander, ed. and trans., *Old Norse Poems: The Most Important Non-Skaldic Verse not Included in the Poetic Edda* (New York: Columbia University Press, 1936), 18–25.

English school or tradition. There is, however, one reason to believe that the *Beowulf* poet's attitude to inherited tradition was more stringent than at least some of his contemporaries: the Old High German *Hildebrandslied*, composed probably within a century of *Beowulf*, appears to be the work of a Christian poet, yet it narrates a spectacular atrocity and illustrates the cruelty of fate.[41] Although the ending is not preserved, the extant fragment plainly sets the stage for a scene in which Hildebrand will be compelled to kill his son Hadubrand (the deed to which he alludes in his death song, discussed above). Hildebrand, recognizing that an atrocity is inevitable once Hadubrand refuses to believe that they are kinsmen, delivers a lament that is unlike anything spoken in *Beowulf*:

> welaga nu, waltant got [quad Hiltibrant],   wewurt skihit.
> ih wallota sumaro enti wintro   sehstic ur lante,
> dar man mih eo scerita   in folc sceotantero:
> so man mir at burc enigeru   banun ni gifasta,
> nu scal mih suasat chind   suertu hauwan,
> breton mit sinu billiu,   eddo ih imo ti banin werdan. (ll. 49–54)

("Ah, now, mighty God!," said Hildebrand, "a woeful fate is being enacted. I have been wandering for thirty years abroad, where I have always been assigned to the company of the spearmen. Whereas at no city has death been inflicted on me, now must my own child strike me with the sword, smite me with his blade, or I become his killer.")[42]

Nowhere in *Beowulf* is there a passage comparable to this one, in which a good-natured hero on the verge of committing a terrible deed cries out for the audience's sympathy. Hildebrand cannot be blamed for what a cruel fate (*wewurt*) has forced him to do: he and his son meet as champions of opposing armies; they are obligated by sworn oaths to fight for their lords; Hadubrand rejects Hildebrand's attempt to dissuade him; the father now must kill or be killed by his own son. Hildebrand finds himself in the standard position of the protagonist

---

41. On the date, context, and literary history of the *Hildebrandslied*, see Bostock, "Lay of Hildebrand"; Siegfried Gutenbrunner, *Von Hildebrand und Hadubrand: Lied, Sage, Mythos* (Heidelberg: Winter, 1976); Rosemarie Lühr, *Studien zur Sprache des Hildebrandliedes* (Frankfurt am Main: Peter Lang, 1982).

42. The text is cited from the edition in Wilhelm Braune, ed., *Althochdeutsches Lesebuch*, rev. Ernst. A. Ebbinghaus, 17th ed. (Tübingen: Max Niemeyer, 1994), 85; the translation is cited from Bostock, "Lay of Hildebrand," 46.

in antecedent legendary tradition, caught between hateful alternatives, not unlike the position in which Hengest finds himself in the Finnsburg digression. Hengest is a wretched hero, obligated to kill his current lord in order to avenge his former lord, but the *Beowulf* poet never grants Hengest the opportunity to deliver a lament calling attention to the cruelty of the fate thrust upon him. Such a lament would demand sympathy for an oath-breaker and shatter the poet's ambition to morally renovate the amoral tradition he inherited. The *Hildebrandslied* poet did not share this ambition. In his work, there are references to the singular "mighty God" (*waltant got*) of Judeo-Christian tradition, but as Brian Murdoch observes, "the whole tone is fatalist, and God has no real role here."[43] The *Beowulf* poet perceived this problem with the tradition he inherited—that is, God's absence from stories about the cruelty of fate—so he composed a radically untraditional poem in which the conventional transgressive protagonists, like Hengest, are consigned to the background, and an unconventional folkloric protagonist, who kills God's monstrous enemies with divine support, dominates the foreground. Directing his audience's sympathy and admiration away from the kin-slayers and oath-breakers of antecedent tradition, the poet sets before them a cast of sanitized characters, unstained by these deeds, who are voices of monotheistic wisdom and exemplars of courtly etiquette. The *Beowulf* poet's moral vision causes his poem to be a world away from the *Hildebrandslied*—not to mention *Hlǫðskviða*, *Vǫlsunga saga*, the *Nibelungenlied*, the *Gesta Danorum*, and every other major witness to migration-period legend discussed thus far.

---

43. Brian Murdoch, "Heroic Verse," in *German Literature of the Early Middle Ages*, ed. Brian Murdoch (Woodbridge, UK: Camden House, 2004), 121–38, at 126. Bostock, "Lay of Hildebrand," similarly observes that although the *Hildebrandslied* is a Christian poem, it still "reflects the pessimistic pagan conception of a merciless and arbitrary fate" (61). Gillespie, "Heroic Lays," likewise writes of the *Hildebrandslied* that "the plot, the conflict between father and son, is amoral, depicting two extremely aggressive characters involved in a situation from which neither can withdraw" (3).

CHAPTER 2

Courtesy and Courtliness

In the previous chapter, it was argued that the *Beowulf* poet consigned the conventional kin-slaying and oath-breaking protagonists of antecedent tradition to his poem's background, while populating its foreground with an unconventional cast of sanitized characters. The poet pays considerable attention to the courteous behavior of these foregrounded characters. His priorities are striking: we are told little about Sigemund and Fitela's "feuds and crimes" ("fǣhðe ond fyrena," l. 879a) and nothing about the circumstances prompting Unferth to kill his brothers, but we are given a careful description of Wealhtheow's ceremonial progress through the hall, in which we are explicitly told that the ring-adorned queen, "versed in courtesies" ("cynna gemyndig," l. 613b), gave the mead cup first to her husband and to other established warriors before eventually passing it to the newcomer, Beowulf, on the evening of his arrival at Heorot (ll. 611–641). Likewise, the accounts of Beowulf's violent interactions with Frankish and Swedish adversaries are terse and vague, comprising fewer than thirty lines (ll. 2359b–2366, 2391–2396, 2501–2509), but the accounts of Beowulf's courteous interactions with the king, the queen, and an array of Danish court personnel are detailed and intricate, running to several hundred lines before the fight against Grendel (ll. 229–702a). Similarly, we are told nothing about the "war success" ("herespēd," l. 64b) that God granted to Hrothgar in his youth, but we are told a great deal about the courtly culture he established at Heorot, which is home to splendid tapestries (ll. 994b–996), wondrous wine vessels (l. 1162a), dutiful attendants (ll. 991–993a, 1161a, 1792–1798), ladies' quarters (l. 921a), poetry recitals (ll. 867b–874a, 1064–1068b), and games on horseback (ll. 853–856a, 864–867a). Yet for all that these striking contrasts suggest about the poet's context and priorities, *Beowulf* has not conventionally been characterized as a work of courtly literature or as one in which ideals of courtesy and courtliness possess central importance.

Is *Beowulf* a courtly poem? Consultation of books on the subject of "courtly literature" suggests a negative answer to this question, since these books tend to exclude *Beowulf* and focus predominantly on French or French-influenced works from the twelfth century onward.[1] In the foreword to a book on *The Legacy of Courtly Literature*, Keith Busby writes: "Courtly literature in English is quite late off the mark, since the audience for courtly literature in England was largely Francophone until the age of Chaucer."[2] His statement asserts what the content of these books implies: namely, that neither *Beowulf* nor anything in Old English is genuinely courtly. The conviction that courtliness is a phenomenon belonging to the later Middle Ages plainly remains widespread in literary studies despite the critique it has received from historians such as C. Stephen Jaeger, Janet L. Nelson, Dominique Barthélemy, and David Crouch. In his book on *The Origins of Courtliness*, Jaeger takes issue with "the idea that *courtoisie* sprang more or less spontaneously to life in France" in the twelfth century and proposes instead that it originated in German courts of the tenth century.[3] Nelson, however, finds evidence of courtliness in

---

1. There is no discussion of *Beowulf*, for instance, in any of the following works: Keith Busby and Erik Kooper, eds., *Courtly Literature: Culture and Context* (Amsterdam: John Benjamins, 1990); Barbara K. Altmann and Carleton W. Carroll, eds., *The Court Reconvenes: Courtly Literature across the Disciplines* (Cambridge: D. S. Brewer, 2003); Albrecht Classen, ed., *Violence in Medieval Courtly Literature: A Casebook* (New York: Routledge, 2004); Deborah Nelson-Campbell and Rouben Cholakian, eds., *The Legacy of Courtly Literature: From Medieval to Contemporary Culture* (Cham, Switzerland: Palgrave Macmillan, 2017). The poem is likewise not mentioned in Norbert Elias, *Die höfische Gesellschaft: Untersuchungen zur Soziologie des Königtums und der höfischen Aristokratie* (Neuwied: Luchterhand, 1969), nor in Joachim Bumke, *Höfische Kultur: Literatur und Gesellschaft im hohen Mittelalter* (Munich: Deutscher Taschenbuch Verlag, 1986), nor in Werner Paravicini, *Die ritterlich-höfische Kultur des Mittelalters* (Munich: Oldenbourg Verlag, 2011). There is, however, brief discussion of *Beowulf* in David Burnley, *Courtliness and Literature in Medieval England* (London: Longman, 1998), 11–14.
2. Keith Busby, foreword to Nelson-Campbell and Cholakian, *Legacy of Courtly Literature*, v–vi, at v.
3. C. Stephen Jaeger, *The Origins of Courtliness: Civilizing Trends and the Formation of Courtly Ideals, 939–1210* (Philadelphia: University of Pennsylvania Press, 1985), 6.

eighth- and ninth-century Carolingian sources, and Barthélemy argues that the courtly phenomena codified under the name of chivalry can be found in sources throughout the first millennium.[4] What distinguishes the twelfth and thirteenth centuries from earlier periods is their more explicit codification of ideals of courtly conduct, though Crouch finds evidence for such codification in eleventh-century references to the figure of the *preudomme*, whose qualities included "courtesy, wisdom, distinguished bearing (*debonaireté*), loyalty, valour, generosity and bravery." Crouch observes that the *preudomme* "was a restrained and courtly man at the time of the *Song of Roland*" and reasons that "the antiquity of *preudommie* betrays the antiquity of courtliness."[5]

An impediment to the characterization of *Beowulf* as a courtly poem is the nebulousness and interchangeability with which terms such as courtesy, courtliness, and chivalry tend to be used. Crouch's work usefully demystifies the terminology by making clear that what we are ultimately dealing with is "an ideal of noble conduct," a more or less codified notion of the restrained and artificial behavior that aristocrats should exhibit at a princely court, where they were expected to display deference toward the powerful and magnanimity toward the powerless. He concludes that "an ideal of noble conduct was in existence long before Chrétien de Troyes wrote, and it arose out of a secular milieu where the princely court modified lay behaviour."[6] Beyond matters of conduct, the terms in question also refer to the culture that emerges in the context of court. James A. Schultz, in a book focusing on courtly literature from the twelfth century onward, provides a definition of courtly culture that can profitably be pondered with respect to *Beowulf*: "Courtly culture elaborated a class-specific ideal of social life that required a certain self-restraint—at table, in speech, in response to insult or challenge—and promised distinction in return. It developed new social forms—the tournament, the festival, the knighting ceremony—that displayed courtly magnificence and refinement, that projected noble

---

4. Janet L. Nelson, "Ninth-Century Knighthood: The Evidence of Nithard," in *Studies in Medieval History Presented to R. Allen Brown*, ed. Christopher Harper-Bill, Christopher J. Holdsworth, and Janet L. Nelson (Woodbridge, UK: Boydell, 1989), 255–66; Janet L. Nelson, "Was Charlemagne's Court a Courtly Society?," in *Court Culture in the Early Middle Ages: The Proceedings of the First Alcuin Conference*, ed. Catherine Cubitt (Turnhout, Belgium: Brepols, 2003), 39–57; Dominique Barthélemy, *La chevalerie: De la Germanie antique à la France du XIIe siècle* (Paris: Fayard, 2007).

5. David Crouch, *The Birth of Nobility: Constructing Aristocracy in England and France, 900–1300* (London: Routledge, 2005), 36, 38.

6. Crouch, *Birth of Nobility*, 30, 41.

power and preeminence, and that heightened the self-regard and co-
hesion of the courtly nobility."[7] The essential courtliness of *Beowulf*
becomes apparent when one considers the extent to which these words,
although formulated with mainstream courtly literature in mind, fit
the poem. From the beginning to the end of *Beowulf*, the poet articu-
lates a class-specific ideal of social life, focusing on the self-restrained
conduct of the noble protagonist and analyzing the social forms of
courtly life that display magnificence, refinement, power, and status.
Far more attention is paid in the poem to the nuances of Beowulf's
behavior at court (and on his way to court) than to the details of his
warfare against human or monstrous adversaries. The argument of the
present chapter is that ideals of courtesy and courtliness were funda-
mental to the composition of *Beowulf*: they pervade the poem, shape the
representation of the protagonist, modify the poet's heroic and folk-
loric inheritances, and inform many passages in subtle ways that have
not been fully appreciated. The *Beowulf* poet appears to have cared far
more about matters of courtesy and courtliness than about many of
the themes that have been thought to lurk beneath the surface of the
poem's narrative. This is not to say that *Beowulf* is exclusively concerned
with the articulation of an ideal of noble conduct, but rather that this
consideration seems to have been as important, if not more so, than
any other consideration that might have guided the poet while com-
posing *Beowulf*. The previous chapter conceived of the *Beowulf* poet as
an artist erasing a great deal from the canvas he inherited; the present
chapter examines what he filled that emptied canvas with, the colors
that dimmed or brightened aspects of the inherited picture.

The pair of terms in this chapter's title, courtesy and courtliness,
have not been very prominently used in *Beowulf* studies, and they
seem in fact to have been consciously avoided by critics concerned
about their potential anachronism. When the material under con-
sideration in the present chapter has been discussed in the critical
literature, it has tended to be analyzed in a piecemeal manner, some-
times with the use of anthropological theories that imply an affin-
ity between the society depicted in *Beowulf* and the tribal societies
of peoples such as the Yanomami.[8] Remarkably, there has been only

---

7. James A. Schultz, *Courtly Love, the Love of Courtliness, and the History of Sexuality* (Chicago:
University of Chicago Press, 2006), xvi.

8. Comparison between the society of *Beowulf* and that of the Yanomami is made, for
example, in John M. Hill, *The Cultural World in Beowulf* (Toronto: University of Toronto Press,

one critic in the history of *Beowulf* studies to write something that contains in its title the pair of terms in the present chapter's title: E. G. Stanley, whose essay on "Courtliness and Courtesy in *Beowulf* and Elsewhere in Medieval English Literature" marks a radical departure from prior criticism, yet one that has exerted minimal influence thus far on subsequent criticism.[9] In this difficult and wide-ranging essay, Stanley has as much to say about other works as he does about *Beowulf*, which he contrasts with several Middle English popular romances. Writing in reference to *Beowulf* and *Waldere*, Stanley asserts: "if we come to them from the rough-and-tumble world of *Havelok* and *Gamelyn*, we sense a higher courtliness, a greater nobility of purpose and achievement." The thrust of his argument is that "the romancers are describing the high world of nobles from below, presumably without having experienced courtliness and high courtesy in the real world."[10] The suggestion, by way of contrast, is that the *Beowulf* poet had firsthand knowledge of courtly life; that whereas the authors of *Havelok* and *Gamelyn* were composing for audiences of laborers in taverns, the *Beowulf* poet was in all likelihood composing for an audience of aristocrats situated at one of the great courts of the Anglo-Saxon period.

Although this is not signaled in his essay, Stanley's conclusion aligns with recent historical thinking on the origins of courtliness. Whereas earlier historians often supposed that courtly life arose in imitation of courtly literature, historians have now generally come to view courtliness as a phenomenon that traveled from the real world of historical courts to the imagined world of courtly literature rather than the other way around. Jaeger, a proponent of this view, credits the sociologist Norbert Elias's *Über den Prozess der Zivilisation* with reversing the tide by disseminating the view that courtliness develops in response

---

1995), 86–88. See also Robert E. Bjork, "Speech as Gift in *Beowulf*," *Speculum* 69, no. 4 (1994): 993–1022; Jos Bazelmans, *By Weapons Made Worthy: Lords, Retainers and Their Relationship in Beowulf* (Amsterdam: Amsterdam University Press, 1999), 37–67.

9. E. G. Stanley, "Courtliness and Courtesy in *Beowulf* and Elsewhere in English Medieval Literature," in *Words and Works: Studies in Medieval English Language and Literature in Honour of Fred C. Robinson*, ed. Peter S. Baker and Nicholas Howe (Toronto: University of Toronto Press, 1998), 67–104. Google Scholar records at present (1 April 2022) only eight citations for Stanley's essay. By comparison, it records 179 citations for Hill, *Cultural World in Beowulf*. Some of Stanley's observations were anticipated in Gabriele Müller-Oberhäuser, "*Cynna Gemyndig*: Sitte und Etikette in der altenglischen Literatur," *Frühmittelalterliche Studien* 30, no. 1 (1996): 19–59, though she tends to analyze the poem in terms of politeness rather than courtliness.

10. Stanley, "Courtliness and Courtesy in *Beowulf*," 83, 96.

to the complex power dynamics of court life.[11] Whether Anglo-Saxon courts of the seventh and eighth centuries actually featured courtesy and courtliness of the sort described in *Beowulf* is a question we are now in a poor position to answer. As James Campbell observes: "The history of the Anglo-Saxon court is largely lost and unknown."[12] Nevertheless, archaeology provides ample reason to believe that the courts of early Anglo-Saxon kings, such as Rædwald of East Anglia (associated with the treasures excavated at Sutton Hoo) or Edwin of Northumbria (associated with the massive hall complex at Yeavering), were centers of wealth, refinement, and culture; it is likely that codes of artificial conduct would develop in such elevated and rarified contexts.[13] The court of Æthelbald of Mercia was probably not a place where aristocrats could behave in a natural and unrestrained manner in the presence of their king. Given the forty-year duration of Æthelbald's reign (716–757), access to the royal person must have been strictly regulated, with aristocrats competing for proximity to the king and the influence that comes with his favor. It is reasonable to think that some form of courtliness developed in such contexts and spread to *Beowulf* therefrom.

Whatever the relationship between life and literature might be, the *Beowulf* poet took pains to infuse his inherited material with a spirit of courtliness and situate the action of his narrative in a world where noble etiquette and courtly procedure are matters of central importance. No other witness to migration-period legend is quite like *Beowulf* in this respect. Thus, whereas the previous chapter considered what the poet omitted and minimized, the present chapter considers what the poet added and emphasized. It will substantiate its arguments by proceeding sequentially through the text of *Beowulf* and identifying the strands of courtesy and courtliness that run through it, but two passages are worth discussing out of sequence in order to introduce the readings developed below. The first occurs in connection with the court official Wulfgar, who is perhaps

11. See Jaeger, *Origins of Courtliness*, 5–8; Norbert Elias, *Über den Prozess der Zivilisation: Soziogenetische und psychogenetische Untersuchungen* (Basel: Haus zum Falken, 1939). See also C. Stephen Jaeger, "Origins of Courtliness after 25 Years," *Haskins Society Journal* 21 (2010): 187–216, at 188–90.

12. James Campbell, "Anglo-Saxon Courts," in *Court Culture in the Early Middle Ages: The Proceedings of the First Alcuin Conference*, ed. Catherine Cubitt (Turnhout, Belgium: Brepols, 2003), 155–69, at 155.

13. See R. L. S. Bruce-Mitford, *The Sutton Hoo Ship Burial: A Handbook*, 3rd ed. (London: British Museum, 1979); Brian Hope-Taylor, *Yeavering: An Anglo-British Centre of Early Northumbria* (London: Her Majesty's Stationery Office, 1977). See also Laurence Marcellus Larson, "The King's Household in England before the Norman Conquest" (PhD diss., University of Wisconsin, 1904).

the most minor character in the foreground to be given both a name and
a speaking role by the poet. After hearing Beowulf's petition to receive an
audience with the king, Wulfgar enters the hall to approach Hrothgar,
and the poet describes his movement in the following terms:

> Hwearf þā hrædlīce   þǣr Hrōðgār sæt
> eald ond anhār   mid his eorla gedriht;
> ēode ellenrōf,   þæt hē for eaxlum gestōd
> Deniga frēan;   cūþe hē duguðe þēaw. (ll. 356–359)

(He turned then quickly to where Hrothgar sat, old and very hoary
with his troop of men, walked boldly till he stood before the shoul-
ders of the lord of the Danes; he knew the custom of the court.)

Considering all of the things that we do not know about the world of *Be-
owulf*, one must marvel at the fact that we know about Wulfgar's correct
bodily comportment. This is not a purple passage; it has not attracted
much commentary; it does not excite critics who are eager to make bold
pronouncements about revenge or heroism or paganism or Christian-
ity. Nevertheless, I would argue that this is an important passage, one
that contributes to the poet's ambition to imbue his work with a quality
that might be termed "courtly realism." Its purpose, and the purpose
of several passages discussed below, is evidently to indicate that *Beowulf*
is set in a realistic and coherent world of migration-period courts that
adheres to standards maintained (or aspired to) in contemporary Anglo-
Saxon courts. It establishes that we are not in the picaresque world of
folklore or fairy tale, where one thing just happens after another. In the
world of *Beowulf*, there are procedures to be followed. Wulfgar displays
the bodily restraint of a proper courtier: he does not shout from the
doorway; he does not run into the hall and startle the king; he does not
invade the king's personal space. Wulfgar knows the custom of the *du-
guð*, the group of established warriors who were presumably granted the
privilege of having the closest proximity to the royal person at court.[14]
Members of the *duguð* know that there are rules governing their access
to the king. They know that a sudden movement near the king could
be interpreted as an attempt on his life. They know that one must take
the time to stand directly in front of the king, before his shoulders (*for
eaxlum*), in order to address him respectfully and make the kind of for-
mal speech that is signaled by the verb *maðelian* (l. 360a). This detail

---

14. On the *duguð*, see Whitelock, *Audience of Beowulf*, 89–90; Peter Clemoes, *Interactions of
Thought and Language in Old English Poetry* (Cambridge: Cambridge University Press, 1995), 7–8.

of courtly realism is not something that has interested *Beowulf* critics, but it certainly interested the *Beowulf* poet, who has more to say about courtly procedure than about most matters that critics would have liked him to address.

The other passage that will introduce the arguments of the present chapter pertains to the characterization of the protagonist. It occurs after Beowulf returns triumphant from his battle against Grendel's mother. Unferth, refusing to undertake the voyage himself, lends Beowulf the famous sword Hrunting, but it turns out to be useless against the monster. Instead of stressing the embarrassing truth about the sword's uselessness or accusing Unferth of sabotage, Beowulf essentially lies to Unferth, telling him that he considers the sword a splendid war-friend, and the poet praises the hero for his courteous behavior:

> Heht þā se hearda   Hrunting beran
> sunu Ecglāfes,   heht his sweord niman,
> lēoflic īren;   sægde him þæs lēanes þanc,
> cwæð, hē þone gūðwine   gōdne tealde,
> wīgcræftigne,   nales wordum lōg
> mēces ecge;   þæt wæs mōdig secg. (ll. 1807–1812)

(The hardy man directed that Hrunting be brought to the son of Ecglaf, told him to take his sword, the valued iron; he offered thanks to him for the loan, said he regarded that war-friend as good, strong in battle, by no means explicitly found fault with the sword's edge; that was a magnanimous man.)

This is a remarkable moment in the poem, in which the courteousness of the hero is so pronounced that the scene would not be out of place in a romance of Perceval or Gawain. Beowulf exhibits here the artificial and restrained behavior of a man who understands the dynamics of court life. Aldo Scaglione, drawing on Elias, defines the terms "courteous and courtesy" as "the results of the civilizing process . . . whereby respect for others' feelings and interests was expected as acceptable behavior and a sign of noble nature."[15] The passage cited above, along with several others discussed below, contributes to the programmatic characterization of Beowulf as a courteous hero. Composing at a time when the standard romance terminology of *courtoisie*

---

15. Aldo Scaglione, *Knights at Court: Courtliness, Chivalry, and Courtesy from Ottonian Germany to the Italian Renaissance* (Berkeley: University of California Press, 1991), 8.

addresses them. Wulfgar is explicitly concerned with the attire and the nobility of the newcomers:

> Þā ðǣr wlonc hæleð
> ōretmecgas   æfter æþelum frægn:
> 'Hwanon ferigeað gē   fǣtte scyldas,
> grǣge syrcan,   ond grīmhelmas,
> heresceafta hēap?   Ic eom Hrōðgāres
> ār ond ombiht.   Ne seah ic elþēodige
> þus manige men   mōdiglīcran.
> Wēn' ic þæt gē for wlenco,   nalles for wræcsīðum
> ac for higeþrymmum,   Hrōðgār sōhton.' (ll. 331b–339)

(Then a proud hero there asked the battle-challengers about their background: "From where are you bringing plated shields, grey shirts, and masked helmets, a host of army-shafts? I am Hrothgar's herald and officer. I have not seen more vigorous outlanders in such numbers. I expect you have come to see Hrothgar out of daring, not on account of exile but out of determination.")

That the poem should contain a speech from a self-described "herald and officer" (*ār ond ombiht*) is a stark reminder that we are in the world of an early medieval court, not in a folktale. Wulfgar begins his inquiry into the newcomers' lineage (*æþelum*) by asking from where they have brought their splendid war gear; in doing so, he acknowledges the role it plays in his estimation of their status. He then remarks that he has never seen so many *mōdiglīcran* foreigners: as noted above in the connection with the description of Beowulf as a *mōdig secg* (l. 1812b) or "magnanimous man," the poet stretches the meaning of *mōdig*; in the present context, it may mean that the official has never seen nobler or more splendid foreigners before. He concludes from their evident wealth that the Geats have come out of daring (*wlenco*) rather than desperation (*wræcsīðum*). Wulfgar, described as a famous prince of the Wendels (ll. 348b–350a), is pleased to find himself welcoming fellow noblemen rather than turning away needy petitioners. Beowulf's response to the official indicates, again, that he understands his status to be the central matter at issue when seeking an audience with a king. He answers the inquiry with the following words:

> Wē synt Higelāces
> bēodgenēatas;   Bēowulf is mīn nama.

> Wille ic āsecgan   sunu Healfdenes,
> mǣrum þēodne   mīn ǣrende,
> aldre þīnum,   gif hē ūs geunnan wile
> þæt wē hine swā gōdne   grētan mōton. (ll. 342b–347)

(We are Hygelac's loyal retainers; Beowulf is my name. I will tell my business to the son of Healfdene, the renowned lord, your leader, if he will be so good as to allow us to approach him.)

The most significant word in Beowulf's response is *bēodgenēatas*, "table-companions," which varies his earlier use of the word *heorðgenēatas* to announce the precise status that he and his men possess. Beowulf informs Wulfgar that he is already the intimate of one king before asking for access to a second king. Furthermore, he refrains again from declaring that he has come to kill a monster; he merely describes himself as a man with a "message" (*ǣrende*) for the king. Finally, with exceptional courtesy, Beowulf does not presume that he will be granted an audience with Hrothgar. He hopes the king will grant him an audience with such a *good* person (*swā gōdne*), another expression where *gōd* evidently refers to status rather than virtue and is therefore used to acknowledge the disparity in status that exists between Hrothgar and Beowulf.

Beowulf's courtly speech and noble appearance impress Wulfgar, who tells Beowulf that he will convey his petition to Hrothgar. Formally approaching his king and standing before his shoulders (the passage discussed above), Wulfgar tells Hrothgar that Geats are at the door and encourages the king to meet with them on account of their attire:

> Nō ðū him wearne getēoh,
> ðīnra gegncwida,   glædman Hrōðgār.
> Hȳ on wīggetawum   wyrðe þinceað
> eorla geæhtlan;   hūru se aldor dēah,
> sē þǣm heaðorincum   hider wīsade. (ll. 366b–370)

(Do not offer them refusal of your audience, gracious Hrothgar. In their war-dress they seem worthy of the esteem of men; indeed, the leader is outstanding who led the militia here.)

Wulfgar's recommendation furnishes a remarkable example of the poet's insistence on depicting Hrothgar's court as a place where realistic court procedures are followed. Wulfgar does not tell his king that the strongest man in the world is at the door, and that he should be invited in on account of his probable ability to kill monsters; instead, Wulfgar recommends that the king meet with Beowulf because he complies with the dress code, that is, because his war garments (*wīggetawum*) make him appear worthy of the attention of noblemen (*eorla geæht-lan*). Hrothgar responds enthusiastically to Wulfgar, explaining that he knew Beowulf as a boy, is aware of his prodigious strength, and hopes that God has sent him here to kill Grendel (ll. 372–389a). Wulf-gar then instructs the Geats to enter Heorot in their war garments but leave their shields and spears at the door—another sign of compliance with realistic court procedure (ll. 395–398). Beowulf is guided inside the hall until "he stood on the hearth" ("þæt hē on heo[r]ðe gestōd," l. 404b). From this location, familiar to a king's *heorðgenēat*, Beowulf introduces himself as Hygelac's "relative and young follower" ("mæg ond magoðegn," l. 408a) and delivers what is perhaps his courtliest speech in the poem.

Beowulf explains to Hrothgar that after word of the Grendel affair (*Grendles þing*) traveled to Geatland, the wise men (*snotere ceorlas*) of the kingdom advised (*gelærdon*) Beowulf to seek out the new monster since they knew that he already had experience in killing monsters in the past (ll. 409b–424a). By attributing his adventure to the advice of the *snotere ceorlas*, Beowulf portrays himself not as a threatening figure ambitious for power or glory but as an obedient youth merely following the in-structions of his elders. He refrains again from boasting that he will kill the monster; he instead states, euphemistically, that he wishes to con-duct a meeting with the monster ("ðing wið þyrse," l. 426a). With these prefatory matters established, Beowulf formally petitions Hrothgar to be permitted to cleanse Heorot:

> Ic þē nūða,
> brego Beorht-Dena,   biddan wille,
> eodor Scyldinga,   ānre bēne,
> þæt ðū mē ne forwyrne,   wīgendra hlēo,
> frēowine folca,   nū ic þus feorran cōm,
> þæt ic mōte āna,   mīnra eorla gedryht,
> ond þes hearda hēap   Heorot fælsian. (ll. 426b–432)

(Now I want to ask you, sovereign of Bright-Danes, defense of the Scyldings, one request, that you, protector of fighters, noble friend of nations, not refuse me, now that I have come thus far, that I myself, the troop of my men and this company of hardy ones be permitted to purge Heorot.)

The hero's vocative use of four complimentary epithets over the course of four lines, unparalleled elsewhere in the poem, appears intended to display his sensitivity to the nuances of court life. Concerned that his request might embarrass the king, who has failed to handle the problem on his own, Beowulf portrays himself as a humble petitioner who asks for a single favor (*ānre bēne*) and cushions his request in constant praise for Hrothgar. As Thomas J. Jambeck observes, Beowulf's petition "is replete with the refined circuity of the courtly gallant," and his "skillful manipulation of syntax would be as appropriate to the rarefied sophistication of Camelot as it is to the more muscular Heorot."[24] Indeed, the petition shows Beowulf at his courtliest, and it is followed by a declaration that Beowulf intends to maintain his commitment to courtesy even during his fight with Grendel:

> Hæbbe ic ēac geāhsod   þæt se æglǣca
> for his wonhȳdum   wǣpna ne recceð;
> ic þæt þonne forhicge,   swā mē Higelāc sīe,
> mīn mondrihten   mōdes blīðe,
> þæt ic sweord bere   oþðe sīdne scyld,
> geolorand tō gūþe,   ac ic mid grāpe sceal
> fōn wið fēonde   ond ymb feorh sacan,
> lāð wið lāþum;   ðǣr gelȳfan sceal
> dryhtnes dōme   sē þe hine dēað nimeð. (ll. 433–441)

(I have also learned that the troublemaker in his heedless way disdains weapons; then I, so that my lord Hygelac may be pleased with me in his heart, scorn that I should bear a sword or a broad shield, a pale buckler to battle, but with my grasp I will grapple with the enemy and compete for survival, foe against foe; there he whom death takes will have to trust in the Lord's judgment.)

---

24. Thomas J. Jambeck, "The Syntax of Petition in *Beowulf* and *Sir Gawain and the Green Knight*," *Style* 7, no. 1 (1973): 21–29, at 25, 28. Translations of this speech are reviewed in John Kenny Crane, "To Thwack or Be Thwacked: An Evaluation of Available Translations and Editions of *Beowulf*," *College English* 32, no. 3 (1970): 321–40. For further discussion, see Michael R. Kightley, "Reinterpreting Threats to Face: The Use of Politeness in *Beowulf*, ll. 407–472," *Neophilologus* 93, no. 3 (2009): 511–20; Thomas Kohnen, "Understanding Anglo-Saxon 'Politeness': Directive Constructions with *Ic Wille / Ic Wolde*," *Journal of Historical Pragmatics* 12, nos. 1–2 (2011): 230–54, at 243; A. Keith Kelly, "Teaching Good Manners: Civil Discourse Patterns in *Beowulf* and *Sir Gawain and the Green Knight*," in *Literary Speech Acts of the Medieval North: Essays Inspired by the Works of Thomas A. Shippey*, ed. Eric Shane Bryan and Alexander Vaughan Ames (Tempe, AZ: ACMRS, 2020), 223–42.

Having already portrayed himself as an obedient youth and a courte-ous politician, Beowulf now alerts us to his devotion to an ideal of fair-ness in combat: he refuses to fight any opponent, even a monster, on unequal terms. If lines with the same import were to be found in a late medieval romance, the word "chivalry" would invariably be used in criti-cal discussion of them. Although the literary codification of chivalric ideals postdates *Beowulf* by several centuries, the existence of a compa-rable code of idealized aristocratic conduct plainly informs Beowulf's announcement. His claim that he will fight unarmed so that Hygelac may be pleased with him suggests, moreover, that his concern for fair play reflects an external norm, not an internally generated imposition. Beowulf concludes the speech by assuring Hrothgar that no funerary expenditure will be necessary if he fails to kill Grendel since the monster will surely consume his corpse if he is defeated (ll. 442–455). This is the grim humor of the conventional Germanic hero, but it is adapted to courtly purposes in the present context, where it is used to underscore the deferential, courteous, and nonboastful character of his entreaty. Beowulf goes to great rhetorical lengths in this speech to signal to the court that he recognizes Hrothgar's superior status, refuses to dishonor or embarrass the king, and wishes to serve him as a nonburdensome, unimposing courtier.

Hrothgar registers his approval of the hero's deferential speech by condescending to address him as "my friend Beowulf" ("wine mīn Bēowulf," l. 457b) and ordering for a bench to be cleared for the Geatish arrivals, who are promptly served drink by a *þegn* and entertained by a *scop* (ll. 491–498). At this point, the poet introduces Unferth, "who sat at the feet of the lord of the Scyldings" ("þē æt fōtum sæt frēan Scyldinga," l. 500). Although he will later be identified as Hrothgar's *þyle* (ll. 1165b, 1456b), the first thing we are told about Unferth is that Beowulf's adventure was a "severe irritation" (*micel æfþunca*) to him, and he resented that any man should be more desirous of glory than himself (ll. 499–505). As noted in the previous chapter, the evident pur-pose of this momentary glimpse into Unferth's mind is to establish that his challenge is not perfunctory. To the contrary, Unferth chal-lenges Beowulf because he is concerned that his prominence at court, visible in his proximity to the royal person, is threatened by the hero's arrival. Whatever the duties of the *þyle* might have been in antecedent tradition, the poet wants the audience to understand the interaction between Beowulf and Unferth within the framework of the "courtly ri-valry," a widespread motif in courtly literature, which was discussed in connection with the *Nibelungenlied* by Katherine DeVane Brown. Within that poem, she persuasively reads Hagen fulfilling "the role of the respected and established courtier," whereas Siegfried "plays the part of his newly arrived and very aggressive younger rival."[25] The same framework fits well onto *Beowulf,* where Unferth is the established court favorite who fears the "encroachment on his former position" made possible by the arrival of the newcomer at court.[26]

Perceiving a courtly rivalry between Beowulf and Unferth clarifies the import of the various passages involving this enigmatic figure. It suggests, first, that Unferth is not a court jester, a licensed fool, an evil counselor, or a ludicrous coward; he is, rather, a serious warrior, the most prominent champion at the Danish court and the nobleman of highest status outside of the royal family (essentially the same position occupied by Hagen in the *Nibelungenlied*).[27] As argued in the previous chapter, Unferth's history of kin-slaying suggests not that he is unusually sinister, but that he is one of the conventional heroes of antecedent legendary tradition, who valiantly committed an egregious transgression when forced to choose between competing ethical imperatives. The poet refuses to valorize characters like Unferth, but he inherited a tradition full of people like him. While consigning most of the kin-slaying and oath-breaking heroes to the poem's background, the poet keeps Unferth in the foreground to serve as a foil to Beowulf, who bests him in both words and deeds, and brings him considerable discomfiture in the process. The diminution of Unferth's standing is suggested first in the reference to him as a "quieter man" (*swīgra secg,* l. 980a) after Beowulf killed Grendel, but then made clearer when the hero prepares to fight Grendel's mother:

> Hūru ne gemunde   mago Ecglāfes,
> eafoþes cræftig,   þæt hē ǣr gespræc

---

25. Katherine DeVane Brown, "Courtly Rivalry, Loyalty Conflict, and the Figure of Hagen in the *Nibelungenlied,*" *Monatshefte* 107, no. 3 (2015): 355–81, at 367. Also relevant is Jaeger's concept of the "courtier narrative," for which see Jaeger, *Origins of Courtliness,* 237–38.

26. Brown, "Courtly Rivalry," 358.

27. For comparable views on Unferth, see Ogilvy, "Unferth: Foil to Beowulf?"; Hughes, "Beowulf, Unferth and Hrunting"; Pope, "*Beowulf* 505"; Leonard Neidorf, "Unferth's Ambiguity and the Trivialization of Germanic Legend," *Neophilologus* 101, no. 3 (2017): 439–54, at 445–47; Neidorf, "On *Beowulf* and the *Nibelungenlied,*" 657–65. For a representative statement of the contrary view of Unferth, see Fred C. Robinson, "Elements of the Marvellous in the Characterization of *Beowulf:* A Reconsideration of the Textual Evidence," in *Old English Studies in Honour of John C. Pope,* ed. Robert B. Burlin and Edward B. Irving Jr. (Toronto: University of Toronto Press, 1974), 119–37.

wīne druncen, þā hē þæs wǣpnes onlāh
sēlran sweordfrecan; selfa ne dorste
under ȳða gewin aldre genēþan,
drihtscype drēogan; þǣr hē dōme forlēas,
ellenmǣrðum. Ne wæs þǣm ōðrum swā,
syðþan hē hine tō gūðe gegyred hæfde. (ll. 1465–1472)

(Certainly, the son of Ecglaf, skillful in his strength, did not re-
call what he had said, intoxicated with wine, when he lent that
weapon to the better swordsman; for his own part, he did not dare
to venture his life under the tumult of waves, engage in bravery;
there he gave up glory, fame from valor. It was not so for the other
after he had readied himself for battle.)

Unferth, willing to lend his sword but unwilling to risk his life, is here
declared to have been defeated in his courtly rivalry with Beowulf: such
is the transparent import of the judgment that "there he gave up glory"
("þǣr hē dōme forlēas") while the other man readied himself to win
lasting glory. The passage would make markedly inferior sense if Un-
ferth were not the most prominent courtier at Heorot and his relation-
ship with Beowulf were not one of courtly rivalry. Part of Beowulf's
achievement in Heorot is that, in addition to killing monsters, he shows
himself to be an able courtier, superior to the established favorite at the
foreign court. The poet gives considerably more attention to this aspect
of Beowulf's achievement, that is, to his successful navigation of the
politics of court life, than to his successful combat against monstrous
adversaries.

After addressing his most courteous speech to Hrothgar, Beowulf
delivers a speech in response to Unferth's challenge that is not particu-
larly courteous, but it is courtly, insofar as it demonstrates that Beowulf
possesses the range of rhetorical talents necessary to thrive at court. As
Peter S. Baker observes, "Beowulf's reply to Unferth is filled with rhe-
torical delights: not only shivering winter imagery and artfully tangled
syntax, but also grim humor, gnomic wisdom, and wry litotes."[28] The
speech reveals Beowulf's capacity to outperform his adversary in the tra-
ditional verbal contest of the flyting by delivering a speech that is mark-
edly different from his earlier speeches.[29] Courteous and deferential

28. Baker, "Beowulf the Orator," 16.
29. On the custom of flyting, see Clover, "Germanic Context"; Harris, "Senna"; Ward
Parks, *Verbal Dueling in Heroic Narrative: The Homeric and Old English Traditions* (Princeton, NJ:

speech being out of place in this context, Beowulf breaks from his earlier habit and finally boasts that he will kill the monster and do what no Dane has managed to do thus far (ll. 590–606). He also displays his ability to level an insult at an opponent when he condemns Unferth to hell for killing his own brothers (ll. 583b–589), a significant passage discussed in the previous chapter. Yet within this variegated speech, a hint of courtesy might still be detected: Graham Williams argues that the vocative address "my friend Unferth" ("wine mīn Ūnferð," l. 530b) is not sarcastic or insulting, and he suggests instead "a reading based in Christian courtliness with links to later developments in courtesy."[30] I would agree that, while the speech itself is not courteous, the initial address of "wine mīn Ūnferð" (paralleling Hrothgar's "wine mīn Bēowulf," ll. 457b, 1704b) is a courteous gesture, which signals to Unferth that after the verbal contest is finished, his friendship will be desired. Certainly, Beowulf's later behavior supports such a reading, as he displays only magnanimity toward his defeated rival. By making a friend out of a potential enemy, Beowulf shows himself to be less grim or ferocious than other heroes in antecedent tradition, who might have insisted on enmity until death for someone who insulted them publicly. Beowulf, achieving victory without necessitating bloodshed, obtains a kind of additional victory through his courteous behavior, which impresses Hrothgar and likely contributes to his high opinion of Beowulf's wisdom and diplomacy (see the discussion of ll. 1841–1845a below).

After noting that Hrothgar is pleased with the "resolute intent" ("fæstrǣdne geþōht," l. 610b) displayed in Beowulf's speech, the poet introduces Wealhtheow, a figure associated in each of her appearances with courtly etiquette and the politics of the court. A more or less unparalleled figure in early Germanic heroic poetry, Wealhtheow is possibly the most original character in *Beowulf*, endowed by the poet with a larger and livelier role than other comparable characters in Germanic legend evidently in order to foreground issues of courtesy and

---

Princeton University Press, 1990); Leslie Katherine Arnovick, "Sounding and Flyting the English Agonistic Insult: Writing Pragmatic History in a Cross-Cultural Context," in *The Twenty-First LACUS Forum 1994*, ed. Mava Jo Powell (Chapel Hill, NC: Linguistic Association of Canada and the United States, 1995), 600–619.

30. Graham Williams, "*Wine Min Unferð*: Courtly Speech and a Reconsideration of (Supposed) Sarcasm in *Beowulf*," *Journal of Historical Pragmatics* 18, no. 2 (2017): 175–94, at 179.

courtliness. Her connection to these concerns is made clear in the passage introducing her:

> Ðǣr wæs hæleþa hleahtor, hlyn swynsode,
> word wǣron wynsume. Ēode Wealhþēo forð,
> cwēn Hrōðgāres cynna gemyndig,
> grētte goldhroden guman on healle,
> ond þā frēolic wīf ful gesealde
> ǣrest Ēast-Dena ēþelwearde,
> bæd hine blīðne æt þǣre bēorþege,
> lēodum lēofne; hē on lust geþeah
> symbel ond seleful, sigerōf kyning. (ll. 611–619)

(There was laughter of heroes, the noise resonated, conversation was cheery. Wealhtheow made an entrance, Hrothgar's queen versed in courtesies, covered in gold, greeted the men in the hall, and then the noble woman gave a cup first to the guardian of the homeland of the East-Danes, told him to be happy at the drinking-rounds, beloved by his men; he partook of the banquet and the hall-cup with pleasure, a king renowned for victories.)

It is conventional in Old English studies to refer to a passage like this as a scene of "joy in the hall," but what is really described here is a scene of idealized court life not unlike those of Camelot in Arthurian literature.[31] Laughter and winsome words are followed by the procession of Wealhtheow, who displays her knowledge of courtly ritual as she passes the ceremonial cup first to the king, then to the established "company of soldiers old and new" ("duguþe ond geogoþe," l. 621a), and then to Beowulf. On greeting him, she thanks God for sending her a warrior she can believe in (ll. 625b–628a); then Beowulf, having drunk from the ceremonial cup, delivers another speech promising to kill Grendel or die in the process (ll. 632–638). Wealhtheow is pleased with his

---

31. See Herbert G. Wright, "Good and Evil; Light and Darkness; Joy and Sorrow in *Beowulf*," *Review of English Studies* 8, no. 29 (1957): 1–11; Kathryn Hume, "The Concept of the Hall in Old English Poetry," *Anglo-Saxon England* 3 (1974): 63–74; Alain Renoir, *A Key to Old Poems: The Oral-Formulaic Approach to the Interpretation of West-Germanic Verse.* (University Park: Pennsylvania State University Press, 1988), 113; Edward B. Irving Jr., *Rereading Beowulf* (Philadelphia: University of Pennsylvania Press, 1989), 133–67; Hugh Magennis, *Images of Community in Old English Poetry* (Cambridge: Cambridge University Press, 1996), 60–81; Paul Battles, "Dying for a Drink: 'Sleeping after the Feast' Scenes in *Beowulf, Andreas,* and the Old English Poetic Tradition," *Modern Philology* 112, no. 3 (2015): 435–57.

words and returns to the seat next to her husband (ll. 639-641). By eliciting this promise in exchange for the drink, Wealhtheow is perhaps now partially entitled to the credit for Beowulf's eventual deed. As later passages indicate, the poet conceives of Wealhtheow as a political entity independent from Hrothgar and not reluctant to advance her own agenda.

Prior to the fight with Grendel, the courtliest section of the poem features a final reiteration of the courtesy theme in the narration of Beowulf removing his war gear, handing it to an "attending officer" (*ombihtþegne*, l. 673b), and then restating his refusal to use weapons against a foe who knows nothing of weaponry (ll. 671-687). After the fight with Grendel, the poet's interest in court life finds renewed expression in descriptions of games on horseback (ll. 853-856a, 864-867a, 916-917a), poetry recited in praise of Beowulf (ll. 867b-874a), and the procession of Hrothgar and Wealhtheow "with a retinue of young women" ("mægþa hōse," l. 924b) toward the hall (ll. 920b-924). In the midst of the celebration, the narrator comments that no one blamed Hrothgar while praising Beowulf (ll. 862-863). The unneeded quality of this comment suggests that it is meaningful: perhaps it hints at the opportunity for a hero in Beowulf's position, a savior of the nation being publicly celebrated, to foment a popular uprising and usurp an old king. Naturally, the courteous Beowulf would not seize power in that manner, and power is, in any event, graciously bestowed on him by Hrothgar in his first speech following the defeat of Grendel. Addressing a crowd outside of Heorot, Hrothgar declares the hero's victory an act of God and promulgates his intention to regard Beowulf henceforth as a son:

> Nū ic, Bēowulf, þec,
> secg bet[e]sta,   mē for sunu wylle
> frēogan on ferhþe;   heald forð tela
> nīwe sibbe.   Ne bið þē [n]ænigre gād
> worolde wilna   þe ic geweald hæbbe. (ll. 946b-950)

(Now, Beowulf, noblest hero, I will cherish you in my heart as a son; henceforth observe well this new kinship. For you there will be no lack of anything desirable in the world that I have at my command.)

The precise import of this passage is a matter of dispute, but I construe it to mean that Hrothgar has formally endowed Beowulf with "new kinship" (*nīwe sibbe*) and thereby made him a potential heir to the throne.[32] The fact that Hrothgar delivers this speech from a *stapol* (l. 926a) supports such a reading, since there are reasons to associate this platform with public announcements related to kingship.[33] Furthermore, Wealhtheow's later speech exhorting Hrothgar to be generous to the Geats with respect to movable property but leave the rule of the kingdom to his own kinsmen indicates that she understood his words to have had sufficient force to make Beowulf an heir to the Danish throne (ll. 1169–1187). It becomes clear with Hrothgar's adoption of Beowulf that the poem is, to a certain extent, a kind of political drama that is as much concerned with the protagonist's path from courtier to king as it is with his capacity for monster-slaying.

Following Hrothgar's speech, there is a passage describing the restoration of Heorot and the gold-plated tapestries that hang on its walls (ll. 991–996). With the hall set in order by servants, the king enters, and the narrator remarks on the superlative conduct of his courtiers:

> Ne gefrægen ic þā mægþe   māran weorode
> ymb hyra sincgyfan   sēl gebǣran. (ll. 1011–1012)

(I have not heard that that nation conducted themselves better in a larger cohort around their wealth-giver.)

This comment introduces the scene of the great banquet at Heorot, which spans several hundred lines (ll. 1008b–1250) and includes the court poet's recitation of the Finnsburg episode (ll. 1063–1159a), the suitability of which for the festive occasion has long been a matter of critical debate. In my view, the legend of Finnsburg is pertinent because it tells of humiliation and nocturnal slaughter that were once inflicted on the Danes and ultimately made right by the death of a responsible

---

32. For comparable interpretations, see John M. Hill, "Beowulf and the Danish Succession: Gift Giving as an Occasion for Complex Gesture," *Medievalia et Humanistica*, n.s., 11 (1982): 177–97; Stephanie Hollis, "Beowulf and the Succession," *Parergon* 1, no. 1 (1983): 39–54; Hill, *Cultural World in Beowulf*, 21; Haruko Momma, "The Education of Beowulf and the Affair of the Leisure Class," in *Verbal Encounters: Anglo-Saxon and Old Norse Studies for Roberta Frank*, ed. Antonina Harbus and Russell Poole (Toronto: University of Toronto Press, 2005), 163–82, at 176–79; Biggs, "Politics of Succession," 726–27; Drout, "Blood and Deeds," 201–2; Leneghan, *Dynastic Drama of Beowulf*, 63–64.

33. See Thomas D. Hill, "Hrothgar's Speech of Adoption: A Danish-Latin Analog," *Notes and Queries* 66, no. 2 (2019): 163–66; Giovanna Princi Braccini, "Perché Hrōðgar Stod on Stapole (*Beowulf* 926a)," in *Echi di Memoria: Scritti di varia filologia, critica e linguistica in recordo di Giorgio Chiarini*, ed. Gaetano Chiappini (Florence: Alinea, 1998), 139–57.

agent after a long period of suffering.[34] The story suits the occasion because Beowulf has just brought relief to the long-suffering Danes by killing Grendel. It is possible, however, that there is also dramatic irony attendant on the recitation of the story, with the focus on Hildeburh's unexpected loss of kinsmen foreshadowing the fate of Wealhtheow, who might lose kinsmen of her own in the political turmoil that will eventually afflict Heorot.[35] Indeed, there is a strong sense of dramatic irony throughout the banquet scene, as the celebrating Danes are ignorant of both the imminent reprisal of Grendel's mother and the eventual strife between members of the Danish royal family. A mere five lines after the narrator's comment that he has never heard of a court with better conduct comes the poem's first mention of Hrothulf (l. 1017a), whose name is immediately followed by the ominous remark that the Scyldings did not perform "treachery" (l. 1018b) at that time. Beowulf thus finds himself in a delicate situation, where there is courtesy and harmony on the surface but danger lurking beneath. One must wonder if his decision to return home to Geatland and not pursue the path to kingship in Denmark is to be interpreted as a sign of the hero's prudence, that is, of his ability to evaluate a political situation and perceive danger where others might perceive only harmony. Certainly, he is characterized as possessing comparable foresight when he predicts that Hrothgar's plan to make peace with the Heathobards through the marriage of Freawaru and Ingeld is doomed to fail (ll. 2020-2069a). Beowulf's perception of the turmoil looming at Heorot might also be registered when he invites Hrethric to spend time at the Geatish court (ll. 1836-1839).[36]

The prospect that Beowulf could become king of Denmark is the subtext throughout the great banquet scene. At the beginning of the banquet, Hrothgar gives Beowulf an assortment of treasures in order to reward him

---

34. Leonard Neidorf, "Hildeburh's Mourning and *The Wife's Lament*," *Studia Neophilologica* 89, no. 2 (2017): 197-204, at 198. See also John M. Hill, *Cultural World in Beowulf*, 25-28; Alexandra Hennessey Olsen, "Gender Roles," in *A Beowulf Handbook*, ed. Robert E. Bjork and John D. Niles (Lincoln: University of Nebraska Press, 1997), 300-324, at 316-18.

35. For a reading along these lines, see Joyce Hill, "'Þæt Wæs Geomuru Ides!': A Female Stereotype Examined," in *New Readings on Women in Old English Literature*, ed. Helen Damico and Alexandra Hennessey Olsen (Bloomington: Indiana University Press, 1990), 235-47, at 242-43.

36. See T. A. Shippey, "Maxims in Old English Narrative: Literary Art or Traditional Wisdom?," in *Oral Tradition, Literary Tradition: A Symposium*, ed. Hans Bekker-Nielsen et al. (Odense: Odense University Press, 1977), 28-46, at 31-33; Susan E. Deskis, *Beowulf and the Medieval Proverb Tradition* (Tempe, AZ: ACMRS, 1996), 126-28.

for his victory over Grendel (ll. 1020–1049). It is significant that Hroth-gar's gifts include a sword possessed by Healfdene ("brand Healfdenes," l. 1020b) and the jewel-adorned saddle that had been used by Hrothgar himself (here identified as "sunu Healfdenes," l. 1040b). The transfer of these family heirlooms evidently symbolizes Hrothgar's intention to make Beowulf a member of the royal family and eventually transfer authority to him. Obstacles in the way of the realization of that intention are pre-sented, however, in the tableau describing the placement at court of Weal-htheow, Hrothulf, and Unferth, each of whom would presumably oppose Beowulf's accession to the throne (ll. 1162b–1168a). Indeed, Wealhtheow makes her opposition clear in her first speech on the occasion, in which she exhorts Hrothgar to leave the throne to his kinsmen and expresses support for Hrothulf to rule after he is gone (ll. 1169–1187). She then turns to Beowulf, whose eligibility for kingship is suggested again in the pregnant detail that he is now sitting next to Hrethric and Hrothmund (ll. 1188–1191), and she offers him alcohol, "friendship" ("frēondlaþu," l. 1192b), and an assortment of her own treasures, including a magnificent torque (ll. 1192–1214). The obligations attendant on his acceptance of these gifts are then made clear in a speech instructing Beowulf to provide her sons with counsel and service (ll. 1215–1231). Her command estab-lishes Beowulf's subordination to her sons and implies that he should not become king before them. The speech ends with a multivalent remark that could be interpreted as a threat to Beowulf:

> Bēo þū suna mīnum
> dǣdum gedēfe,   drēamhealdende.
> Hēr is ǣghwylc eorl   ōþrum getrȳwe,
> mōdes milde,   mandrihtne hol[d];
> þegnas syndon geþwǣre,   þēod eal gearo;
> druncne dryhtguman   dōð swā ic bidde. (ll. 1226b–1231)

(Be just in your actions toward my sons, you who are key to our contentment. Here every man is true to the other, kindly of heart, loyal to his lord; the thegns are in harmony, the people completely ready; the reveling men of the corps do as I ask.)

Her remarks can be read, first, as a restatement of her confidence that there is no longer anything to worry about. As she earlier told Hroth-gar, "Heorot is purged" ("Heorot is gefǣlsod," l. 1176b): the monster is dead, so there is no need for us to continue hosting a monster-slaying hero. The arrival of Grendel's mother will prove Wealhtheow to be mistaken in this respect, just as the eventual strife between kinsmen will prove wrong her belief that a harmonious transfer of power will occur following Hrothgar's death. Yet in addition to restating Weal-htheow's confidence, her concluding remarks can be read as a warning to Beowulf. She says not merely that each man is loyal to the other, but that they are loyal to her: the men of the war band, who have consumed alcohol from her ceremonial cup (*druncne dryhtguman*), will do what she tells them (*dōð swā ic bidde*). The implication would seem to be that if her will should differ from the will of Hrothgar, she has the capacity to enforce her will, presumably because she has secured the loyalty of various individuals through the distribution of her own property. The message to Beowulf is that if she does not want him on the throne, she has the power to place obstacles in the way of his accession. Another message is that since there is already unity and harmony here, it would be unfortunate if an outsider were to pursue the throne and disturb the courtly serenity of Heorot.

Later speeches from Beowulf and Hrothgar indicate that they have understood the import of the queen's words and have come to accept that it will not be feasible for Beowulf to become king of Denmark. Prior to his fight with Grendel's mother, Beowulf reminds Hrothgar of his adoption, but only to articulate what it should entail in the event of his untimely demise:

> Geþenc nū, se mǣra   maga Healfdenes,
> snottra fengel,   nū ic eom sīðes fūs,
> goldwine gumena,   hwæt wit geō sprǣcon,
> gif ic æt þearfe   þīnre scolde
> aldre linnan,   þæt ðū mē ā wǣre
> forðgewitenum   on fæder stǣle. (ll. 1474–1479)

(Think now, renowned son of Healfdene, wise sovereign, now that I am on the verge of this exploit, gold-friend of men, about what we two discussed earlier, if in your service I should part with my life, that you would always occupy for me, once departed, the place of a father.)

Beowulf then makes three postmortem requests of Hrothgar: to assume lordship over his lordless men, to send to Hygelac the treasures he won in Denmark, and to give Hrunting back to Unferth (ll. 1480–1491). Returning to the courteous style of his earlier speech of petition (ll. 407–455), Beowulf considers only what Hrothgar should do if he were to be killed; neither here nor in any later speech does Beowulf raise the issue of what his adoption should oblige of Hrothgar following a victory over Grendel's mother. Subsequent interactions between the two men show them crafting a new relationship, not one between father and son or king and heir, but one between two kings of cooperating nations. After examining the sword hilt that Beowulf recovered from the lair of Grendel's mother, Hrothgar has an epiphany, which he expresses in the long speech that has come to be known as his "sermon." The speech, however, is not quite a sermon: it is a prophecy that Beowulf will become the king of the Geats, accompanied by advice about how to rule well and righteously. Hrothgar's new vision for Beowulf's future is announced at its beginning:

> Þæt, lā, mæg secgan   sē þe sōð ond riht
> fremeð on folce,   feor eal gemon,
> eald ēþelweard,   þæt ðes eorl wære
> geboren betera.   Blæd is ārǣred
> geond wīdwegas,   wine mīn Bēowulf,
> ðīn ofer þēoda gehwylce.   Eal þū hit geþyldum healdest,
> mægen mid mōdes snyttrum.   Ic þē sceal mīne gelǣstan
> frēode, swā wit furðum sprǣcon.   Ðū scealt tō frōfre weorþan
> eal langtwīdig   lēodum þīnum,
> hæleðum tō helpe. (ll. 1700–1709a)

(He who practices truth and right among his people, remembers all from far back, an old defender of the homeland, can well say that this man was born superior. Your glory is upraised, my friend Beowulf, through the world's wide ways over every nation. You will keep hold of all of it steadily, strength and discernment of intellect. I shall fulfill my friendship with you, as we two discussed a short time ago. You shall be a very long-lasting comfort to your people, a help to heroes.)

In declaring that Beowulf is *geboren betera*, Hrothgar might be saying that the hero is superior to him, but in view of the poet's use of *gōd* to mean "noble," the king is likelier announcing that Beowulf must be a man of exceptionally noble birth who was destined to achieve fame and rule a kingdom. Significantly, Hrothgar now envisions this outcome occurring not among the Danes but among Beowulf's own people (*lēodum þīnum*). His new perspective is likewise reflected when he describes the relationship he has established with Beowulf as one of "friendship" (*frēode*) rather than the "new kinship" (*nīwe sibbe*, l. 949a) of which he earlier spoke. Hrothgar evidently intends to "fulfill" (*gelǣstan*) the obligations of this friendship not by making Beowulf a future king of Denmark but by making his kingship in Geatland an inevitability through the transfer of treasures that effectively elevate his status to that of a king. At the end of the sermon, such treasures are promised (ll. 1782–1784), and they are delivered on the following day (ll. 1866–1869); the intervening sermon takes Beowulf's future kingship as a foregone conclusion, as it advises him to rule generously, not like Heremod (ll. 1709b–1724a), and to be mindful of the unpredictable reversals of fortune that will inevitably befall even the most fortunate men, whether a hypothetical nobleman granted earthly joy in his own country ("on ēþle eorþan wynne," l. 1730) or Hrothgar himself, who experienced a reversal of fortune in his own country ("on ēþle edwenden cwōm," l. 1774). The repetition of the word for "homeland" (*ēþel*) in these exempla, following Hrothgar's reference to himself as "an old defender of the homeland" (*eald ēþelweard*), reflect his newfound recognition that Beowulf must, for better or worse, return to his homeland and realize his royal destiny there.

Following Hrothgar's speech, the poet reiterates the courtly realism of life at Heorot by mentioning a hall attendant who escorts Beowulf to his sleeping quarters:

> Gēat unigmetes wēl,
> rōfne randwigan,   restan lyste;
> sōna him seleþegn   sīðes wērgum,
> feorrancundum   forð wīsade,
> sē for andrysnum   ealle beweote*de*
> þegnes þearfe,   swylce þȳ dōgor
> heaþolīðende   habban scoldon. (ll. 1792b–1798)

(It pleased the Geat ever so much, the vigorous shield-warrior, to retire; at once a hall-officer led him away, the visitor from afar weary of his exploit; he reverently tended to all the thegn's needs, such as battle-mariners should have in those days.)

The inclusion of this minor detail seems intended to serve as a final reminder of the high standard of courtly etiquette established by Hrothgar. The courteous behavior of the *seleþegn* on Beowulf's final night in Heorot recalls the courtliness of Wulfgar encountered in his first moments there; the consistency suggests that Hrothgar maintained a dignified court in times of both adversity and triumph. The next morning, Beowulf returns Hrunting to Unferth and courteously praises the failed weapon (ll. 1807–1812) in the passage discussed at the beginning of this chapter, and then delivers his final speech addressed to Hrothgar. After announcing his intention to depart (ll. 1818–1820a), Beowulf thanks the king for his hospitality and proposes the continuation of their relationship:

> Wǣron hēr tela
> willum bewenede;   þū ūs wēl dohtest.
> Gif ic þonne on eorþan   ōwihte mæg
> þīnre mōdlufan   māran tilian,
> gumena dryhten,   ðonne ic gȳt dyde,
> gūðgeweorca,   ic bēo gearo sōna. (ll. 1820b–1825)

(Here we were hosted well and to our liking; you have done well by us. If, then, I can cultivate any more on earth of your affection, of martial deeds, lord of men, than I have already done, I will be ready at once.)

Beowulf then exemplifies his vision for their future relationship by proposing that he would furnish military support, in the form of a thousand warriors, if he ever hears that Hrothgar is under attack, and he trusts that Hygelac will support the expedition (ll. 1826–1835). Beowulf concludes his speech by proposing that if Hrethric should like to visit the Geatish court, he would find friends there (ll. 1836–1839). The invitation, which implies that Hrethric might find himself in need of friends someday, subtly reveals the hero's awareness of the peril facing Hrothgar's eldest son once the question of succession arises. In his final words to Hrothgar, Beowulf displays the education in diplomacy that he has received at Heorot. He speaks now as an experienced courtier with the authority of a king. His euphemistic use of "affection" (*mōdlufu*) to describe Hrothgar's contribution to his proposed military and diplomatic relationship anticipates the courtly language of renaissance literature, where patronage relationships are often framed in the language of love.[37]

---

37. See, for example, Michael Schoenfeldt, "The Sonnets," in *The Cambridge Companion to Shakespeare's Poetry*, ed. Patrick Cheney (Cambridge: Cambridge University Press, 2007), 125–43, at 128, where it is said that in the language of Shakespeare's Sonnets 78–90, "literary patronage and erotic relations are blurred."

Hrothgar, in his response, recognizes the hero's maturation and perceives divine intervention in his precocious display of diplomatic skill:

> Þē þā wordcwydas   wigtig drihten
> on sefan sende;   ne hȳrde ic snotorlicor
> on swā geongum feore   guman þingian.
> Þū eart mægenes strang   ond on mōde frōd,
> wīs wordcwida. (ll. 1841–1845)

(God in his wisdom put those remarks into your head. I have never heard a man at such a young age conduct diplomacy more perceptively. You are physically strong and acute of mind, judicious of speech.)

Hrothgar is evidently amazed that Beowulf, after only two days at the Danish court, is able to perceive both the peril facing Hrethric and the unfeasibility of Hrothgar's original plan to make Beowulf an heir to the Danish throne. This passage offers an important insight into the characterization of Beowulf. There is more to the peculiar protagonist crafted by the *Beowulf* poet than wisdom (*sapientia*) and bravery (*fortitudo*);[38] this hero is also to be admired for his exceptional courtesy and for his uncanny ability to conduct diplomacy (*þingian*), which allows him to make his way through the perilous world of the court. Hrothgar follows his assessment of the hero by expressing his "expectation" (*wēn*, l. 1845b) that if Hygelac should die prematurely in battle, the Geats would choose Beowulf to be their next king, should he be willing to rule (ll. 1845b–1853a). Hrothgar then comments again on the hero's progression:

> Mē þīn mōdsefa
> līcað leng swā wēl,   lēofa Bēowulf. (ll. 1853b–1854)

(Your character pleases me, the longer the better, dear Beowulf.)

Such a remark seems to indicate that an element of *bildung* is intended in the poem's narrative: Beowulf has grown on Hrothgar through the progressive revelation and development of his character. Hrothgar concludes his speech by declaring that Beowulf has firmly established a relationship of peace and trade between the Danes and the Geats, which will last as long as Hrothgar lives (ll. 1855–1865). The king alludes to

---

38. On this pair of traits, see R. E. Kaske, "*Sapientia et Fortitudo* as the Controlling Theme of *Beowulf*," *Studies in Philology* 55, no. 3 (1958): 423–56.

prior conflicts between the two peoples, which suggests that the arrangement brought about by Beowulf is no small achievement. Beowulf cleansed Heorot by killing its monsters, but Hrothgar appears in the end to be no less impressed by his political performance than his monster-slaying.

Following the exchange of speeches and treasures, there is a poignant description of the two men embracing. In this scene, the hero goes well beyond the achievement of one of his original goals when he first approached Heorot: namely, to gain access to the king and be granted the privilege of proximity to the royal person. Having announced himself as the "hearth-companion" (heorðgenēat) and "table-companion" (bēodgenēat) of his own king, Beowulf leaves Heorot as a physical intimate of a second king. The passage is pregnant with implications:

> Gecyste þā   cyning æþelum gōd,
> þēoden Scyldinga   ðegn bet[e]stan
> ond be healse genam;   hruron him tēaras
> blondenfeaxum.   Him wæs bēga wēn
> ealdum infrōdum,   ōþres swīðor,
> þæt h[ī]e seoðða(n nō)   gesēon mōston,
> mōdige on meþle.   (W)æs him se man tō þon lēof
> þæt hē þone brēostwylm   forberan ne mehte,
> ac him on hreþre   hygebendum fæst
> æfter dēorum men   dyrne langað
> born wið blōde. (ll. 1870–1880a)

(Then that king of noble lineage, lord of the Scyldings, kissed the best thegn and held him by the neck; the grey-haired one dropped tears. Old and immensely wise, he had two expectations—but one stronger, that they would not be permitted to see each other again, brave men in meeting. The man was so dear to him that he could not suppress the turmoil in his breast, but in his heart, fixed in the manacles of his mind, a close-held yearning for the beloved man burned in his blood.)

The poet calls attention to the disparity in status between the two men in order to hint at the extraordinary nature of the gesture: Hrothgar is a "king of noble lineage" (cyning æþelum gōd) and Beowulf is merely "the best thegn" (ðegn bet[e]stan), yet Hrothgar considers it no insult to his own dignity to kiss and embrace this great man of lower status. An implication is that Hrothgar has come to consider Beowulf an equal; the elevation of the hero to quasi-royal status is again insinuated here. When Beowulf arrived at Heorot, he was a young and unproven hero, but he leaves Heorot as both an accomplished monster-slayer and a future king. Furthermore, while the poet makes it clear that Hrothgar feels genuine affection for Beowulf, the scene's poignancy is elevated by the possibility that Hrothgar can foresee the misfortune that lies ahead for the Danish royal family. Knowing that his own death is imminent, Hrothgar burns with an "unexpressed desire" or "secret longing" (*dyrne langað*): the phrase is intentionally mysterious, but I would construe it as a final allusion to Hrothgar's thwarted desire for Beowulf to become his heir, accede to the Danish throne, and prevent the looming civil war. At the moment of their parting, Hrothgar presumably wishes to exhort Beowulf to remain in Denmark, but like the speaker of *The Wanderer* (ll. 11b–14), he knows it is a noble custom to conceal one's deepest thoughts and allow decorum to govern what can be expressed. Nevertheless, the tears that he could not suppress (*forberan ne mehte*) indicate the profundity of the considerations coursing through his mind at that moment.

When Beowulf parts from Hrothgar, he is described as a "gold-stately warrior" ("gūðrinc goldwlanc," l. 1881a) who is "reveling in his rewards" ("since hrēmig," l. 1882b). He leaves with treasures that command frequent admiration (ll. 1884–1885a) and ensure his eventual kingship, yet he remains an exemplar of courtesy, as indicated in his one last interaction with an official of the Danish court:

> Hē þǣm bātwearde   bunden golde
> swurd gesealde,   þæt hē syðþan wæs
> on meodubence   māþme þȳ weorþra,
> yrfelāfe. (ll. 1900–1903a)

(He gave the boat-watch a sword bound with gold, so that after that on the mead-bench he was the worthier for that precious thing, that rich legacy.)

Minor though the passage may seem, it contributes to the characterization of Beowulf as a courteous hero and reminds the audience that he has successfully managed relationships with many potentially hazardous characters at the Danish court. He earned the respect of the coast-guard and Wulfgar, having defused their concerns about his status and intentions; he turned Unferth from a decided foe to at least an apparent friend; he received splendid treasures from Wealhtheow and avoided her animosity by not pursuing the Danish throne; and he so impressed Hrothgar with his words and deeds that he managed to earn the firm friendship of the poem's wealthiest king as well as an assortment of treasures and heirlooms that are fit only for the possession of a king. The passage also reiterates the connection between treasure and status by stating that the coastguard was *māþme þȳ weorþra*, that is, made worthier, or ennobled, in the eyes of his peers on the mead-bench by means of the weapon. The comment about the coastguard's elevation raises a question: if this official is made worthier by one treasure, how much more formidable is Beowulf now that he possesses an array of royal treasures? This is the central question that informs his interaction with Hygelac once he returns to Geatland.

When Beowulf enters Hygelac's hall, he is asked by a pious and concerned Hygelac to report what transpired in Heorot (ll. 1987-1999). In response, Beowulf delivers the longest speech in the poem (ll. 2000-2151, 2155-2162). Though long regarded as a crude summary of the Danish adventure reflecting composite authorship or serial performance, several critics in recent decades have perceived considerable subtlety and artistry in this speech.[39] I concur with them and regard the speech as the culmination of the poet's interest in courtliness, in which the narrative of Beowulf's rise to kingship is concluded and his transition from courtier to king is effected. In this speech, Beowulf does not merely provide a summary of his struggles against Grendel and Grendel's mother. Rather, the speech appears to be intended primarily to allow Beowulf to display his education in courtliness, to announce the elevation of his status, and to demonstrate to the Geatish court that he is no longer the unpromising nobleman that he was once thought to be. Less than ten lines into the speech, it becomes clear that the hero

---

39. See Edward B. Irving Jr., "Beowulf Comes Home," in *Acts of Interpretation: The Text in Its Contexts, 700–1600: Essays on Medieval and Renaissance Literature in Honor of E. Talbot Donaldson*, ed. Mary J. Carruthers and Elizabeth D. Kirk (Norman, OK: Pilgrim Books, 1982), 129–43; Robin Waugh, "Competitive Narrators in the Homecoming Scene of *Beowulf*," *Journal of Narrative Technique* 25, no. 2 (1995): 202–22; John W. Schwetman, "Beowulf's Return: The Hero's Account of His Adventures among the Danes," *Medieval Perspectives* 13 (1998): 136–48; Momma, "Education of Beowulf," 179–81; John M. Hill, *Narrative Pulse of Beowulf*, 65–69; Leneghan, *Dynastic Drama of Beowulf*, 129–34. For the older view of the homecoming speech as a sign of composite authorship, see Levin Ludwig Schücking, *Beowulfs Rückkehr: Eine kritische Studie* (Halle: Max Niemeyer, 1905). For arguments against those of Schücking, see Chambers, *Beowulf: An Introduction*, 117–20.

is concerned as much with matters of status and state as he is with monsters. He reports:

> Ic ðǣr furðum cwōm
> tō ðām hringsele   Hrōðgār grētan;
> sōna mē se mǣra   mago Healfdenes,
> syððan hē mōdsefan   mīnne cūðe,
> wið his sylfes sunu   setl getǣhte.
> Weorod wæs on wynne;   ne seah ic wīdan feorh
> under heofones hwealf   healsittendra
> medudrēam māran. (ll. 2009b–2016a)

(There first I came to the ring-hall to meet Hrothgar; the famous son of Healfdene, after he understood my intentions, immediately assigned me a seat by his own sons. The company was in contentment; never in all my life have I seen under heaven's vault greater mead-revelry of hall-occupants.)

Beowulf boldly communicates two important points to Hygelac here: first, that Hrothgar correctly perceived Beowulf's nobility and treated him like one of his own sons; second, that the court of Heorot was more impressive in its conduct and celebration than any court that Beowulf had previously been acquainted with. There are subtle implications for Hygelac inherent in both of these points: first, that Hygelac, like Hrothgar, ought to recognize Beowulf's worth; second, that Beowulf has returned with knowledge of the customs of a court that is superior to the Geatish court, and he could use this knowledge to rule well in Geatland.

Beowulf then develops his impression of the grandeur of the Danish court by commenting on the noble etiquette of the royal women he encountered there:

> Hwīlum mǣru cwēn,
> friðusibb folca   flet eall geondhwearf,
> bǣdde byre geonge;   oft hīo bēahwriðan
> secge (sealde)   ǣr hīe tō setle gēong.
> Hwīlum for (d)uguðe   dohtor Hrōðgāres
> eorlum on ende   ealuwǣge bær,
> þā ic Frēaware   fletsittende
> nemnan hȳrde,   þǣr hīo (næ)gled sinc
> hæleðum sealde. (ll. 2016b–2024a)

(From time to time the famous queen, peace-pledge of peoples, roamed all through the building, urged on the young men; she often gave a wrought ring to a warrior before she went to her seat. At times in the company's presence Hrothgar's daughter conveyed ale-cups to the men from end to end, whom I heard the hall-occupants name Freawaru, where she brought a studded vessel to heroes.)

That Beowulf, asked to report the outcome of his battle with Grendel, should bother to mention the presence of these noble ladies at all is yet another striking indicator of the priorities of the *Beowulf* poet. In relating the ideal conduct that he witnessed at Hrothgar's court, the hero implies that a strict sense of decorum governed relationships between the sexes there. Beowulf indicates he knew Wealhtheow through her official capacities and that he was never actually introduced to Freawaru, whose name he learned from overhearing others in the hall. By mentioning the women strictly in connection with their public functions, the hero suggests that he had no private interactions with them and that Heorot, consequently, is a court where excessive familiarity between the sexes was not to be found.[40] Beowulf follows his notice of the royal ladies by predicting the failure of Freawaru's diplomatic marriage to Ingeld:

> Sīo gehāten (is),
> geong goldhroden, gladum suna Frōdan;
> (h)afað þæs geworden wine Scyldinga,
> rīces hyrde, ond þæt ræd talað,
> þæt hē mid ðȳ wīfe wælfǣhða dǣl,
> sæcca gesette. Oft seldan hwǣr
> æfter lēodhryre lȳtle hwīle
> bongār būgeð, þēah sēo brȳd duge. (ll. 2024b–2031)

(She is promised, young and gold-bangled, to the gracious son of Froda; the friend of the Scyldings, caretaker of the realm, has determined and counts it advisable that by means of that woman he should settle a sum of fatal feuds and conflicts. As a rule, the murderous spear will rest idle only a little while after a national calamity, no matter how good the bride.)

---

40. *Beowulf* is not unique in this respect. See Hugh Magennis, "'No Sex Please, We're Anglo-Saxons'? Attitudes to Sexuality in Old English Prose and Poetry," *Leeds Studies in English* 26 (1995): 1–27.

Beowulf then spends nearly forty lines envisioning a scenario in which an aged Heathobard, mindful of Danish triumph in the past, prods a young man to violate the peace, and this eventually leads Ingeld to dissolve the marriage and avenge his father (ll. 2032–2069a). The evident reason for the inclusion of this digression in the midst of the homecoming speech must be to allow Beowulf to display the political wisdom he has acquired. Since the analogues confirm the accuracy of Beowulf's prediction, it appears that his understanding of foreign policy surpasses even that of the old and wise Hrothgar.[41] The Ingeld digression, far from being out of place in this context, recalls Hrothgar's earlier assessment ("ne hȳrde ic snotorlicor / on swā geongum feore guman þingian," ll. 1842b–1843) and reinforces the characterization of Beowulf as a hero whose talents include the ability to conduct diplomacy well at a young age. The passage contributes to the general aim of Beowulf's speech, which is to announce his maturation and demonstrate his readiness to rule.

Another striking detail that Beowulf provides without provocation materializes when he reveals that Hrothgar himself performed various poems at the banquet in celebration of the victory over Grendel:

> Þǣr wæs gidd ond glēo; gomela Scilding,
> felafricgende   feorran rehte;
> hwīlum hildedēor   hearpan wynne,
> gome(n)wudu grētte,   hwīlum gyd āwræc
> sōð ond sārlic,   hwīlum syllic spell
> rehte æfter rihte   rūmheort cyning;
> hwīlum eft ongan   eldo gebunden,
> gomel gūðwiga   gioguðe cwīðan,
> hildestrengo;   hreðer (in)ne wēoll
> þonne hē wintrum frōd   worn gemunde. (ll. 2105–2114)

(There was storytelling and entertainment; the ancient Scylding, well informed, recounted from far back; at times the battle-bold man touched the lyre with pleasure, the diverting wood; at times he pursued a tale, true and tragic; at times the big-hearted king duly offered an unusual account; at times, in turn, hobbled by age, the old war-maker sang dirges to his youth, his war powers; the breast welled up inside him when, made wise by the years, he called many things to mind.)

---

41. On the analogues, see Malone, "Tale of Ingeld." On the characterizing function of Beowulf's prediction, see Momma, "Education of Beowulf," 179.

In this account, Beowulf informs the Geatish court that Hrothgar, in addition to being a wealthy and generous king, is also a man of culture who could personally ensure that over the course of one evening his court would experience three of the main literary genres of traditional Germanic culture. The three clauses beginning with *hwīlum* describe three recognizable genres: the first, referring to a "true and tragic" (*sōð ond sārlic*) tale, evidently describes a heroic-legendary poem, since such poetry tends to focus on a tragic moment for a historical or pseudo-historical personage from the migration period; the second, referring to an "unusual account" (*syllic spell*), evidently describes the folktale or wonder story, the genre to which a hero's contests against monstrous adversaries would belong; and the third, referring to a lamentation on the king's loss of youth, appears to describe the elegiac and autobiographical monologue, a form made familiar by *The Wanderer*, *The Wife's Lament*, and many other monuments of early Germanic poetry.[42] By characterizing Hrothgar as a man of poetic aptitude and cultivated sensibility, Beowulf continues to impress on his countrymen the superior refinement of the foreign court where his talents were recognized and rewarded. The young king Hygelac, who has not yet been "made wise by years" (*wintrum frōd*), presumably lacks the knowledge and experience required to deliver a comparable performance.

A notable feature of Beowulf's homecoming account of his fights against the two monsters at Heorot is that he attributes neither of his victories to divine intervention.[43] The omission results in a salient contrast with the earlier accounts that Beowulf provided in Heorot, where he repeatedly stressed that God was ultimately responsible for his victory and survival. The difference reflects Beowulf's ability to calibrate his speech based on his context and purpose. In Denmark, where he found himself before a court that was not entirely friendly, he spoke as a humble courtier who did not desire the throne but merely sought advancement by earning the friendship of Hrothgar and the elevation

---

42. For discussion of the generic terms used, see David R. Howlett, "Form and Genre in *Beowulf*," *Studia Neophilologica* 46, no. 2 (1974): 309–25. On the elegiac genre, see Anne L. Klinck, *The Old English Elegies: A Critical Edition and Genre Study* (Montreal: McGill-Queen's University Press, 1992); Joseph Harris, "Elegy in Old English and Old Norse: A Problem in Literary History," in *The Old English Elegies: New Essays in Criticism and Research*, ed. Martin Green (Rutherford, NJ: Fairleigh Dickinson University Press, 1983), 46–56; Joseph Harris, "Hadubrand's Lament: On the Origin and Age of Elegy in Germanic," in *Heldensage und Heldendichtung im Germanischen*, ed. Heinrich Beck (Berlin: Walter de Gruyter, 1988), 81–114.

43. This observation is registered and discussed in Robert D. Stevick, "Christian Elements and the Genesis of *Beowulf*," *Modern Philology* 61, no. 2 (1963): 79–89, at 81–83.

in status that came with it. In Geatland, however, where Beowulf is confidently displaying his suitability for kingship, excessive humility would undermine the aim of his speech. In this context, Beowulf takes full credit for his victories over monstrous foes, stressing to Hygelac the honor brought to the Geatish people—"there, my lord, I brought honor to your people by acting" ("þǣr ic, þēoden mīn, þīne lēode / weorðode weorcum," ll. 2095–2096a)—and the ample rewards that he received from Hrothgar. The hero's confidence is manifest in the remark that punctuates his account of his victory over Grendel's mother:

> næs ic fǣge þā gȳt,
> ac mē eorla hlēo   eft gesealde
> māðma menigeo,   maga Healfdenes. (ll. 2141b–2143)

(I was not yet fated to die, but the protector of men again gave me many valuables, Healfdene's son.)

Beowulf says nothing to undercut the impression that he alone performed these unprecedented deeds and merited the treasures that resulted from them. Having already made several references to treasure and reward (ll. 2101–2104, 2134b, 2143a), Beowulf concludes his speech with a final reference to the treasures and an announcement that he intends to present the entirety of his winnings to Hygelac:

> Swā se ðēodkyning   þēawum lyfde
> nealles ic ðām lēanum   forloren hæfde,
> mægnes mēde,   ac hē mē (māðma)s geaf,
> sunu Healfdenes   on (mīn)ne sylfes dōm;
> ðā ic ðē, beorncyning,   bringan wylle,
> ēstum geȳwan.   Gēn is eall æt ðē
> lissa gelong;   ic lȳt hafo
> hēafodmāga   nefne, Hygelāc, ðec. (ll. 2144–2151)

(Thus, the king lived up to his usual ways; by no means had I forfeited the prize, the reward of my strength, but he gave me treasures, Healfdene's son, of my own choosing; I will bring them to you, your majesty, present them with goodwill. All favors are still dependent on you; I have few close relatives, except, Hygelac, for you.)

There is, perhaps, an element of suspense surrounding this conclusion. Beowulf has made it clear to the Geatish court that his accomplishments surpass those of the young king Hygelac, who was famous at the time only for being the bane of one notable human adversary. Hygelac's status as "the slayer of Ongentheo" ("bonan Ongenþeoes," l. 1968a) is mentioned in the passage leading up to Beowulf's arrival at court, though it is later revealed that he earned this title not through his own action but through the combined action of two of his men (ll. 2961–2984). Beowulf, in contrast, is personally responsible for the extermination of two monsters, and he has earned the admiration of a rich and powerful neighboring king as a result. He is in a position where he could, like Hlǫðr in *Hlǫðskviða*, demand from his kinsman rule over half of the kingdom, if not more.[44] A comment following the interaction that praises the hero for not contriving the death of his uncle appears to acknowledge that he is in such a position:

> Swā sceal mǣg don,
> nealles inwitnet   ōðrum bregdon
> dyrnum cræfte,   deað ren(ian)
> hondgesteallan.   Hygelāce wæs
> nīða heardum,   nefa swȳðe hold
> ond gehwæðer ōðrum   hrōþra gemyndig. (ll. 2166b–2171)

(That is what a kinsman ought to do, not to weave a web of malice around another with covert craftiness, plot the death of a comrade. To Hygelac, firm in adversity, his nephew was very loyal, and each watched out for the benefit of the other.)

There would be little point to this comment if the audience were not aware of scenarios in which a hero's arrival at court led to strife between kinsmen rather than the peaceful sharing of wealth. The comment highlights the courteousness of Beowulf, who manages to strike a balance in his artful speech: he is assertive about his achievements, yet he refrains from openly coercing Hygelac into granting him royal authority. By placing himself entirely at the mercy of his kinsman, Beowulf allows Hygelac to appear generous rather than vulnerable. Should Hygelac choose to grant Beowulf such authority, his decision would be seen, on account of Beowulf's perfect courtesy, as a sign of magnanimity rather than weakness.

---

44. See Hollis, "*Beowulf* and the Succession," 46–50. Rather than likening Beowulf to Hlǫðr, Hollis proposes that he is being contrasted with Hrothulf in this scene (under the assumption that Hrothulf will eventually seize power).

Although Beowulf's concluding gesture displays his usual courtesy and restraint, he does not refrain in this context from acknowledging that Hrothgar wished to make him an heir to the Danish throne. In Denmark, Beowulf had the circumspection to mention his adoption only in connection with the possibility that he might die prematurely. In Geatland, Beowulf openly draws the connection between the transfer of royal heirlooms and succession to the Danish throne in an enigmatic postscript to his lengthy speech. Having ordered his winnings to be brought forward (ll. 2152–2154), Beowulf relates the history of one of the treasures to Hygelac:

> Mē ðis hildesceorp   Hrōðgār sealde
> snotra fengel;   sume worde hēt
> þæt ic his ǣrest ðē   ēst gesægde:
> cwæð þæt hyt hæfde   Hiorogār cyning,
> lēod Scyldunga   lange hwīle;
> nō ðȳ ǣr suna sīnum   syllan wolde,
> hwatum Heorowearde,   þēah hē him hold wǣre,
> brēostgewǣdu.   Brūc ealles well! (ll. 2155–2162)

(Hrothgar gave me this war gear, the wise monarch; he enjoined that I should first explain to you in a few words his goodwill: he said that King Heorogar owned it, that man of the Scyldings, for a long while; yet he did not care to give the breast-covering to his son, bold Heoroweard, though he was dear to him. Enjoy all of it well!)

The narrator labels this history of the royal war gear a *gyd* (2154b), a word often applied in other sources to parables and riddles.[45] The generic label essentially indicates that there is a layer of significance in the speech that resides beneath the surface of what is being directly stated. In this case, the riddle is not difficult to solve, as the hidden meaning is rather transparent: since Heorogar passed the royal war gear to Hrothgar rather than to his own son and the throne likewise passed to Hrothgar rather than to Heoroweard, then Hrothgar's gifting of these treasures to Beowulf effectively designates Beowulf as the person whom Hrothgar wishes to succeed him on the throne. Beowulf

---

45. See Scott Gwara, "Paradigmatic Wisdom and the Native Genre *Giedd* in Old English," *Studi Medievali* 53, no. 2 (2012): 783–852; Roscoe E. Parker, "*Gyd, Leoð,* and *Sang* in Old English Poetry," *University of Tennessee Studies in the Humanities* 1 (1956): 59–63; Richard North, *Pagan Words and Christian Meanings* (Amsterdam: Rodopi, 1991), 39–62.

is not so indiscreet as to say directly to Hygelac that his elevation in Denmark merits commensurate elevation in Geatland and that he expects to be granted royal authority in exchange for these supremely valuable treasures. Nevertheless, Hygelac plainly comprehends the import of Beowulf's courteous yet subtly coercive gesture, which demands an equally grand gesture in return. Hygelac reciprocates by sharing royal authority with Beowulf and making him the subordinate king of Geatland:

Hēt ðā eorla hlēo   in gefetian,
heaðorōf cyning,   Hrēðles lāfe
golde gegyrede;   næs mid Gēatum ðā
sincmāðþum sēlra   on sweordes hād;
þæt hē on Bīowulfes   bearm ālegde,
ond him gesealde   seofan þūsendo,
bold ond bregostōl.   Him wæs (b)ām samod
on ðām lēodscipe   lond gecynde,
eard ēðelriht,   ōðrum swīðor
sīde rīce   þām ðær sēlra wæs. (ll. 2190–2199)

(Then the men's protector, the war-strong king, directed that Hrethel's legacy, trimmed with gold, be fetched in; there was not then among the Geats a better jeweled treasure in the form of a sword; he laid it in Beowulf's lap and gave him seven thousand hides of land, a hall, and a lord's throne. The land in that nation was proper to both of them together, the country and ancestral domain, the broad rule more especially to one of them, who was superior in rank.)

In exchange for Heorogar's war gear, Hygelac places into Beowulf's lap the sword of Hrethel, the greatest treasure in the kingdom and an heirloom symbolizing the possession of royal authority. While in previous cases the poet had refrained from spelling out the implications attendant on the transfer of royal heirlooms, in this case the result is made clear: Beowulf has been made the coruler of Geatland, subordinate in authority to Hygelac, but possessing for himself a kingdom equivalent in size to that of the South Saxon kingdom at the time of the Tribal Hidage.[46]

---

46. See Frederick M. Biggs, "*Beowulf* and Some Fictions of the Geatish Succession," *Anglo-Saxon England* 32 (2003): 55–77; Biggs, "Politics of Succession," 731–34. For the observation

At line 2199, the narrative of Beowulf's transition from courtier to king reaches its end. Beowulf is not yet the sole ruler of Geatland—he will wait for both Hygelac and Heardred to die before agreeing to possess that status—but he has been made a king, and that is sufficient for the poet to consider the first portion of his epic poem to have satisfactorily concluded. That the poet conceived of his work possessing a bipartite structure, with its first part focusing on the hero's path to kingship and its second part focusing on the hero's death, seems clear from the fact that both parts are punctuated by eulogistic assessments of the hero's character. Immediately prior to the passage just cited, the poet provides an overview of Beowulf's life, which begins by distinguishing his general conduct from that of a conventional hero:

> Swā b(eal)dode   bearn Ecgðeowes,
> guma gūð(um) cūð,   gōdum dǣdum,
> drēah æfter dōme;   nealles druncne slōg
> heorðgenēatas;   næs him hrēoh sefa
> ac hē mancynnes   mǣste cræfte
> ginfæstan gife   þe him God sealde
> hēold hildedēor. (ll. 2177–2183a)

(Ecgtheo's offspring had thus shown himself brave, a man renowned in war, by his good deeds, had acted in accordance with honor; by no means did he strike down close associates as they drank; he did not have a fierce temperament, but, brave in battle, with the greatest of human skill he managed the abundant gifts that God had granted him.)

What makes Beowulf special, the poet stresses here, is his courtesy and self-restraint, his ability to manage the prodigious endowments that distinguish any hero from an ordinary human being. Critics have occasionally supposed that the poet is contrasting Beowulf specifically with Heremod here, but most heroes in Germanic legend have a "fierce temperament" (*hrēoh sefa*) and would insist on killing anyone, even an inebriated companion, who leveled a real or perceived insult at their personal honor (recall that Rosimund contrived the death of Alboin on

---

about the size of Beowulf's kingdom, see Martin Welch, "The Kingdom of the South Saxons: The Origins," in *The Origins of Anglo-Saxon Kingdoms*, ed. Steven Bassett (London: Leicester University Press, 1989), 75–83, at 75.

account of words he spoke while drunk).⁴⁷ The *Beowulf* poet makes explicit in this overview his intention to construct an untraditional hero who does not prioritize personal honor over everything else. Whereas other heroes might have killed Unferth for words spoken while drunk, Beowulf is willing to forgive Hrothgar's *heorðgenēat* and pursue friendship at Heorot. The hero managed his endowments well by using them to kill monsters rather than his fellow noblemen; through a combination of brave deeds and courteous behavior, Beowulf became a king without killing kinsmen, breaking oaths, or spilling unnecessary blood. The second half of the overview of Beowulf's life makes his rise to power all the more remarkable by revealing that he was considered unpromising as a youth:

> Hēan wæs lange
> swā hyne Gēata bearn   gōdne ne tealdon,
> nē hyne on medobence   micles wyrðne
> (dry)hten Wedera   gedōn wolde;
> swȳðe (wēn)don   þæt hē slēac wære,
> æðeling unfrom.   Edwenden cwōm
> tīrēadigum menn   torna gehwylces. (ll. 2183b–2189)

(For a long time he had been lowly, as the sons of the Geats had not thought him good, nor had the lord of the Weders cared to put him in possession of much on the mead-bench; they had rather thought that he was shiftless, a slack lordling. A reversal of fortune for all his troubles came to the man blessed with glory.)

This passage has often been considered problematic, since it is thought to create an inconsistency with other passages concerning Beowulf's youthful achievements and happy upbringing.⁴⁸ Conventional explanations for the alleged inconsistency suppose that the poet has either carelessly preserved a folk motif from traditions about Beowulf that

47. For the supposition of a contrast with Heremod specifically, see Adrien Bonjour, "Young Beowulf's Inglorious Period," *Anglia* 70 (1951): 339–44, at 340; Klaeber, *Beowulf,* 162.

48. For discussion of this minor crux and a sense of its critical history, see Kemp Malone, "Young Beowulf," *Journal of English and Germanic Philology* 36, no. 1 (1937): 21–23; Bonjour, "Young Beowulf's Inglorious Period"; George J. Engelhardt, "On the Sequence of Beowulf's *Geogoð,*" *Modern Language Notes* 68, no. 2 (1953): 91–95; Norman E. Eliason, "Beowulf's Inglorious Youth," *Studies in Philology* 76, no. 2 (1979): 101–8; Raymond P. Tripp Jr., "Did Beowulf Have an 'Inglorious Youth'?," *Studia Neophilologica* 61, no. 2 (1989): 129–43; Momma, "Education of Beowulf," 168–70; Leneghan, *Dynastic Drama of Beowulf,* 103.

he inherited or carelessly added this common motif to such traditions. I would argue, however, that no serious inconsistency emerges from the passage if it is understood to mean only that Beowulf was not considered in his youth to be the most promising candidate for kingship: out of the pool of Geatish *æðelingas*, Beowulf was not being groomed for kingship because there were several others who possessed a more immediate claim to the throne than the son of Ecgtheow.[49] Beowulf was not despised or mistreated; he was merely lower in the hierarchy of noblemen, not considered as "good" (*gōdne*) or as "worthy" (*wyrðne*) as his peers, because his extraordinary abilities had not yet been made apparent. Whether inherited or invented, the poet has evidently adapted this common folktale motif to his courtly narrative in order to make Beowulf's accession to the throne more impressive and lend further validation to the hero's conduct. Had Beowulf been the designated heir to the Geatish throne all his life, there would be little reason for him to undertake a dangerous adventure and win fame in a foreign court in order to forge his path to the throne.

When *Beowulf* is viewed through the lens of courtesy and courtliness, the bipartite structure of the poem becomes more starkly apparent, as the poet's interest in these two phenomena finds most of its expression in lines 1–2199, being expressed far less often in lines 2200–3182. The reason for the disparity is rather clear: courtesy and courtliness are associated in *Beowulf* with life, with society, with thriving and rising, and are thus suited to a narrative about a hero's coming of age; by the same token, these themes are correspondingly unsuited to a narrative about a hero's death, where the selection of material in the background appears designed to enhance the poignancy in the foreground of the world's loss of this peerless hero. Indeed, the possibility for the poet to describe scenes of courtly life is largely eliminated after lines 2324–2332, in which we are told that the dragon burned down the Geatish court and that this loss caused Beowulf to experience uncharacteristically dark thoughts. Of course, Beowulf is not characterized as a *discourteous* hero in the poem's second part, but opportunities for displaying courteous behavior become rather limited in a world without a court. There is, however, one significant reminder of the hero's courteousness

---

49. For comparable readings, see Biggs, "Politics of Succession," 725; North, "Hrothulf's Childhood and Beowulf's," 233–35.

in a speech he delivers while preparing to fight the dragon. Beowulf restates his characteristic concern for fair play:

> Nolde ic sweord beran,
> wǣpen tō wyrme,   gif ic wiste hū
> wið ðām āglǣcean   elles meahte
> gylpe wiðgrīpan,   swā ic giō wið Grendle dyde;
> ac ic ðǣr heaðufȳres   hātes wēne,
> [o]reðes ond *āttres*;   forðon ic mē on hafu
> bord ond byrnan. (ll. 2518b–2524a)

(I would not bear a sword, a weapon against the reptile, if I knew how I could otherwise honorably grapple with the troublemaker, as I once did with Grendel; but I expect hot war-flame there, exhalations and poison; therefore I have on me shield and mail-shirt.)

Along with his insistence on fighting the dragon alone (ll. 2532b–2535a), this passage indicates that Beowulf's commitment to fair and honorable combat, having been demonstrated in his youth, persists into his old age. His elderly reminiscence of his refusal to use weapons against Grendel creates an element of unity between the three monster fights, insofar as each fight affords the hero an opportunity to express his commitment to an ideal of noble conduct while also testing that commitment. Against Grendel, he completely lived up to his ideal; against Grendel's mother, he largely lived up to his ideal, with the exception of a hair pull employed in desperation (ll. 1537–1540);[50] and against the dragon, he lived up to his ideal not by abstaining from weaponry or refusing additional help—the foe was too powerful and dangerous for a genuinely equal fight to take place—but by sacrificing himself in order to protect his people from a national threat. In each fight, Beowulf shows himself to be conscientious about norms of conduct even when forced, in mortal danger, to relax the strictness with which he adheres to these norms.

Courtesy and courtliness, though necessarily minimized in the elegiac and foreboding poetry constituting the second part of *Beowulf*, are stressed again in the poem's concluding lines. Describing the hero's funeral, the poet becomes as attentive to matters of status and conduct as

---

50. On the passage in question, see E. G. Stanley, "Did Beowulf Commit 'Feaxfeng' against Grendel's Mother?," *Notes and Queries* 23, no. 8 (1976): 339–40.

he was during the scenes of courtly life in Heorot, while simultaneously reminding the audience that courtesy ranked among the most commendable traits of his protagonist. Having constructed a burial mound for Beowulf, his retainers ride around it and lament their beloved king:

> Þā ymbe hlǣw riodan   hildedīore,
> æþelinga bearn,   ealra twelf(e),
> woldon (care) cwīðan   (ond c)yning mǣnan,
> wordgyd wrecan,   ond ymb w(er) sprecan;
> eahtodan eorlscipe   ond his ellenweorc
> duguðum dēmdon—   swā hit gedē(fe) bið
> þæt mon his winedryhten   wordum herge,
> ferhðum frēoge,   þonne hē forð scile
> of l(ī)chaman   (lǣ)ded weorðan.
> Swā begnornodon Gēata lēode
> hlāfordes (hry)re,   heorðgenēatas;
> cwǣdon þæt hē wǣre   wyruldcyning[a]
> manna mildust   ond mon(ðw)ǣrust,
> lēodum līðost   ond lofgeornost. (ll. 3169–3182)

(Then battle-brave sons of nobles rode around the mound, twelve in all, wanted to voice their grief and lament their king, express it in words and speak of the man; they praised his manliness and honored his acts of heroism with glory—just as it is proper for a man to commend his friend and lord in speech, cherish him in his soul when he must be led forth from the flesh. Just so the Geatish people, his retinue, bemoaned the fall of their lord; they said that of worldly kings he was the most benevolent of men and the kindest, most generous to his people and most honor-bound.)

It is significant that the men who perform the funerary ritual on horseback are described as the "sons of nobles" (*æþelinga bearn*) and the king's "hearth-companions" (*heorðgenēatas*). The noble birth and high rank of the men are made unambiguously clear in order to indicate that every aspect of the hero's funeral is "proper" (*gedēfe*). The hearth-companions, the men who had been granted the most intimate access to the royal person when he lived, are the same men granted the privilege of proximity to his symbolic remains. Beowulf is fittingly honored to have these men ceremoniously grieve and eulogize him. The poem's final words recall the overview of the hero's character that had punctuated the conclusion of the poem's first part: he is praised for being not the greatest monster-slayer ever to live but the kindest, gentlest, and mildest king (*mildust, monðwærust, liðost*) as well as the most eager for fame (*lofgeornost*). Of the four superlatives constituting the final eulogy, only one of them (*lofgeornost*) appears to reflect on the hero's monster-slaying; the other three have nothing to do with the monster fights and instead recall the courteous behavior that Beowulf consistently displayed toward others. The emphasis on the hero's gentleness recalls the significant comment in the earlier overview that "he did not have a fierce temperament" ("næs him hrēoh sefa," l. 2180b). Such reiteration confirms that an ambition to construct a notably untraditional hero—lower in bellicosity and higher in courtesy—was central to the poem's design.

The uniqueness of *Beowulf* reflects its poet's delicate fusion of two distinct sets of inherited material: heroic-legendary poetry, which told of semi-historical heroes forced by circumstances to kill kinsmen or break oaths, and folkloric narratives, which told of supernatural heroes and their monster-slaying adventures. With the former material, the poet evidently appreciated its historical and aristocratic dimensions while objecting to its amoral vision. The previous chapter demonstrated that the poet made a concerted effort to sanitize the heroic inheritance and avoid valorizing heroes who were known to have killed kinsmen or broken oaths. With the folkloric material, the poet evidently appreciated its freedom from moral ambiguity, while objecting to its unrealistic and non-aristocratic character. Although folktales might tell of kings and princes, they tend to "describe the high world of nobles from below," to borrow an apt phrase from Stanley,[51] and pay minimal attention to the nuances of court life. The *Beowulf* poet, trained in an aristocratic poetic tradition and composing in all likelihood for a courtly audience, appears to have considered this absence of courtliness a serious problem. The present chapter has demonstrated that the poet went to great lengths to remedy that problem and endow his folkloric inheritance with a quality of courtly realism. At the same time, the poet uses the behavioral restraint associated with courtliness to temper the unrelenting ethos conventionally celebrated in the heroic-legendary tradition. The first 2,199 lines of *Beowulf* feature a hero's victory over two monsters, but they apportion considerably more attention to the courteous and courtly behavior that the hero displays as he experiences hospitality

---

51. Stanley, "Courtliness and Courtesy in *Beowulf*," 96.

and hostility at the Danish court and then makes the transition from courtier to king on arrival in Geatland.

The previous chapter concluded by contrasting *Beowulf* with the *Hildebrandslied* and observing that there is nothing in *Beowulf* comparable to the agonized depiction of a father forced by a cruel fate to kill his own son. The present chapter will conclude by suggesting that the extent to which *Beowulf* differs from its folkloric inheritance with respect to courtliness might be apprehended by contrasting the poem with *Hrólfs saga kraka*.[52] Although the saga was composed after *courtoisie* became a major literary and cultural phenomenon throughout Europe, it is far less concerned with courtliness than *Beowulf*. In the saga, when the ursine hero Bǫðvarr Bjarki arrives at the Danish court from Geatland, he simply enters it "without asking anyone's permission" and proceeds to gain the king's attention by killing one of his retainers; the king then requires Bǫðvarr to recompense the killing by taking the dead retainer's place in his retinue.[53] What transpires fantastically over a single page in the saga transpires more realistically (and rather differently) over several hundred lines in *Beowulf*, where the arriving Geatish hero is not the son of a bear but a kinsman and hearth-companion of the historical king Hygelac, who must interact courteously with a series of officials before he is deemed worthy (on account of his noble war gear) of an audience with the Danish king. The author of the saga has allowed his folkloric inheritance to retain its magical quality, evidently finding no need to alter narratives where a hero simply walks into a court unannounced and quickly finds himself in the service of the king. The *Beowulf* poet must have inherited such narratives, but he clearly found them in need of substantial revision in order for them to become compatible with his ambition to compose a sophisticated poem set in a plausible courtly environment.

The contrast between the extensive attention paid to court procedure in *Beowulf* and the disregard for it in *Hrólfs saga kraka* recalls the penetrating remarks with which T. A. Shippey concluded the study that pioneered the analysis of *Beowulf* through the lens of Vladimir Propp's *Morphology of the Folktale*. Proppian analyses of *Beowulf*, which have been

---

52. Much has been written about the relationship between *Beowulf* and *Hrólfs saga kraka*, though not about the relative courtliness of the two works. See Friedrich Kluge, "Der Beowulf und die Hrolfs saga kraka," *Englische Studien* 22 (1896): 144–45; Oscar Ludvig Olson, "The Relation of the *Hróſs Saga Kraka* and the *Bjarkarímur* to *Beowulf*," *Publications of the Society for the Advancement of Scandinavian Study* 3, no. 1 (1916): 1–104; Shippey, "*Hrólfs saga kraka*."

53. Jesse L. Byock, *The Saga of King Hrolf Kraki* (London: Penguin, 1998), 48–49.

carried out by several others following the publication of Shippey's study, facilitate the identification of folktale functions both included in the poem and excluded or obscured.[54] Pondering the functions that the *Beowulf* poet has deliberately omitted from his folkloric inheritance, Shippey arrives at a paradoxical conclusion:

> Propp's analysis . . . remind[s] us that fairy-tales are not adventures enriched and complicated by magic, but stories about magic, with their illogical and "inadvertent" nature always a part of them, not a corruption. So, one insight that we gain into *Beowulf* is that it is this magic element that the poet likes least, for he can be seen not only disguising his hero's bear-nature and converting waterfall-caves into submarine halls, but also trying to blot out the typical features of the magical object of search and the magic property that helps in the search. . . . *Beowulf* is a fairy-tale with all the magic removed, as far as possible—a paradox worth considering.[55]

A similar paradox emerges from the present chapter, which has been arguing for the deliberate realism of a medieval poem that must strike any modern reader as manifestly unrealistic, peopled as it is by a preternaturally strong hero and several fantastical monsters. The realism of *Beowulf* is obviously not the realism of the nineteenth-century novel: the poem is far less realistic, in any sense of the term, than a novel by Flaubert, yet that should not prevent us from recognizing that *Beowulf* is significantly more realistic, at least with respect to the details of court life, than *Hrólfs saga kraka* and probably all of the folktales the poet inherited. Moral as much as aesthetic considerations probably motivated the poet's insistence on courtly realism: the protagonist would not be a very effective model of commendable behavior if he seemed to exist in an ahistorical, dreamlike, fairy-tale world. In order for Beowulf to be a persuasive exemplar of courtesy and courtliness, he must be a mortal man rather than a bear's son, and he must be placed in a historical setting at plausibly structured courts, where noble birth, aristocratic war gear, and nuances of status mattered; where disputes arose between courtiers vying for position; where grievances over succession

---

54. See V. Propp, *Morphology of the Folktale*, trans. Laurence Scott, rev. Louis A. Wagner (Austin: University of Texas Press, 1968); T. A. Shippey, "Fairy-Tale Structure of *Beowulf*"; Barnes, "Folktale Morphology"; Rosenberg, "Folktale Morphology"; Gould, "*Beowulf* and Folktale Morphology"; Stitt, *Beowulf and the Bear's Son*.

55. Shippey, "Fairy-Tale Structure of *Beowulf*," 10–11.

were aired through gracious words and subtle gestures; and where the spatial arrangement of personnel at court was deeply significant. The poet's interest in courtesy and courtliness might seem to be expressed in sundry details, but when these details are viewed cumulatively, they can be seen to be fundamental to the poet's aspiration to construct a moving, edifying, and relatively realistic poem around a stainless protagonist whose death is such a tragic event that it merits the extended elegy with which the poem concludes.

CHAPTER 3

Monotheism and Monstrosity

An argument developed throughout the preceding chapters is that the peculiar design of *Beowulf* reflects a poet's plan to morally renovate the amoral tradition of heroic-legendary poetry that he inherited. In the antecedent tradition, circumstances conventionally compel a protagonist to kill a kinsman or break an oath against his or her inclinations; the cruelty of fate drives a good-natured hero to commit a dishonorable transgression in order to escape from an equally dishonorable situation. Moral ambiguity pervades nearly every extant witness to migration-period legend, from the *Hildebrandslied* to the *Nibelungenlied*, as these works tell of conflicts not between good and evil but between justified participants motivated by irreconcilable ethical imperatives. A different moral vision prevails in *Beowulf*, where the focus is placed on a benevolent protagonist, who kills no kinsmen, breaks no oaths, behaves courteously, believes in God, and receives the support of God in struggles against monstrous adversaries. This protagonist is surrounded in the poem's foreground not by the kin-slayers and oath-breakers of antecedent tradition, who are consigned to the digressions, but by a set of similarly virtuous and sanitized characters, who also abstain from the major transgressions, display courteous behavior, and express monotheistic convictions. In the previous chapter, I argued that the courtesy displayed by these characters, far from being an incidental feature of the poem, is actually fundamental to its design and connected to the poet's broader aim to lend a quality of courtly realism to the folkloric traditions from which the unstained protagonist derives. The argument of the present chapter is that the monotheism of the foregrounded characters is similarly fundamental, as it forms a coherent and consistent feature of the poem that contributes to the moral renovation of an amoral heroic tradition.

The monotheism of *Beowulf* has received far more attention than its courtliness in the critical literature, though it has usually been analyzed through the distorting lens of "Christian and pagan elements," which generations of critics have imagined as coexisting uneasily within the poem.[1] The notion that there is tension between Christianity and paganism in *Beowulf* appears to stem less from the poem itself, where the foregrounded characters are consistently represented as pious monotheists, than from scholarly contemplation of the following consideration: the fifth- and sixth-century inhabitants of the poem's world, contemporaries of the historical king Hygelac (who died around 525), should be pagan practitioners of a polytheistic religion, whereas the author of *Beowulf*, displaying familiarity with scripture and composing after the conversion of the Anglo-Saxons, must be a Christian. This consideration, while unobjectionable in itself, has led to many extrapolations about the characters' paganism and the poet's Christianity that contradict what is actually stated in the poem. Critics have often assumed that since the poet is a Christian, he must have taken seriously the Augustinian doctrine that there is no salvation outside the church (*extra ecclesiam nulla salus*) and consequently considered his cast of pagan characters to be damned on account of their ignorance of the Christian revelation.[2] Fred C. Robinson, for instance,

---

1. See the overview of the critical history in Edward B. Irving Jr., "Christian and Pagan Elements," in *A Beowulf Handbook*, ed. Robert E. Bjork and John D. Niles (Lincoln: University of Nebraska Press, 1997), 175–92. See also Brodeur, *Art of Beowulf*, 182–219; Betty S. Cox, *Cruces of Beowulf* (The Hague: Mouton, 1971), 12–32; Orchard, *Critical Companion*, 130–68.

2. See Stanley, *Hæþenra Hyht*; Larry D. Benson, "The Pagan Coloring of *Beowulf*," in *Old English Poetry: Fifteen Essays*, ed. Robert P. Creed (Providence: Brown University Press, 1967), 193–213; Goldsmith, *Mode and Meaning*; W. F. Bolton, *Alcuin and Beowulf: An Eighth-Century View* (New Brunswick, NJ: Rutgers University Press, 1978); A. J. Bliss, "*Beowulf*, Lines 3074–3075," in *J. R. R. Tolkien, Scholar and Storyteller: Essays in Memoriam*, ed. Mary Salu and Robert T. Farrell (Ithaca, NY: Cornell University Press, 1979), 41–63; Robinson, *Beowulf and the Appositive Style*; Fidel Fajardo-Acosta, *The Condemnation of Heroism in the Tragedy of Beowulf: A Study in the Characterization of the Epic* (Lewiston, ME: Edwin Mellen Press, 1989); Richard North, "Gold and the Heathen Polity in *Beowulf*," in *Gold in der Europäischen Heldensage*, ed. Wilhelm Heizmann (Berlin: De Gruyter, 2019), 72–114.

argues on the basis of this assumption that an ambivalent *Beowulf* poet "wants to acknowledge his heroes' damnation while insisting on their dignity."[3] Arguments of this sort, while attractive for their historical plausibility, run contrary to the poem itself, where there is no clear acknowledgment of the damnation of the foregrounded characters.

The Augustinian words written by Alcuin of York in the year 797, probably within a century of the composition of *Beowulf*, have often figured into critical discussion of the nature of the poet's Christianity and the relative orthodoxy of his doctrinal perspective. Exhausted though the passage may seem, Alcuin's words remain worthy of consideration, as their relationship to the views expressed in *Beowulf* might be clarified in the context of the argument developed throughout the present book. In a letter to a correspondent pseudonymously named Speratus, likely to be identified as Bishop Unwona of Leicester, Alcuin writes:

> Verba Dei legantur in sacerdotali convivio. Ibi decet lectorem audiri, non citharistam; sermones patrum, non carmina gentilium. Quid Hinieldus cum Christo? Angusta est domus; utrosque tenere non poterit. Non vult rex celestis cum paganis et perditis nominetenus regibus communionem habere; quia rex ille aeternus regnat in caelis, ille paganus perditus plangit in inferno.

> (Let God's words be read at the episcopal dinner table. It is right that a reader should be heard, not a harpist, patristic discourse, not pagan song. What has Ingeld to do with Christ? The house is narrow and has no room for both. The Heavenly King does not wish to have communion with lost, pagan kings listed name by name: for the eternal King reigns in Heaven, while the lost, pagan king wails in Hell.)[4]

Many critics have cited these words in order to suggest that the *Beowulf* poet concurred with Alcuin and considered his historically pagan

---

3. Robinson, *Beowulf and the Appositive Style*, 13.

4. The text is cited from Ernst Dümmler, ed., *Epistolae Karolini Aevi II*, Monumenta Germaniae Historica, Epistolae 4 (Berlin: Weidmann, 1895), 183; the translation follows Donald A. Bullough, "What Has Ingeld to Do with Lindisfarne?," *Anglo-Saxon England* 22 (1993): 93–125, at 124. The identification of Speratus with Unwona is likewise made by Bullough. For further discussion of Alcuin's letter, see Mary Garrison, "'Quid Hinieldus cum Christo?'" in *Latin Learning and English Lore: Studies in Anglo-Saxon Literature for Michael Lapidge*, ed. Katherine O'Brien O'Keeffe and Andy Orchard, vol. 1 (Toronto: University of Toronto Press, 2005), 237–59.

characters condemned, while other critics have cited these words to suggest that the *Beowulf* poet disagreed with Alcuin and composed his epic poem as a dissenting reaction to the kind of sentiments that Alcuin expressed.[5] I will put forward an alternative view, one that differs from the standard positions but is supported by the poet's systematic refusal to valorize the kin-slayers and oath-breakers of antecedent tradition: the *Beowulf* poet did not consider all pagans to be damned, but he might have considered Ingeld and others like him to be probable candidates for damnation. Moreover, the *Beowulf* poet appears to have agreed with Alcuin about the essential impiety of the conventional legends of kin-slayers and oath-breakers, and that is why he sought to compose an unconventional poem focused on an unconventional hero. In the legend of Ingeld, the protagonist is compelled to break his oath and attack his in-laws in order to escape the humiliation of letting his father lie unavenged. The *Beowulf* poet evidently agreed with Alcuin that a poem dwelling on Ingeld's predicament would be unsuitable for a Christian audience, that it would be impossible to compose a morally edifying Christian epic focused on a wretched hero such as Ingeld, Hengest, Hildebrand, Angantýr, or Signý, among others. For in these stories, where protagonists are driven to commit grievous transgressions contrary to their inclinations, an inextricably amoral vision is expressed, as we are presented only with desperate human resistance to the cruelty of fate in an unjust world. In such stories, there is beauty and pathos, but there is no room for a poet to insist repeatedly on the eternal reign of divine providence or to place instructive exemplars of courtesy and piety before a Christian audience.

Of all the migration-period legends, the story of Ingeld was perhaps particularly offensive to the sensibilities of a censorious churchman because of the prominent role played in it by the larger-than-life figure of Starkaðr. In many respects, Starkaðr is the embodiment of everything that the *Beowulf* poet found objectionable about the antecedent legendary tradition, everything that he sought to minimize, obscure, or invert during the composition of his unconventional epic. Starkaðr is a kin-slayer, an oath-breaker, a *þulr* (like Unferth), a devotee of Óðinn—indeed, he kills Víkarr, his lord and foster brother, at the instigation of Óðinn—and an inveterate opponent of courtesy and courtliness in all

---

5. For an example of the former, see Robinson, *Beowulf and the Appositive Style*, 8–9; for an example of the latter, see Hill, "Christian Language," 69–70. See also J. R. R. Tolkien, "*Beowulf*: The Monsters and the Critics," 266.

of its manifestations.[6] In Saxo's account of the speech that breaks the peace in the Ingeld legend, this crucial speech is delivered by Starkaðr, and it contains expressions of vulgarity, xenophobia, and anti-courtly sentiment (directed toward Ingeld's foreign bride) that are unlike anything found in the decorous world of *Beowulf*. Starkaðr, of course, is not mentioned in *Beowulf*, where the inciting speech is instead delivered by an anonymous "old ash-fighter, who remembers all" ("eald æscwiga, sē ðe eall geman," l. 2042). The description of this bellicose old warrior, who lived through the old wars and insists on vengeance for the dead, might allude to the supernaturally extended lifespan of Starkaðr, who carries the sobriquet "the old" (*hinn gamli*) in Old Norse tradition.[7] If the old Heathobard were not already Starkaðr in the legendary tradition that the *Beowulf* poet inherited, it would seem that this character must have developed into him and that he already possessed some of the qualities that the poet (and Alcuin) would have found repugnant. Indeed, if Starkaðr seems in many ways to be the antithesis of Beowulf, the contrast might well have been apparent to the poet, who attributes to the old Heathobard a fierce temperament ("him bið grim sefa," l. 2043b) while attributing the opposite to the protagonist ("næs him hrēoh sefa," l. 2180b) in parallel formulaic language.[8]

The *Beowulf* poet, like Alcuin, evidently recognized that the legend of Ingeld, with the prominence it accorded either to Starkaðr or the figure who developed into him, is not a promising vehicle for moral instruction within a Christian framework. The amorality of the antecedent tradition is too firmly woven into the plot attached to Ingeld, as it is with any plot that is structured around conflicting ethical

---

6. On the figure of Starkaðr and his place in legendary tradition, see Ciklamini, "Problem of Starkaðr"; Georges Dumézil, "The Three Sins of Starcatherus," in *The Destiny of the Warrior*, trans. Alf Hiltebeitel (Chicago: University of Chicago Press, 1970), 82–95; Jan de Vries, "Die Starkadsage," *Germanisch-Romanisch Monatsschrift* 36 (1955): 281–97; Poole, "Some Southern Perspectives"; William Layher, "Starkaðr's Teeth," *Journal of English and Germanic Philology* 108, no. 1 (2009): 1–26. For a discussion of Starkaðr's hostility to courtliness, see Kemp Malone, "Primitivism in Saxo Grammaticus," *Journal of the History of Ideas* 19, no. 1 (1958): 94–104.

7. For arguments in favor of the identification of the old Heathobard with Starkaðr, see de Vries, "Die Starkadsage," 283–84; Turville-Petre, *Myth and Religion*, 210; Poole, "Some Southern Perspectives," 155–56; Edward Currie, "Political Ideals, Monstrous Counsel, and the Literary Imagination in *Beowulf*," in *Imagination and Fantasy in the Middle Ages and Early Modern Time: Projections, Dreams, Monsters, and Illusions*, ed. Albrecht Classen, vol. 24 (Berlin: De Gruyter, 2020), 275–302, at 295–301.

8. For a suggestion that Beowulf is characterized as an "anti-Odinic hero," see Frank, "Skaldic Verse," 133. See also Thomas D. Hill, "Confession of Beowulf"; Momma, "Education of Beowulf," 163–65.

imperatives and the catastrophes that result from their collision. Ingeld, as an integral figure in the cycle of legends associated with the pious king Hrothgar, can be mentioned in a digression that showcases Beowulf's political shrewdness and lends historical depth to the poem, but he cannot be the protagonist of a poem like *Beowulf*, where a poet attempts to bring to life the world of migration-period legend without concentrating the narrative on the amoral plots traditionally attached to it. To place the world of legend within a moral framework, the *Beowulf* poet relegates the problematic aspects of tradition to his poem's background while concentrating on a virtuous monotheist and his struggle against monstrous adversaries in the foreground. The present chapter, on monotheism and monstrosity, examines in tandem the two aspects of *Beowulf* that actualize the poet's plan for moral renovation and enable him to make migration-period legend palatable for a Christian audience. It aims to establish the precise nature and function of the monotheistic vision expressed by the characters and the narrator while also exploring the relationship of the monsters to the poem's insistent monotheism. An attempt to unravel the ostensibly complex web of references to God and providence is also made in the following discussion. The poet appears, ultimately, to have sought to introduce greater polarity into his inherited materials: Beowulf is represented as more pious and benevolent than other migration-period heroes, while the monsters are represented as more sinister and malevolent than other monsters found in medieval Germanic literature. Such polarization functions to endow *Beowulf* with a sense of moral clarity that is not found in other works concerned with migration-period legend.

To assess the role that monotheism plays in the poem, it is worthwhile to establish who is and who is not represented as a monotheist in *Beowulf*. In addition to Hrothgar and Beowulf, whose numerous references to the singular deity will be analyzed below, several other major and minor characters in the poem's foreground are casually characterized as monotheists. Wealhtheow makes reference to "the decree of Providence" ("metodsceaft," l. 1180a) in one of her speeches and the narrator reports that she "thanked God" ("Gode þancode," l. 625b) when she greeted Beowulf. Hygelac, in his only speech in the poem, says, "I give thanks to God" ("Gode ic þanc secge," l. 1997b) on account of the hero's safe return. In his few speeches, Wiglaf twice mentions God (2650b, 2874b), describes God as the "wielder of victories" ("sigora waldend," l. 2875a), and asserts that the dead Beowulf will dwell "in the ruler's covenant" ("on ðæs waldendes wǣre," l. 3109). Further-more, the Danish coastguard is incidentally revealed to be a monotheist when he parts from the Geats and says to them: "may the all-powerful father with generosity keep you safe in your travels" ("fæder alwalda / mid ārstafum ēowic gehealde / sīða gesunde," ll. 316b–318a). The Geatish arrivals are likewise made out to be monotheists, as the narra-tor reports that they "thanked God that their passage over the waves had been easy" ("Gode þancedon / þæs þe him ȳþlāde ēaðe wurdon," ll. 227b–228) on arrival in Denmark; later in the poem, the same Geatish troop "thanked God" ("Gode þancodon," l. 1626b) for their leader's safe return from the mere of Grendel's mother. Finally, a monotheistic vision of creation is expressed by the anonymous court poet at Heorot, who tells how a single god, "the Almighty" ("se ælmihtiga," l. 92a), cre-ated the earth, the sun, the moon, and every form of life.

Monotheistic language is not used, however, by every character granted a speaking role in the poem. Wulfgar, in his series of short speeches, uses no monotheistic language, though it seems doubt-ful that the poet intended this omission to reflect negatively on him. Wulfgar's terse speech, focused entirely on the business at hand, char-acterizes him as a diligent and conscientious official who knows the custom of the court and admirably recognizes the worthiness of the Geatish petitioner. The 128-line speech of the Geatish messenger (ll. 2900–3027), the second longest speech in the poem, is also devoid of monotheistic language. In this case as well, the omission seems unlikely to reflect negatively on this character, about whom we are told noth-ing besides the accuracy of his predictions (ll. 3028–3030a). The more significant insight revealed by the case of the Geatish messenger is that monotheistic language is not something that would inevitably appear in any Beowulfian speech of sufficient length; this kind of language was not so integral to the poetic tradition that a poet could not avoid using it thoughtlessly to fill out lines with alliteration and adequate metrical weight.[9] Rather, the presence or absence of monotheistic lan-guage in a character's speech appears to be a deliberate and purposive feature of the poem that characterizes its speakers and might possess other functions. Comparable to courtesy and courtliness, monotheism is an insistent feature of Beowulf, an aspect of the poem that need not be present and might therefore be significant when it is present. This

---

9. For a similar claim, see J. R. R. Tolkien, "Beowulf: The Monsters and the Critics," 284–88.

conclusion is strengthened on recognition that monotheistic language is absent from the speeches of Unferth (ll. 506–528), the old Heathobard (ll. 2047–2056), and the last survivor (ll. 2247–2266), three characters whom the poet had good reason to avoid characterizing as pious monotheists.

Unferth is the most prominent character in the poem's foreground who neither uses monotheistic language nor is made out to be a monotheist in the narration concerning him. The omission is consistent with the poet's moral vision and his programmatic refusal to valorize the transgressive heroes of antecedent tradition: Unferth is a kin-slayer condemned to hell by the protagonist, who is consistently depicted in a negative light by the narrator, and his status as the court's *þyle* might indicate a connection to the worship of Woden.[10] The old Heathobard, if identified with Starkaðr, would also happen to be a transgressive *þulr* with ties to Óðinn, but even if the identification were rejected, this character would still be responsible for delivering the speech that leads to Ingeld's eventual oath-breaking. Yet of these three characters, it is the last survivor who possesses the clearest ties to paganism: the treasure he deposits in the earth is described as "heathen gold" ("hæðen gold," l. 2276b) constituting the "heathen treasury" ("hæðnum horde," l. 2216a) over which the dragon presides; his apostrophe to the "earth" ("hrūse," l. 2247a) might be a vestige of pre-Christian animistic belief; and his very act of burying treasure appears to have been regarded by the poet as a misguided pagan practice.[11] Additionally, G. V. Smithers has identified reasons to believe that in the tradition the poet inherited, the last survivor was posthumously reincarnated as the dragon.[12] Naturally, in this case and in all of the cases of pagan associations pertaining to these and other characters, the *Beowulf* poet's systematic tendency is to obscure such associations rather than emphasize then. A poet

10. See Hardy, "Christian Hero Beowulf and Unferð Þyle," 63–66; Hollowell, "Unferð the *Þyle*"; Jan de Vries, *Altgermanische Religionsgeschichte*, 2nd ed., 2 vols. (Berlin: De Gruyter, 1956), 1:402–4.

11. See Joseph Harris, "Heroic Poetry and Elegy: *Beowulf*'s Lay of the Last Survivor," in *Heldenzeiten—Heldenräume: Wann und wo spielen Heldendichtung und Heldensage?*, ed. Johannes Keller and Florian Kragl (Wien: Fassbaender, 2007), 27–41.

12. G. V. Smithers, *The Making of Beowulf: Inaugural Lecture of the Professor of English Language Delivered in the Appleby Theatre on 18 May, 1961* (Durham: University of Durham, 1961). See also H. R. Ellis Davidson, *Gods and Myths of Northern Europe* (Harmondsworth, UK: Penguin, 1964), 161; Raymond P. Tripp Jr., *More about the Fight with the Dragon: Beowulf, 2208b–3182: Commentary, Edition, and Translation* (Lanham, MD: University Press of America, 1983), 60; Peter C. Braeger, "Connotations of (Earm) Sceapen: *Beowulf* II. 2228-2229 and the Shape-Shifting Dragon," *Essays in Literature* 13, no. 2 (1986): 327–28.

concerned about the morality of the traditional amoral plot must have been no less concerned about objectionable forms of paganism in the originally pagan tradition that he inherited.

While assessing who is and who is not a monotheist in *Beowulf*, the poet's five uses of the word *hǣðen* are worth considering. In addition to its two occurrences in connection with the dragon's hoard, the word is used twice with reference to Grendel: when he dies, we are told that hell received his "heathen soul" ("hǣþene sāwle," l. 852a); and the nails on his severed hand are described as "hand-vestiges of the heathen" ("hǣþenes handsporu," l. 986a). The application of the term *hǣðen* to Grendel is sensible within the moral framework of *Beowulf*, where a heathen is not a practitioner of a particular form of pagan religion, but anyone who fails to recognize the authority of the one true God by opposing him, consorting with his enemies, or worshipping false gods. Although the *Beowulf* poet had historical grounds for depicting every character as a heathen, he decided to characterize Grendel as the only inveterate heathen in his narrative, while characterizing Beowulf, Hrothgar, and the other virtuous characters in the foreground as pious monotheists who are never described as "heathens." The fifth use of the term *hǣðen* is applied not to the foregrounded characters but to an unspecified group of Danes who turn to idol worship in a misguided attempt to gain supernatural assistance against Grendel. This controversial passage must be considered at length:

> Hwīlum hīe gehēton   æt hærgtrafum
> wīgweorþunga,   wordum bǣdon
> þæt him gāstbona   gēoce gefremede
> wið þēodþrēaum.   Swylc wæs þēaw hyra,
> hǣþenra hyht;   helle gemundon
> in mōdsefan,   metod hīe ne cūþon,
> dǣda dēmend,   ne wiston hīe drihten God,
> nē hīe hūru heofena   helm herian ne cūþon,
> wuldres waldend.   Wā bið þǣm ðe sceal
> þurh slīðne nīð   sāwle bescūfan
> in fȳres fæþm,   frōfre ne wēnan,
> wihte gewendan;   wēl bið þǣm þe mōt
> æfter dēaðdæge   drihten sēcean
> ond tō fæder fæþmum   freoðo wilnian. (ll. 175–188)

(At times they pledged honors to idols, prayed explicitly that a soul-slayer would lend them assistance against that countrywide disaster. Such was their way, the hope of heathens; they minded hell in their heart of hearts; they did not recognize Providence, the arbiter of all things done; they did not know the Lord God, nor did they even know to praise heaven's helm, the master of magnificence. Woe to one who has to thrust his soul through dire affliction into the fire's embrace, expect no comfort, experience no change at all; well to one who is permitted after his death-day to seek the Lord and sue for peace in the father's embrace.)

This passage has widely been considered one of the most problematic in the poem. Indeed, some critics have considered it to be so fundamentally irreconcilable with the rest of the poem that they would regard it as an interpolation composed by an individual who was not the author of the surrounding textual matrix.[13] I would argue, however, that the passage is consistent with the theological vision expressed elsewhere in the poem, and that the problems surrounding this passage emerge only when it is made to state more than it actually does. The passage never states that damnation is the inevitable end awaiting all of the poem's characters; it never states that all Danes were hopeless and incorrigible heathens on account of their ignorance of the Christian revelation. It states, rather, that some Danes, in their ignorance and desperation, "occasionally" (hwīlum) turned to idol worship in the erroneous belief that the entity to which they were praying—who is, in actuality, the devil, the "soul-slayer" (gāstbona)—would fortify them against their national calamity. The ancient custom (þēaw) of idol worship expresses "the hope of heathens" (hǣþenra hyht) because it denies the sole authority of the one true God. While engaged in idol worship, the relevant Danes are aptly described as "heathens," according to the logic of the poem, since they are exhibiting the same failure to recognize God's authority as Grendel, who opposes God, and the last survivor, who appears to believe that the earth possesses supernatural powers of its own.[14]

---

13. See J. R. R. Tolkien, "*Beowulf*: The Monsters and the Critics," 287–89; J. R. R. Tolkien, *Beowulf: A Translation and Commentary; Together with Sellic Spell*, ed. Christopher Tolkien (London: HarperCollins, 2014), 169–81; Whitelock, *Audience of Beowulf*, 77–79; Thomas D. Hill, "Christian Language," 68–69; Thomas D. Hill, "*Beowulf* and Conversion History," in *The Dating of Beowulf: A Reassessment*, ed. Leonard Neidorf (Cambridge: D. S. Brewer, 2014), 191–201. See also Cox, *Cruces of Beowulf*, 102–30.

14. For other readings of lines 175–188 that defend its integrity, see Karl P. Wentersdorf, "*Beowulf*: The Paganism of Hrothgar's Danes," *Studies in Philology* 78, no. 5 (1981): 91–119; Dennis Cronan, "*Beowulf*, the Gaels, and the Recovery of the Pre-Conversion Past," *Anglo-Saxon* 1 (2007): 137–80; Geoffrey Russom, "Historicity and Anachronism in *Beowulf*,"

There is no thematic tension within *Beowulf* between "Christian and pagan elements." The only significant theological distinction in the world of the poem, made clear in lines 175–188, is between monotheism and polytheism, not Christianity and paganism. The poet imagines that the sixth-century Germanic peoples, who have received neither the Mosaic law nor the Christian revelation, were nonetheless capable of possessing intuitive knowledge of the singular deity of Judeo-Christian religion.[15] Consequently, the principal theological obligation that befell them was to follow their better intuitions and worship this one true God rather than myriad false gods. The poet does not represent his foregrounded characters as benighted heathens destined for an eternity in hell simply because the gospel had not reached them yet. Rather, the poet considers it possible for these characters to obtain salvation by worshipping God, recognizing his rule over the world, and trying to live in a manner that would be pleasing to him. This set of convictions forms a coherent intellectual framework within which every theological passage in *Beowulf*, including lines 175–188, can be shown to be sensible and internally consistent. A plausible doctrinal basis for this framework has been identified in St. Paul's Epistle to the Romans (1:19–23, 2:6–7, 13–15), where the apostle insists on the ability of pagans both to infer the existence of God from his creation and to live in accordance with divine law by following the natural law inscribed on the heart of every person.[16] In addition to Paul's epistle, there are several other conceivable theological and literary traditions to which the theological framework of *Beowulf* might be indebted.[17] Whatever the poet's sources might have been, he created an intellectually coherent poem where the

---

in *Epic and History*, ed. David Konstan and Kurt A. Raaflaub (Malden, MA: Wiley-Blackwell, 2010), 243–61.

15. Much has been written about the religious outlook of the poem's characters. I consider the most persuasive accounts to be those put forward by Charles Donahue and other scholars influenced by him. See Charles Donahue, "*Beowulf*, Ireland and the Natural Good," *Traditio* 7 (1951): 263–77; Donahue, "*Beowulf* and Christian Tradition"; Marijane Osborn, "The Great Feud: Scriptural History and Strife in *Beowulf*," *PMLA* 93, no. 5 (1978): 973–81; Thomas D. Hill, "Christian Language"; Cavill, "Christianity and Theology"; Cronan, "*Beowulf* . . . Pre-Conversion Past"; Russom, "Historicity and Anachronism"; Thomas D. Hill, "*Beowulf* and Conversion History."

16. See A. D. Horgan, "Religious Attitudes in *Beowulf*," in *Essays and Poems Presented to Lord David Cecil*, ed. W. W. Robson (London: Constable, 1970), 9–17. See also Donahue, "*Beowulf* and Christian Tradition," 59–63; Osborn, "Great Feud," 978–80.

17. For the suggestion that ideas of Celtic theologians might have influenced the *Beowulf* poet's perspective, see Donahue, "*Beowulf*, Ireland"; Donahue, "*Beowulf* and Christian Tradition"; Cronan, "*Beowulf* . . . Pre-Conversion Past." For other parallels, see Thomas D. Hill, "*Beowulf* and Conversion History."

theology expressed by the principal characters is best conceptualized neither as paganism nor as Christianity but as intuitive monotheism.

The poet acknowledges the intuitive nature of his characters' piety in the various passages constituting what Marijane Osborn calls "the two levels of knowledge": the direct references to scriptural events—Cain's killing of Abel, God's punishment of sin with the flood—are restricted to the poem's narration and kept out of the mouths of the characters, who know nothing of Grendel's ancestry or God's feud with Cain's descendants.[18] Their ignorance of scripture is likewise acknowledged in lines 180b–183a, where it is stated that the Danes neither know God (*metod hīe ne cūþon*) nor how to praise him (*herian ne cūþon*). Though often regarded as an inconsistency, the passage merely makes explicit the epistemological predicament that is implied throughout the poem. The poet laments the Danes' lack of formal theological instruction only at this point because their ignorance threatens here to imperil their souls: Grendel's depredations have caused them to deviate from their monotheistic intuitions and revert in desperation to the temporal expediency of polytheistic idol worship. Yet even this erroneous practice, undertaken occasionally (*hwīlum*), does not peremptorily ensure their damnation. The contrast between the woe that awaits the damned and the bliss that awaits the saved in lines 183b–188 implies not that the relevant Danes are inevitably damned but that their chances of salvation are jeopardized by engaging in idol worship. In doing so, the contrast simultaneously suggests that salvation could be attained by these Danes if they followed their nobler intuitions and prioritized the eternal over the transient.[19] The same idea appears to inform Hrothgar's exhortation to Beowulf to choose "eternal counsels" ("ēce rǣdas," l. 1760a): he warns the hero not to allow temporal prosperity to jeopardize his long-term spiritual prospects. Common to both passages, then, is a notion that salvation is possible for the poem's characters as long as they follow their better intuitions and never allow circumstances to induce them to worship wealth, power, or idols instead of the one true God. Far from being an aberration, lines 175–188 articulate a theological perspective that is perhaps unorthodox but is nevertheless consistent with the rest of the poem.

---

18. Osborn, "Great Feud," 973. See also Rafael J. Pascual, "Material Monsters and Semantic Shifts," in *The Dating of Beowulf: A Reassessment*, ed. Leonard Neidorf (Cambridge: D. S. Brewer, 2014), 202–18.

19. See Cronan, "*Beowulf* . . . Pre-Conversion Past," 171–80.

The foregoing discussion has aimed to establish that a doctrine of intuitive monotheism provides the *Beowulf* poet with a coherent theological framework and a tool for the characterization of the exemplary figures in the poem's foreground. The poet, having inherited an amoral tradition where heroes had little choice but to curse the Norns and bemoan the cruel fates thrust upon them, uses the doctrine of intuitive monotheism to create non-Christian characters who are far more palatable for a Christian audience than Ingeld or Hildebrand ever could have been. To arrive at a fuller understanding of the nature of the poem's monotheism, the discussion will now proceed sequentially through the uses of monotheistic language first by Hrothgar and then by Beowulf. In the course of doing so, it becomes apparent that there is an element of spiritual drama in *Beowulf*. In his first speech, Hrothgar establishes himself to be one of the more spiritually minded characters in the poem. Responding to Wulfgar's announcement of the arrival of Beowulf, who has not yet revealed his intention to fight Grendel, Hrothgar infers that God has sent Beowulf to eradicate Grendel:

> Hine hālig God
> for ārstafum   ūs onsende,
> tō West-Denum,   þæs ic wēn hæbbe,
> wið Grendles gryre. (ll. 381b–384a)

(The blessed Lord in his mercy has sent him to us, to the West-Danes, I think, against the terror of Grendel.)

In this first expression of monotheistic piety, Hrothgar exhibits a characteristic tendency to associate divine intervention with good fortune rather than ill fortune, with reward rather than punishment. God, in Hrothgar's conception, is a merciful figure whose providence is responsible not for inflicting Grendel's depredations on the Danes but for providing the Danes with the hero who will save them from Grendel. In his next speech, Hrothgar describes the suffering and humiliation that he has endured on account of Grendel's incursions, and then he exclaims: "God can easily hinder the mad ravager from these deeds!" ("God ēaþe mæg / þone dolscaðan dæda getwæfan!," ll. 478b–479). In both speeches, Hrothgar does not express the thought that his suffering might have been divinely inflicted; he assumes that divine intervention would be manifest only in the merciful elimination of his suffering. As we will see below, Hrothgar's conception of an exclusively benevolent God is largely shared by the poem's narrator, who tends also to associate divine intervention with reward and relief rather than punishment and suffering.

The next speech in which Hrothgar uses monotheistic language occurs after Beowulf's victory over Grendel. Standing on the *stapol* (926a) and looking at *Grendles hond* (927b), Hrothgar provides his people with a lesson in intuitive monotheism and exhorts them to infer God's miraculous providence from its visible manifestations:

> Ðisse ansȳne   alwealdan þanc
> lungre gelimpe.   Fela ic lāþes gebād,
> grynna æt Grendle;   ā mæg God wyrcan
> wunder æfter wundre,   wuldres hyrde. (ll. 928–931)

(For this sight let thanks be raised at once to the all-wielder. I have suffered much grief, misfortunes at the hands of Grendel; God can ever work miracle after miracle, herder of glory.)

Hrothgar here instructs his people, who have been celebrating Beowulf's victory, to direct their expressions of thanksgiving to the single all-powerful God. Perhaps implicit in his words is an instruction not to direct their gratitude toward any other spiritual entities through sacrifices or other superstitious rituals. Indeed, Hrothgar insists that the intervention of the singular deity pervaded every aspect of the elimination of Grendel, extending from Beowulf's latest deed to the moment that he was first conceived in his mother's womb:

> Nū scealc hafað
> þurh drihtnes miht   dǣd gefremede
> ðē wē ealle   ǣr ne meahton
> snyttrum besyrwan.   Hwæt, þæt secgan mæg
> efne swā hwylc mægþa   swā ðone magan cende
> æfter gumcynnum,   gyf hēo gȳt lyfað,
> þæt hyre ealdmetod   ēste wǣre
> bearngebyrdo. (ll. 939b–946a)

(Now a youngster has through the power of the Lord accomplished a deed that we all in our cleverness had not been able to contrive. Yes, whatsoever woman among the human race gave birth to this son, if she is still living, can say that Providence was gracious to her in her childbearing.)

Hrothgar declares that "the power of the Lord" (*drihtnes miht*) was expressed in Beowulf's performance of a deed that no amount of Danish "cleverness" (*snyttrum*) was able to effect. In making this statement, he is perhaps expressing regret for the errant course of action, namely, idol worship, that Danish counselors had previously advocated. He then announces, in a possible echo of statements about the birth of Christ made in the Gospel of Luke (1:42, 11:27), that the mother of Beowulf must have been blessed by God when she conceived him.[20] By suggesting that the elimination of Grendel had been planned before Grendel's ravages began, Hrothgar articulates a conception of providence not unlike that possessed by the narrator, who asserts in several passages (discussed below) that God has always ruled and continues to rule over all humankind. Having claimed that Beowulf is divinely supported, Hrothgar then announces that he will adopt the hero, offering him the highest conceivable reward and promising him access to everything in the kingdom (ll. 946b–950). Hrothgar concludes the speech as it began, with an acknowledgment of God's role in what transpired: "May the all-wielder reward you with good, as he has already done" ("Alwalda þec / gōde forgylde, swā hē nū gȳt dyde," ll. 955b–956). Hrothgar here implies that even his own behavior, in the form of his generosity to the hero, was providentially ordained. The speech as a whole thus conveys Hrothgar's confidence in the pervasive, eternal, and benevolent nature of God's presence in the world.

Hrothgar's confidence is shaken, however, when Grendel's mother avenges the death of her son by killing Æschere, Hrothgar's beloved counselor and closest companion. In his next speech, delivered on the morning after this event transpired, Hrothgar speaks for sixty lines (ll. 1322–1382) yet does not make a single reference to God or providence. The absence of monotheistic language suggests that Hrothgar has plunged into a state of deep despair on account of Æschere's death. Prior to the speech, the narrator hints at a crisis of faith within Hrothgar by noting that the king awaited "whether the all-wielder would ever effect a change for him after that period of affliction" ("hwæþer him

---

20. On the possible biblical echoes here, see Daniel F. Pigg, "Cultural Markers in *Beowulf*: A Re-Evaluation of the Relationship between Beowulf and Christ," *Neophilologus* 74, no. 4 (1990): 601–7. For a skeptical view, see Fred C. Robinson, "*Beowulf* in the Twentieth Century," *Proceedings of the British Academy* 94 (1997): 45–62, at 59–60; but see Cavill, "Christianity and Theology," 24–25.

alwalda æfre wille / æfter wēaspelle wyrpe gefremman," ll. 1314–1315). In his despondency, Hrothgar does not mention God, whose intervention he associates only with positive developments. He instead describes to Beowulf the horrific reports he has received about Grendel and his mother, two monsters of uncertain origin, and the terrifying conditions in which these monsters live (ll. 1345–1366a). Hrothgar concludes his speech not by expecting a divine remedy but by placing his hope entirely in Beowulf: "Now the course of action is again dependent on you alone" ("Nū is se rǣd gelang / eft æt þē ānum," ll. 1376b–1377a). A significant change has taken place within Hrothgar in the time that has elapsed since his previous speech: with his confidence in God's benevolent presence shaken, he has become a frightened king describing a world of malevolent supernatural beings ("ellorgǣstas," l. 1349a) and expressing uncertainty as to whether even Beowulf will be able to return alive from it. The final words of the speech—"if you get away" ("gyf þū on weg cymest," l. 1382b)—punctuate it with a reminder of the king's bleak outlook.

Yet Hrothgar's faith is restored after he hears Beowulf's forceful response, in which the young hero exhorts his wise elder not to grieve ("Ne sorga, snotor guma," l. 1384a) and to pursue instead immediate vengeance for his fallen friend.[21] The narrator states that Hrothgar made a sudden gesture of thanksgiving after hearing Beowulf's stirring words:

> Āhlēop ðā se gomela,   Gode þancode,
> mihtigan drihtne,   þæs se man gespræc. (ll. 1397–1398)

(Then the old man leapt up, thanked God, the mighty Lord, for what the man had said.)

It is clear from this narration that the poet intended a kind of spiritual drama to be attached to the figure of Hrothgar, who had been in a state of godless despair moments earlier. His expressions of piety are neither static nor perfunctory; they alter and develop in step with the poem's narrative. The next significant episode in this spiritual drama occurs after Beowulf presents Hrothgar with the hilt of the gigantic sword that he discovered (due to divine intervention) in the underwater dwelling

---

21. Thijs Porck observes that the *Beowulf* poet here creates "a complete reversal of the typical scene in the Germanic heroic tradition where an elderly warrior spurs on the young." See Porck, *Old Age in Early Medieval England: A Cultural History* (Woodbridge, UK: Boydell, 2019), 204.

of Grendel's mother. Before Hrothgar articulates his epiphanic reaction to the hilt in his sermon, he is described examining the hilt and apparently arriving at a new understanding of his predicament from it:

Hrōðgār maðelode;   hylt scēawode,
ealde lāfe.   On ðǣm wæs ōr writen
fyrngewinnes;   syðþan flōd ofslōh,
gifen gēotende   gīganta cyn,
frēcne gefērdon;   þæt wæs fremde þēod
ēcean dryhtne;   him þæs endelēan
þurh wæteres wylm   waldend sealde.
Swā wæs on ðǣm scennum   scīran goldes
þurh rūnstafas   rihte gemearcod,
geseted ond gesǣd,   hwām þæt sweord geworht,
īrena cyst   ǣrest wǣre,
wreoþenhilt ond wyrmfāh.   Ðā se wīsa sprǣc
sunu Healfdenes;   swīgedon ealle (ll. 1687–1699)

(Hrothgar made a speech; he examined the hilt, the ancient legacy. On it was incised the beginning of ancient strife; afterward the flood, the cascading ocean, struck down the race of giants; they fared terribly; that was a race foreign to the eternal Lord; the ruler gave them final retribution for that through the surging of water. Thus on the sword-guard of luminous gold it was rightly indicated through runic characters, set down and declared, for whom that sword had first been made, choicest of irons, with a wrapped hilt and serpent-patterned. Then the sage son of Healfdene spoke; all were hushed)

This enigmatic passage does not make clear exactly what Hrothgar learns from his examination of the sword hilt, but it suggests that the hilt enables him to break through the "two levels of knowledge" and acquire some of the understanding that had previously been possessed only by the poem's narrator.[22] From the hilt, Hrothgar becomes aware of "the origin of ancient strife" (ōr fyrngewinnes), a probable reference to Cain's killing of Abel, as well as the flood (flōd) with which God later punished the "race of giants" (gīganta cyn) that had descended from Cain. The narrator does not reveal the name of the individual "for

---

22. See Dennis Cronan, "Hroðgar and the Gylden Hilt in Beowulf," Traditio 72 (2017): 109–32.

whom that sword had first been made" (*hwām þæt sweord geworht*), and scholarship has never arrived at a convincing identification, but Hrothgar appears to learn from this inscription and from everything carved on the hilt that there is a much larger dimension to the suffering he received at the hands of Grendel. The past twelve years were not random or senseless; Grendel's persecution of Heorot involved Hrothgar in an ancient feud between the eternal lord and a monstrous people who were alienated from him (*þæt wæs fremde þeod / ēcean dryhtne*) because they violated natural law and failed to recognize God's authority. Learning from the flood narrative that God uses natural phenomena to punish even his most powerful and prodigious creations, Hrothgar comes to think of the downfall of Heremod, whom he turns into an exemplar in the sermon that follows his examination of the hilt.

God appears in Hrothgar's sermon, however, not as the stern punisher of overweening men but as the benevolent agent who had initially endowed these errant men with strength, wealth, and distinction. A man such as Heremod is envisioned in the sermon as reaching a bad end in this life, and presumably in the afterlife as well, not because God punished him but because he voluntarily alienated himself from human society ("hē āna hwearf / mǣre þēoden mondrēamum from," ll. 1714b–1715). Heremod, according to Hrothgar, mismanaged the gifts God gave him and violated natural law by rejecting the norms of reciprocity that structure human society:

> Ðēah þe hine mihtig God   mægenes wynnum,
> eafeþum stēpte   ofer ealle men,
> forð gefremede,   hwæþere him on ferhþe grēow
> brēosthord blōdrēow,   nallas bēagas geaf
> Denum æfter dōme;   drēamlēas gebād
> þæt hē þæs gewinnes   weorc þrōwade,
> lēodbealo longsum. (ll. 1716–1722a)

(Though mighty God exalted him with the delights of power and strength over all, furthered him on his way, his breast-hoard nonetheless grew bloodthirsty in spirit, by no means gave rings to Danes for their glory; estranged from contentment, he lived to see it that he suffered the pain of that struggle, a long-lived bane to the people.)

Although Hrothgar might have learned of God's punishment of the giants from the hilt, he maintains his conviction that God is responsible

only for the good things in life, while human beings are responsible
for the disasters that befall them. In Hrothgar's theology, God has no
inherent animosity toward any of his creations; he endowed them all
with life, and he had actually favored Heremod, whose worldly success
is interpreted as a sign of divine support. Hrothgar's conception of God
as a benevolent and magnanimous giver of gifts is reiterated in his next
exemplum, which moves from the particular case of Heremod to the
general case of an exceptionally fortunate nobleman:

> Wundor is tō secganne
> hū mihtig God   manna cynne
> þurh sīdne sefan   snyttru bryttað,
> eard ond eorlscipe;   hē āh ealra geweald.
> Hwīlum hē on lufan   lǣteð hworfan
> monnes mōdgeþonc   mǣran cynnes,
> seleð him on ēþle   eorþan wynne,
> tō healdanne   hlēoburh wera,
> gedēð him swā gewealdene   worolde dǣlas,
> sīde rīce,   þæt hē his selfa ne mæg
> for his unsnyttrum   ende geþencean. (ll. 1724b–1734)

(It is a wonder to say how mighty God in magnanimous spirit
distributes wisdom to the human race, property and rank; he has
control of everything. Sometimes he lets the designs of a man of
good family wander in delight, gives him in his own country the
pleasures of the earth, to rule the sheltering stronghold of men,
makes portions of the world thus subject to him, a broad king-
dom, so that he himself in his ignorance cannot imagine an end.)

Consistent with Hrothgar's earlier remarks and with various state-
ments by the poem's narrator, God is imagined here as being actively
responsible for the good fortune that this hypothetical nobleman
experiences. God wondrously distributes mental qualities (*snyttru*), ma-
terial possessions (*eard*), and social status (*eorlscipe*) to men, and he oc-
casionally lends direct support to the ambitions (*mōdgeþonc*) of a man
of noble birth (*mǣran cynnes*). God's involvement ends, however, with
the distribution of gifts; the recipient of those gifts bears all the re-
sponsibility for managing them well and conscientiously. The failure
of the prosperous nobleman to recognize that there will eventually be
an end to his prosperity seems at first glance, in light of the Heremod
exemplum, to suggest his vulnerability only to a bad end in this life. Yet

as Hrothgar develops his second exemplum, he alters the significance of the first exemplum, proposing that the arrogance of the prosperous nobleman puts him in a state of spiritual danger that is more perilous than mere physical decay:

> him eal worold
> wendeð on willan;   hē þæt wyrse ne con—
> oð þæt him on innan   oferhygda dǣl
> weaxe(ð) ond wrīdað;   þonne se weard swefeð,
> sāwele hyrde;   bið se slǣp tō fæst,
> bisgum gebunden,   bona swīðe nēah,
> sē þe of flānbogan   fyrenum scēoteð.
> Þonne bið on hreþre   under helm drepen
> biteran strǣle   —him bebeorgan ne con—
> wōm wundorbebodum   wergan gāstes;
> þinceð him tō lȳtel   þæt hē lange hēold,
> gȳtsað gromhȳdig,   nallas on gylp seleð
> fǣtte bēagas,   ond hē þā forðgesceaft
> forgyteð ond forgȳmeð,   þæs þe him ǣr God sealde,
> wuldres waldend,   weorðmynda dǣl. (ll. 1738b–1752)

(all the world bends to his will; he does not recognize the worse—until a measure of overconfidence sprouts and grows, when the watch sleeps, the soul's overseer; the slumber is too deep, tied up with cares, the killer very near, who shoots fiercely with his bow. He is then struck in the breast under helmet with a bitter dart—he does not know how to protect himself—with the perverse, astonishing directives of an accursed spirit; what he has held for long seems to him too little; bitter-minded, he is miserly, by no means gives plated rings with pomp, and he forgets and neglects his condition of life, what God had granted him, wielder of glory, his share of honors.)

This passage, with its evocation of spiritual turmoil between the soul's guardian (*sāwele hyrde*) and an accursed demon (*wergan gāstes*) or spectral assassin (*bona*), differs significantly from everything that Hrothgar has thus far said both in the sermon and in the poem as a whole. With this passage, it becomes clear that the sword hilt, the ancient heirloom, has inspired Hrothgar to recognize that there is an eternal and spiritual dimension to mortal life. There is more than mere mortal danger facing the arrogant nobleman who becomes dissatisfied with the gifts God gave him and then, like Heremod, refuses to distribute treasure to his men. Heremod suffered a premature death for killing his retainers and hoarding his wealth, but death is inevitable for all men, as Hrothgar later emphasizes to Beowulf in his catalogue of possible ends (ll. 1761b–1768). The real danger facing Heremod and the hypothetical nobleman is spiritual danger, as their violations of natural law jeopardize their prospects in the afterlife. To be mindful of the eternal consequences of mortal life is the lesson that Hrothgar communicates to Beowulf in his sermon's critical moment of direct exhortation:

> Bebeorh þē ðone bealonīð,   Bēowulf lēofa,
> secg bet[e]sta,   ond þē þæt sēlre gecēos,
> ēce rǣdas;   oferhӯda ne gӯm,
> mǣre cempa. (ll. 1758–1761a)

(Safeguard yourself against that deadly affliction, beloved Beowulf, finest warrior, and choose what is better for you, lasting prudence; give no consideration to self-conceit, celebrated champion.)

Like his earlier references to an accursed spirit and a demonic assassin, Hrothgar's reference to "eternal counsels" (*ēce rǣdas*) recasts the content of his sermon in a spiritual light and indicates that it is no mere exhortation to be mindful of the inevitability of death. He stresses to Beowulf that death will eventually come to urge vigilance not against potential threats to his mortal life but against spiritual corruption in the form of *oferhӯgd*, the vice attributed to the hypothetical nobleman (and by implication Heremod). This term, associated with Lucifer's disobedience in *Genesis A* (ll. 22b, 29a), can be translated as "overconfidence" or "self-conceit," but within the context of the poem's theology, the more essential quality it connotes is a failure to recognize God's authority and live in accordance with natural law.[23] The man who allows *oferhӯgd* to corrupt his soul occupies the same perilous position as the idol worshippers condemned in lines 175–188, though for opposite reasons: while temporal suffering causes the idol worshippers to embrace polytheism in desperation, temporal prosperity causes the hypothetical nobleman to live an impious and unnatural life in arrogance. Both

---

23. For extensive analysis of *oferhӯgd* in *Beowulf* and other Old English poems, see Gwara, *Heroic Identity*, 181–238. See also Hans Schabram, *Superbia: Studien zum altenglischen Wortschatz* (Munich: Wilhelm Fink, 1965). For *Genesis A*, see A. N. Doane, ed., *Genesis A: A New Edition, Revised* (Tempe, AZ: ACMRS, 2013).

follow the wrong intuitions, fail to recognize their subordination to the one true God, and allow the temporal to jeopardize the eternal.

Hrothgar's sermon illustrates the development of his moral intuitions and reveals the spiritual progress that has taken place within this character. Prior to his sermon, Hrothgar showed himself to be a pious king, keen to attribute good fortune to the intervention of God, but he made no references to the soul or the afterlife. The inscription on the sword hilt evidently causes him to become mindful of the eternal dimension of mortal life. Hrothgar's recognition that he is part of an ancient and mysterious feud prompts him to reflect, like King Edwin's counselor in Bede's account of the Northumbrian conversion, on his ignorance of all that comes before and after his brief period of life on earth.[24] In this inspired and reflective state, Hrothgar prophesizes that Beowulf will become king of the Geats (ll. 1700–1709a; also ll. 1845b–1853a) and then urges him to rule in a pious manner, guard his soul against the devil, and be similarly mindful of eternity. Hrothgar still maintains his characteristic tendency to attribute good fortune to divine intervention, and he concludes the sermon by restating his conviction that the will of God is expressed in Beowulf's monster-slaying:

> Þæs sig metode þanc,
> ēcean dryhtne,   þæs ðe ic on aldre gebād
> þæt ic on þone hafelan   heorodrēorigne
> ofer ealdgewin   ēagum starige. (ll. 1778b–1781)

(Thanks be to Providence for that, to the eternal Lord, that in my lifetime I have experienced it that I can see with my own eyes this sword-bloody head after an age-old struggle.)

Significantly, in this restatement, Hrothgar now refers to God as the "eternal lord" ("ēce dryhten"), a pair of words he had not previously used when speaking of the deity. In fact, the phrase *ēce dryhten* had been kept out of the mouths of all characters until this point, having appeared thus far only in two narrative passages (ll. 108, 1692a) concerning God's feud with Cain. After line 1779a, *ēce dryhten* is placed in the mouth of a character on only one subsequent occasion: it appears in the dying words of Beowulf (l. 2796a), who has evidently taken Hrothgar's

---

24. See Colgrave and Mynors, *Bede's Ecclesiastical History*, 182–85. For a comparison between Edwin's counselor and the *Beowulf* poet, see Eric John, "*Beowulf* and the Margins of Literacy," *Bulletin of the John Rylands Library* 56, no. 2 (1974): 388–422, at 417.

words to heart, to judge from his use of this phrase and from his pious concern that he might have offended God (ll. 2329–2331a), which shows that he has not allowed *oferhȳgd* to corrupt his soul.[25] In the context of Hrothgar's utterance, *ēce dryhten* resonates with the sermon's emphasis on time and eternity, and it contributes to the suggestion that the king now possesses insights that had previously been restricted to the poem's narrator. With the end of the sermon, Hrothgar's spiritual journey is complete: he feels relief and gratitude at the sight of Grendel's severed head, and he has learned an invaluable lesson from his long ordeal.

There is a less marked emphasis on spiritual development in the characterization of Beowulf, who is represented from the outset as possessing a wider range of theological intuitions, which he casually expresses in many of his speeches. In his first speech addressed to Hrothgar, the protagonist states a characteristic belief that God decides every outcome: in reference to his upcoming fight with Grendel, he declares that "there he whom death takes will have to trust in the Lord's judgment" ("ðær gelȳfan sceal / dryhtnes dōme sē þe hine dēað nimeð," ll. 440b–441). In his response to Unferth, Beowulf refers to the sun as "God's bright beacon" ("beorht bēacen Godes," l. 570a) and then reveals his awareness of the afterlife and posthumous judgment when he asserts that Unferth will suffer damnation in hell for killing his own brothers ("þæs þū in helle scealt / werhðo drēogan," ll. 588b–589a). In his final speech before the fight with Grendel, Beowulf restates his conviction that "wise God" ("wītig God," l. 685b), the "holy Lord" ("hālig dryhten," l. 686b), will decide the outcome of the fight "as it seems fitting to him" ("swā him gemet þince," l. 687b). The omniscient narrator confirms that these are no mere words, informing the audience prior to the speech of the genuineness of Beowulf's belief:

> Hūru Gēata lēod   georne truwode
> mōdgan mægnes,   metodes hyldo. (ll. 669–670)

(Certainly, the man of the Geats trusted deeply in his prideful strength, the favor of Providence.)

Following his victory over Grendel, Beowulf delivers a speech in which he continues to express the conviction that "Providence" ("metod," l.

---

25. On the phrase *ēce dryhten*, see James Cahill, "Reconsidering Robinson's *Beowulf*," *English Studies* 89, no. 3 (2008): 251–62.

967b) governed every aspect of the fight, including his failure to secure more corporeal evidence of his victory than the monster's hand, arm, and shoulder. He concludes the speech with a striking reference to "the great judgment" ("miclan dōmes," l. 978b) that awaits the mortally wounded Grendel, who will posthumously discover "how radiant Providence will prescribe for him" ("hū him scīr metod scrīfan wille," l. 979).

The impression created by Beowulf's use of monotheistic language throughout the first thousand lines is that he entered the poem in a spiritually advanced state: in his references to hell and the last judgment, he shows an awareness of the eternal dimensions of mortal life before Hrothgar; he also exhibits a firmer and more unshakable faith in the providential support of the singular deity. The narrator, when introducing Grendel's mother, reviews what transpired between Beowulf and her son, and here states clearly that Beowulf's faith in God was instrumental in his victory:

> Þǣr him āglǣca   ǣtgrǣpe wearð;
> hwæþre hē gemunde   mægenes strenge,
> gimfæste gife   ðe him God sealde,
> ond him tō anwaldan   āre gelȳfde,
> frōfre ond fultum;   ðȳ hē þone fēond ofercwōm,
> gehnǣgde helle gāst. (ll. 1269–1274a)

(There the troublemaker laid hold of him; nonetheless, he kept in mind the force of his strength, the ample gift that God had granted him, and trusted in the ruler's favor for him, his support and aid; thereby he overcame the enemy, subdued the creature of hell.)

Beowulf reasserts his faith in God's support in the speech he delivers after defeating Grendel's mother. He declares that it was a difficult struggle, and that "the battle would have been cut off immediately if God had not shielded me" ("ǣtrihte wæs / gūð getwǣfed, nymðe mec God scylde," ll. 1657b–1658). He then informs the Danish court that "the ruler of mortals" (ylda waldend, l. 1661a) intervened in the battle by directing his attention to the supernatural sword with which he killed the monster. While describing the same conflict in his homecoming speech, however, Beowulf makes no mention of divine intervention. In this lengthy speech, spiritual language is limited to casual references to "heaven's vault" ("heofones hwealf," l. 2015a), "heaven's gem" ("heofones gim," l. 2072b), and "devil's devices" ("dēofles cræftum," l. 2088a). There is no mention here of God, as Beowulf refrains from ascribing the victories over Grendel and his mother to divine support. Instead of interpreting this omission as a sign of waning spirituality in the protagonist, I argue (in the previous chapter) that the assertive quality of this speech is connected to the crucial role it plays in the narrative of Beowulf's transition from courtier to king. The protagonist is here demonstrating his aptitude for kingship by displaying worldly wisdom and making plain the extraordinary nature of his achievement; he reveals his knowledge of a culturally superior court and shows that he has won the favor of a wealthier and more powerful king. In this speech, which leaves Hygelac little choice but to invest Beowulf with royal authority, the humble gesture of ascribing victory to God would be out of place. Accordingly, the contrast between Beowulf's speeches corroborates the claim that the poet did not place monotheistic language thoughtlessly into the mouths of his characters, and that there is a genuine connection between the use of such language and the characterization of the poem's principal actors.

As an elderly king, Beowulf retains his characteristic tendency to reveal the profound extent of his spiritual knowledge in a casual manner. Recounting the death of Hrethel, who succumbed to grief when he refused to avenge one son by killing the other, Beowulf states that his grandfather "chose God's light" ("Godes lēoht gecēas," l. 2469b). The hero's use of this phrase, which would plainly refer to salvation in any other context, suggests that he has intuitively arrived at a conception of heaven as well as hell.[26] Beowulf's belief in posthumous judgment, articulated earlier in reference to Unferth and Grendel, is reaffirmed in his dying words in reference to himself, when he rejoices that "the ruler of men" ("waldend fīra," l. 2741b) need not punish him for kin-slaying or oath-breaking once life leaves his body. Furthermore, as the hero prepares to die, he once again thanks God for a favorable outcome, but this time with more marked piety than before:

Ic ðāra frætwa   frēan ealles ðanc
wuldurcyninge   wordum secge,
ēcum dryhtne,   þē ic hēr on starie,
þæs ðe ic mōste   mīnum lēodum
ær swyltdæge   swylc gestrȳnan. (ll. 2794–2798)

---

26. See Donahue, "*Beowulf* and Christian Tradition," 103; Thomas D. Hill, "Variegated Obit," 119–20; Thomas D. Hill, "Christian Language," 70–71; Cavill, "Christianity and Theology," 38. See also the discussion of Hrethel in chapter 1.

(I will express in words thanks to the Lord of all, the king of glory, the eternal ruler, for this gear that I look on here, for allowing me to acquire such for my people before my day of death.)

The hero's use of three epithets for God over the course of three lines is significant: it is not a common phenomenon in direct discourse, and it recalls Beowulf's speech of petition to Hrothgar, where the density of epithets characterizes the protagonist as a distinctly courteous speaker.[27] Beowulf's use here of three terms for the deity that he had not previously used, including *ēce dryhten*, reminds the audience of the protagonist's salient piety before he exits the poem. Beowulf dies not in an embittered or pessimistic state; he is grateful to God for the treasure he won for the benefit of the Geats. The speech illustrates again the firmness of Beowulf's faith in God's benevolent providence, and it raises the gravest doubts about interpretations wherein Beowulf is viewed as a spiritually corrupt or hopelessly condemned character who is about to spend eternity in hell.[28] *Beowulf* is not the kind of literature where a character might feign piety in his speech while harboring impiety in his soul.[29] Arguments for the spiritual corrosion of the hero in his old age rest in part on the following passage, in which Beowulf learns of the dragon's destruction and wonders if he has offended God:

Þā wæs Bīowulfe   brōga gecȳðed
snūde tō sōðe,   þæt his sylfes hām,
bolda sēlest,   brynewylmum mealt,
gifstōl Gēata.   Þæt ðām gōdan wæs
hrēow on hreðre,   hygesorga mǣst;
wēnde se wīsa   þæt he wealdende
ofer ealde riht,   ēcean dryhtne
bitre gebulge;   brēost innan wēoll
þēostrum geþoncum,   swā him geþȳwe ne wæs. (ll. 2324–2332)

(Then Beowulf was soon informed for certain about the terror, that his own home, the best of halls, had melted in surging flames,

27. See Jambeck, "Syntax of Petition." See also the discussion of this speech in chapter 2.
28. See, for example, Stanley, "*Hæþenra Hyht*"; Goldsmith, *Mode and Meaning*; Bliss, "*Beowulf*, Lines 3074–3075"; Fajardo-Acosta, *Condemnation of Heroism*; North, "Gold and the Heathen Polity."
29. On the nature of speech in Old English poetry in general, see Elise Louviot, *Direct Speech in Beowulf and Other Old English Narrative Poems* (Cambridge: D. S. Brewer, 2016).

the throne of the Geats. To the good man that was heartfelt distress, the severest mental affliction; the wise one imagined that he had bitterly enraged the ruler contrary to old law, the eternal Lord; dark thoughts welled up in his breast, as was not usual for him.)

This passage is undoubtedly an important one. It offers perhaps the clearest depiction in the poem of the relationship that obtains between the intuitive monotheists and God. Living without Mosaic law and the Christian revelation, these characters nonetheless possess an intuitive ethical code, here labeled the "old law" ("ealde riht"), that they aspire to follow in order to please the singular deity and receive his benevolent support both in this life and in the afterlife.[30] With the destruction of the Geatish court, the center of civilization, the hero intuitively considers it possible that he has transgressed against the "old law" (or natural law) and thereby offended God. The poem offers no reason to believe that the hero has actually transgressed; he simply does not yet know the origin of the dragon's enmity, though he learns it later on (l. 2403). He is characterized here in a manner comparable to an Old Testament monarch, who displays humility by wondering if the lord has had reason to forsake him.[31] The passage thus indicates not that Beowulf has succumbed to vice and is duly punished by God, but rather that he has followed Hrothgar's advice and prevented *oferhygd* from corrupting his spirit. He remains spiritually vigilant; he is not too arrogant to rule out the possibility that he has transgressed. Furthermore, he does not allow the temporal to jeopardize the eternal: when the dragon destroys the Geatish court, Beowulf does not turn to idol worship in despair. In prosperity and adversity, he maintains his intuitive covenant with God, never doubting that the singular deity is the sole governor of all that transpires.

An insight that emerges from the careful examination of the monotheistic language used by Hrothgar and Beowulf is that their theological convictions are not substantially different from the convictions articulated by the poem's narrator. Hrothgar repeatedly expresses the belief that God mercifully bestows gifts on humankind; he asserts that God

---

30. On the phrase *ealde riht*, see Donahue, "*Beowulf*, Ireland," 275; Donahue, "*Beowulf* and Christian Tradition," 98–99; Morton W. Bloomfield, "Patristics and Old English Literature: Notes on Some Poems," *Comparative Literature* 14, no. 1 (1962): 36–43, at 39–41.

31. See Leneghan, *Dynastic Drama of Beowulf*, 215–16. See also Joseph L. Baird, "The Uses of Ignorance: *Beowulf* 435, 2330," *Notes and Queries* 14, no. 1 (1967): 6–8.

was directly responsible for the elimination of Grendel; and his speech contains references to the soul (*sāwele*), the devil (*bona*), demonic adversaries (*wergan gastes*), and eternal counsels (*ēce rǣdas*), all of which suggest an awareness of the spiritual and eternal dimensions of mortal life on earth. Beowulf repeatedly expresses the belief that God decides every martial outcome; he asserts that God was directly responsible for his victory over Grendel's mother; and his speech contains references to heaven (*heofones*), hell (*helle*), the devil (*deofles*), damnation (*werhðo*), God's light (*Godes lēoht*), and the last judgment (*miclan dōmes*), all of which fill out the picture of his expectation that God will eventually sit in judgment over Unferth, Grendel, and himself. Turning now to the narrator's monotheism, we can observe that it is doctrinally consistent with that of Hrothgar and Beowulf. The narrator says nothing to contradict the intuitions of the poem's two most vocal monotheists, while saying much to confirm the rectitude of their intuitions. The alignment between Hrothgar, Beowulf, and the narrator suggests that some critics have carried the implications of "the two levels of knowledge" into unfounded territory. The distinction between the narrator's theological knowledge and that of the characters is largely limited to the matter of Grendel's ancestry and God's feud with Cain's descendants. As far as doctrine is concerned, the presence of two levels of knowledge does not function to create an ironic or pathetic perspective on the beliefs of the intuitive monotheists. The characters are not viewed as "heathen, noble, and hopeless"; rather, like Abraham and the patriarchs, they have intuitively arrived at pious views that the Christian poet of *Beowulf* could endorse without hesitation.[32]

The doctrinal alignment for which I argue could be substantiated in various ways, one being to note that the narrator, like Hrothgar and Beowulf, also alludes to salvation, damnation, heaven, hell, the soul, the devil, demonic adversaries, and eternal counsels, while never alluding to Christ or the saints. Additionally, like Hrothgar, the narrator frequently highlights God's role in the giving of gifts, talents, and forms of relief (rather than punishment) to his human subjects. Such theological overlap suggests that we do not have a Christian narrator looking with condescension on pagan characters. Although the narrator is aware of various Old Testament events, which are matters of scriptural history rather than doctrine, he appears otherwise to inhabit the same

---

32. The quotation is taken from J. R. R. Tolkien, "*Beowulf*: The Monsters and the Critics," 264. This conception of the poem's characters underlies the arguments of Robinson, *Beowulf and the Appositive Style*.

theological plane as the foregrounded monotheists. Perhaps the most striking alignment between the narrator and the characters material-izes in the two passages concerning God's intervention into Beowulf's struggle against Grendel's mother. The narrator gives the following ac-count of Beowulf's comeback:

> Hæfde ðā forsīðod   sunu Ecgþeowes
> under gynne grund,   Gēata cempa,
> nemne him heaðobyrne   helpe gefremede,
> herenet hearde,   ond hālig God.
> Gewēold wīgsigor   wītig drihten,
> rodera rǣdend;   hit on ryht gescēd
> ȳðelīce,   syþðan hē eft āstōd.
> Geseah ðā on searwum   sigeēadig bil,
> ealdsweord eotenisc   ecgum þȳhtig . . . (ll. 1550–1558)

(Ecgtheo's son would have gone missing then under the cavern-ous ground, champion of the Geats, if his war-armor had not given him help, the hard combat-net, and holy God. The Lord in his wisdom, architect of the skies, held in his power victory in battle; he settled it with justice, effortlessly, after he stood again. Then he saw among the arms a victory-blessed weapon, an ancient ogreish sword firm in its edges . . .)

In the omniscient narration of the fight, God's intervention is registered immediately prior to Beowulf's realization that there is an ancient and otherworldly sword in the vicinity, which he could try to wield against his monstrous adversary. In Beowulf's narration of the fight on his return to Heorot, he perceives the intervention of God at precisely the same moment:

> Ne meahte ic æt hilde   mid Hruntinge
> wiht gewyrcan,   þēah þæt wǣpen duge;
> ac mē geūðe   ylda waldend
> þæt ic on wāge geseah   wlitig hangian
> ealdsweord ēacen. (ll. 1659–1663a)

(With Hrunting I could not accomplish anything in the fight, though the weapon is good; but the ruler of mortals granted me that I saw hanging handsome on the wall an immense old sword.)

The agreement between the accounts of Beowulf and the omniscient nar-rator indicates that the characters are intuitively capable of arriving at a correct understanding of God's presence in the world. The characters' reliance on intuition and inference rather than revealed scripture does not put them at an insurmountable disadvantage; they are not benighted pagans grasping poignantly and fruitlessly at spiritual truths. Earlier in the poem, prior to Beowulf's victory over Grendel, the narrator confirmed that "the Lord granted weavings of war-success" ("dryhten forgeaf / wīgspēda gewiofu," l. 696b–697a) to Beowulf in this venture. In doing so, the narration confirms that all of Hrothgar's subsequent statements about divine intervention in the elimination of Grendel, as well as all of Beowulf's statements about God deciding every outcome, stem from accurate intuitions. Their theological perspective is endorsed by the omniscient narrator.

Although there are subtle allusions to various aspects of Christian doctrine in the poem's narration, there is one doctrinal conviction that the narrator articulates more frequently and unequivocally than any other: namely, that the one true God rules and has always ruled over all humankind. There are no fewer than four statements to this effect in the poem's narration:

> Sōð is gecȳþed
> þæt mihtig God   manna cynnes
> wēold (w)īdeferhð. (ll. 700b–702a)

(The truth is plain that mighty God has always ruled the human race.)

> Metod eallum wēold
> gumena cynnes,   swā hē nū gīt dêð. (ll. 1057b–1058)

(Providence governed all of the human race, as it still does.)

> sē geweald hafað
> sǣla ond mǣla;   þæt is sōð metod. (ll. 1610b–1611)

(who has the governance of hours and seasons; that is the true Providence.)

> wolde dōm Godes   dǣdum rǣdan
> gumena gehwylcum,   swā hē nū gēn dêð. (ll. 2858–2859)

(God's judgment would govern the doings of all men, just as it now still does.)

In addition to these four statements, various localized remarks about God permitting or refusing to permit a certain event could be added (e.g., ll. 967–970b).[33] The narrator's persistent emphasis on God's eternal governance establishes a further degree of alignment between his theological perspective and that of the foregrounded monotheists, who likewise express trust in the governance of God more frequently and unequivocally than they express any other theological conviction. The shared emphasis of both the narrator and the characters on this one particular doctrine has not generally been treated by critics as a peculiar or remarkable feature of the poem, but I would argue that it is. Such an emphasis is hardly inevitable: one can imagine a different version of *Beowulf*, where instead of repeatedly stressing God's providence, the narrator and characters constantly meditate on salvation and damnation, with elaborate passages on the joy of the former and the misery of the latter. Posthumous judgment is a matter of interest to the narrator and the characters, but it is treated by them in an incidental manner and usually with some degree of subtlety or ambiguity. In contrast, there is no such subtlety or ambiguity attached to the numerous passages concerning God's providence and divine intervention, which are as firm and unequivocal as any statement made in the poem.

Like many other features of *Beowulf* that have been discussed in previous chapters of this book, the persistent emphasis on God's providence can be understood as part of the poet's programmatic reaction to the amoral tradition of heroic-legendary poetry that he inherited. In the antecedent tradition, the conventional plot illustrated the cruelty of fate by pitting a protagonist against an individual to whom he or she is tied by bonds of oath or kinship. In the poetry relating such plots, in which characters commit one transgression in order to avoid committing a different transgression, an unwavering emphasis on God's benevolent, eternal, and just governance of all human affairs would appear rather discordant. What instead suits such narratives are remarks on the cruelty of fate in a world that is apparently not governed by a benevolent providential plan. Such remarks are indeed found throughout the extant witnesses to migration-period legend: Hildebrand, in the *Hildebrandslied*, decries the "cruel fate" ("wewurt") befalling him as he prepares to kill his own son; Angantýr, in the final words of *Hlǫðskviða*, laments that "the Norns' doom is evil" ("illr er dómr Norna") as he stands over the corpse of his kinsman.[34] In the *Nibelungenlied*, Dietrich von Bern exclaims after learning that his friends have killed his retainers:

---

33. See Deskis, *Beowulf*, 12–21, 26–29, 35–36.
34. See the discussion of these poems in the introduction and chapter 1.

"If all my men are dead, then God has forgotten me, wretched Diet-
rich!" ("unde sint erstorben alle mîne man, sô hât mîn got vergezzen,
ich armer Dieterîch," 2316.2–3); he proceeds to decry his "ill-fortune"
("mîn ungelücke," 2317.4) and his "evil fate" ("mîn unsælde," 2318.1).[35]
In *Sigurðarkviða in skamma*, the narrator and the characters are aligned
not in their trust in providence but in their belief that fate has wrought
an outrageous tragedy: the poem's narrator states, "The terrible fates
intervened in this" ("Gengo þess á milli grimmar urðir," 5.4), and Bryn-
hild concurs shortly thereafter that "the hateful norns decreed this
long torment for us" ("liótar nornir scópo oss langa þrá," 7.3).[36] The
emphasis on the cruelty of fate in such temporally and geographically
scattered sources suggests that it was an archaic feature that had likely
been present in the traditions that the *Beowulf* poet knew concerning
the wretched predicaments of Ingeld, Hengest, Sigemund, Eormenric,
and other migration-period heroes.

In many respects, the peculiarity of *Beowulf* relative to other wit-
nesses to migration-period legend appears to reflect the poet's dis-
comfort with the fundamental amorality of the antecedent tradition.
The insistence throughout *Beowulf* on God's exclusive control of hu-
man events, voiced repeatedly by the narrator and the characters, is one
rather salient expression of the poet's desire to revise what he inherited.
Composing for an audience that was familiar with this inheritance, the
poet wishes to leave no doubt that in his unconventional poem the
power to shape human events is possessed only by the one true God, by
"true Providence" ("sôð metod"), and that this power is not shared with
any other supernatural forces such as "terrible fates" ("grimmar urðir")
or "hateful norns" ("liótar nornir"). In *Beowulf*, "the Wyrd of the old
religion becomes a mere body-snatcher," its former place having been
taken over by God.[37] To effect this revision in a convincing manner,

---

35. The text is cited from Hermann Reichert, *Das Nibelungenlied: Text und Einführung* (Ber-
lin: De Gruyter, 2017), 312; the translation is cited from Cyril Edwards, trans., *The Nibelungen-
lied: The Lay of the Nibelungs* (Oxford: Oxford University Press, 2010), 209.

36. The text is cited from Neckel, *Edda*, 207–8; the translation is cited from Larrington,
Poetic Edda, 178.

37. Phillpotts, "Wyrd and Providence," 21. Though *wyrd* probably referred in pagan times
to the cruel and inexorable fate that governed all human affairs, it appears to have been largely
shorn of such associations in *Beowulf*, where the repeated insistence on divine providence es-
tablishes, in any event, the absolute superiority of God in the poem's cosmology. For critical
discussion of *wyrd*, see B. J. Timmer, "Wyrd in Anglo-Saxon Prose and Poetry," *Neophilologus*
26, nos. 1 and 3 (1941): 24–33, 213–28; Weber, *Wyrd*; G. V. Smithers, "Destiny and the Heroic
Warrior in *Beowulf*," in *Philological Essays: Studies in Old and Middle English Literature in Honour of
Herbert Dean Meritt*, ed. J. L. Rosier (The Hague: Mouton, 1970), 65–81; F. Anne Payne, "Three

the poet necessarily refrains from focusing his narrative on any of the traditional plots wherein circumstances compel an innocent protagonist to kill kinsmen or break oaths. Such plots, if not fundamentally rooted in a pagan worldview, nevertheless create an unpromising environment for sincere expressions of trust in divine justice. To compose a migration-period epic consistent with his providential vision, the poet instead focuses his narrative on the monster fights of a hero derived from originally distinct folkloric traditions. Unstained by the conventional wretchedness and transgression, this hero can convincingly believe in God's benevolent providence. Alongside a Danish king famous for a long reign spent at home, the folkloric protagonist can plausibly be depicted as an intuitive monotheist who earns God's support, merits salvation, and gives voice to a theological perspective endorsed by the poem's narrator.

The *Beowulf* poet's ambition to morally renovate an amoral tradition is expressed partially in the refusal to valorize heroes known to have killed kinsmen or broken oaths; partially in the emphasis on courtesy and courtliness; partially in the insistent monotheism of the narrator and the foregrounded characters; and partially in the selection of monsters as the hero's principal adversaries. As noted in the introductory chapter of this book, early critics recognized that the centrality of the monsters in *Beowulf* constituted a salient departure from heroic-legendary tradition, where the killing of a monster would not be positioned as the pivotal episode in a protagonist's life. Other migration-period heroes were known to have killed monsters, but they were known primarily for their involvement in tragic plots culminating in one of the standard heroic transgressions. The *Beowulf* poet's decision to focus on three monster fights, which might have formed minor episodes in an epic of Dietrich or Siegfried, was regarded by early critics as a regrettable decision, a sign of bad taste, which undermined the dignified style and moral seriousness otherwise admirably maintained in the poem.

Aspects of Wyrd in *Beowulf*," in *Old English Studies in Honour of John C. Pope*, ed. Robert B. Burlin and Edward B. Irving Jr. (Toronto: University of Toronto Press, 1974), 15–35; Jon C. Kasik, "The Use of the Term *Wyrd* in *Beowulf* and the Conversion of the Anglo-Saxons," *Neophilologus* 63, no. 1 (1979): 128–35; Susanne Weil, "Grace under Pressure: 'Hand Words,' 'Wyrd,' and Free Will in *Beowulf*," *Pacific Coast Philology* 24 (1989): 94–104; E. G. Stanley, *Imagining the Anglo-Saxon Past: The Search for Anglo-Saxon Paganism and Trial by Jury* (Cambridge: D. S. Brewer, 2000), 85–109; Augustyn, "Semiotics of *Fate*," 71–93; David Pedersen, "*Wyrd ðe Warnung* . . . or God: The Question of Absolute Sovereignty in *Solomon and Saturn II*," *Studies in Philology* 113, no. 4 (2016): 713–38.

Their views went on to be countered by Tolkien, who argued that the monsters invest the poem with greater profundity and universality, and thereby provide it with those qualities that his predecessors admired. Critics after Tolkien have tended to take the centrality of the monsters for granted, treating them as if it were normal for poetry rooted in migration-period legend to concentrate on a hero's struggle against monsters.[38] Yet prior to Tolkien, Phillpotts's comparison of *Beowulf* with the antecedent legendary tradition established the essential peculiarity of its construction, and she arrived at the argument that has been developed and substantiated throughout the present book: the poet's decision to concentrate on monster fights, rather than on one of the traditional plots, is part of his broader plan for the moral renovation of the amoral tradition he inherited.

If the *Beowulf* poet sought to relate a narrative that pitted good against evil, there is reason to believe that he would have found remarkably little to work with in the multitude of migration-period legends known to him and his contemporaries. In the vast majority of the extant witnesses to this legendary tradition, we do not find narratives in which the protagonist is decidedly virtuous and the antagonist is decidedly vicious. In Eddic poems such as *Hlǫðskviða*, *Atlakviða*, *Sigurðarkviða*, and *Hamðismál*, no character is as benevolent as Beowulf or as malevolent as Grendel.[39] The same can be said for the *Hildebrandslied* and the *Nibelungenlied*, both of which elicit sympathy for characters guilty of the gravest transgressions. Furthermore, when one surveys the archaic plots preserved in legendary compendia such as *Vǫlsunga saga*, *Þiðreks saga*, and Saxo's *Gesta Danorum*, or in scattered witnesses such as Paul the Deacon's *Historia Langobardorum*, one consistently finds plots structured around conflicting ethical imperatives, not around good versus evil. By all appearances, the tradition had no place for characters displaying saintly benevolence or inexplicable malevolence. The line between right and wrong is normally blurred, and it is often

---

38. In even the most insightful recent criticism dealing with the poem's monsters, there is little sense that the poet's decision to concentrate on monsters was unusual. See, for example, Andy Orchard, *Pride and Prodigies: Studies in the Monsters of the Beowulf-Manuscript* (Cambridge: D. S. Brewer, 1995); Megan Cavell, "Constructing the Monstrous Body in *Beowulf*," *Anglo-Saxon England* 43 (2014): 151–81; Paul S. Langeslag, "Monstrous Landscape in *Beowulf*," *English Studies* 96, no. 2 (2015): 119–38; Michael Bintley, "*Hrinde Bearwas*: The Trees at the Mere and the Root of All Evil in *Beowulf*," *Journal of English and Germanic Philology* 119, no. 3 (2020): 309–26.

39. Although Iǫrmunrekkr (Ermanaric) and Atli (Attila) are depicted as unsympathetic figures in *Hamðismál* and *Atlakviða*, respectively, the poets responsible for these works neither dwell on the evil nature of these men nor seize the opportunity to frame their narratives as conflicts between good and evil. An amoral framework is maintained in both works.

unclear whether the victor or the victim is more deserving of the audience's sympathy. Certainly, there is no plot attached to a migration-period hero that exhibits the stark contrast found in *Beowulf*, where the protagonist receives God's support and his first antagonist is described as "God's adversary" ("Godes andsaca," ll. 786b, 1682b). Had the *Beowulf* poet not turned to monsters, and had he sought to remain within the confines of legendary tradition, it appears that he would have had little choice but to relate narratives in which the protagonist is not much more virtuous or morally justified than his antagonists. These antagonists, moreover, would not be unambiguously evil; they would most likely be the kinsmen or sworn friends of the protagonist, opposing him not out of sheer malice but out of a high-minded sense of societal duty or personal honor.

Monsters provided the *Beowulf* poet with a solution to the problem voiced by Alcuin. Like Alcuin, the poet evidently accepted that the traditional poetry on the cruelty of fate and compelled transgressions had nothing to do with Christ—that it was fundamentally amoral, impious, and unsuitable for sustained narration before a Christian audience. Yet the poet managed to preserve as much as he could from this venerable tradition by having it form an allusive background to three foregrounded fights between a benevolent protagonist and his monstrous adversaries. Of the three adversaries, it is Grendel in particular whom the poet uses to establish a clear moral vision at the outset of his epic narrative. The narrator makes it unambiguously clear that Grendel's malice has no credible justification, that he is inherently and unalterably evil, and that his death is a positive development for every human concerned. In addition to being "God's adversary," Grendel is described as "the enemy of humankind" ("fēond mancynnes," l. 164b; "mancynnes fēond," l. 1276a), whose essentially evil nature is registered in epithets such as "villainous raider" ("mānscaða," ll. 712a, 737b), "criminal marauder" ("synscaða," l. 801b), and "herder of crimes" ("fyrena hyrde," l. 750b). Grendel is also associated in various phrases with hell: he is one of "hell's intimates" ("helrūnan," l. 163a), who is apparently both a perennial denizen of hell—a "hellish foe" ("fēond on helle," l. 101a), a "captive of hell" ("helle hæft," l. 788a), and a "creature of hell" ("helle gāst," l. 1274a)—as well as a heathen sinner destined to return to hell at the end of his mortal life ("þær him hel onfēng," l. 852b).[40] Unlike a

---

40. On Grendel as a denizen of hell, see Geoffrey Russom, "At the Center of *Beowulf*," in *Myth in Early Northwest Europe*, ed. Stephen O. Glosecki (Tempe, AZ: ACMRS, 2007), 225–40; Sarah Lynn Higley, "*Aldor on Ofre*, or the Reluctant Hart: A Study of Liminality in *Beowulf*,"

conventional adversary in heroic legend, who is merely committed to a different ethical imperative, Grendel is committed to opposing God: he is one of the monstrous descendants of Cain, who have already "struggled against God" ("þā wið Gode wunnon," l. 113b), and he himself is in a state of hostility with God ("hē wæs fāg wið God," l. 811b). Lest it could be thought that there is some conceivable justification for his actions, the narrator states without equivocation that Grendel "made war on justice" ("wið rihte wan," l. 144b).

Consideration of the various terms applied to Grendel indicates that the poet intended to create a loathsome antagonist with whom no member of his Christian audience could mistakenly sympathize. The poet, recognizing that it was conventional for each combatant in heroic-legendary narrative to be relatively sympathetic, took pains to obviate this interpretive possibility by creating a situation where sympathy for the antagonist would amount to outright impiety, since it would place one on the side of God's enemies. The construction of such an unsympathetic and malevolent antagonist is perhaps the poet's most radical departure from the antecedent legendary tradition. Affinities observed between Grendel and monstrous adversaries in Icelandic sagas (trolls, *draugar*, *haugbúar*), as well as the attestation of Grendel's name in English place-names, suggest that the monster himself was not an invention of the *Beowulf* poet.[41] The decision to connect this notorious monster to Cain's kin, however, might originate with our poet. Whether it originated with him or one of his immediate predecessors, the connection might well have formed the kernel out of which *Beowulf* developed, providing the poet with the belief that he could compose a legendary epic that could conceivably have something to do with Christ and be performed before a Christian audience without concern about

---

Neuphilologische Mitteilungen 87, no. 3 (1986): 342–53; Kemp Malone, "Grendel and His Abode," in *Studia Philologica et Litteraria in Honorem L. Spitzer*, ed. Anna G. Hatcher and K. L. Selig (Bern: Francke, 1958), 297–308.

41. On the connections between Grendel, Grendel's mother, and monsters in medieval Scandinavian literature, see Nora K. Chadwick, "Norse Ghosts (A Study in the *Draugr* and the *Haugbúi*)," *Folklore* 57, no. 2 (1946): 50–65; Nora K. Chadwick, "The Monsters and Beowulf," in *The Anglo-Saxons: Studies in Some Aspects of Their History and Culture Presented to Bruce Dickins*, ed. Peter Clemoes (London: Bowes & Bowes, 1959), 171–203; Jorgensen, "Two-Troll Variant"; Jorgensen, "Additional Icelandic Analogues"; Stitt, *Bear's Son*; Fjalldal, "*Beowulf*." On Grendel's name in English place-names, see R. E. Zachrisson, "Grendel in *Beowulf* and in Local Names," in *A Grammatical Miscellany Offered to Otto Jespersen on His Seventieth Birthday*, ed. N. Bøgholm, Aage Brusendorff, and C. A. Bodelsen (Copenhagen: Levin & Munksgaard, 1930), 39–44; Michael Lapidge, "*Beowulf*, Aldhelm, the *Liber Monstrorum* and Wessex," *Studi Medievali* 23, no. 1 (1982): 151–92, at 179–84.

its moral implications. In any event, the representation of Grendel as an embodiment of pure and irrational evil does not appear to have possessed any representational precedent within the tradition of poetry associated with migration-period legend. Just as the poet derived Beowulf from originally distinct folkloric traditions, he appears to have derived the characterization of Grendel from hagiographical literary tradition, which was certainly distinct from the antecedent legendary tradition.[42] In hagiography, there is absolute moral clarity, with the Christlike saint depicted as purely good and the saint's demonic adversaries depicted as purely evil. Having constructed an antagonist who would fit comfortably into any hagiographical narrative, the *Beowulf* poet thrusts this diabolical creature onto center stage in the sixth-century world of Danes and Geats—a feat performed in no other extant witness to migration-period legend.

After Grendel is killed, the poet relaxes the demonization of the hero's monstrous adversaries. No subsequent monster is made out to be quite as evil as Grendel. Whereas Grendel's hostility is apparently inborn and irrational, there is an intelligible motive both for the hostility of his mother, who "wanted to avenge her child" ("wolde hire bearn wrecan," l. 1546b), and for the hostility of the dragon, who sought to avenge the theft of treasure from his hoard. Whereas Grendel brought death and humiliation to the Danes for a period of twelve years, the enmity of the subsequent monsters is expressed in a matter of days. While satanic associations swirl around the figure of Grendel, diabolical language is not used in reference to Grendel's mother or the dragon: unlike Grendel, neither of the latter monsters is described as an adversary of God (*Godes andsaca*), an enemy of mankind (*fèond mancynnes*), a fiend in hell (*fèond on helle*), or a shepherd of sin (*fyrena hyrde*).[43] Furthermore, the dragon is never made out to be one of the descendants of Cain locked in a state

---

42. For criticism that discerns patristic or hagiographical influence in the poet's treatment of Grendel, see Goldsmith, *Mode and Meaning*, 97–145; Lars Malmberg, "Grendel and the Devil," *Neuphilologische Mitteilungen* 78, no. 3 (1977): 241–43; Judson Boyce Allen, "God's Society and Grendel's Shoulder Joint: Gregory and the Poet of the *Beowulf*," *Neuphilologische Mitteilungen* 78, no. 3 (1977): 239–40; Malcolm Andrew, "Grendel in Hell," *English Studies* 62, no. 5 (1981): 401–10; Kenneth Florey, "Grendel, Evil, 'Allegory,' and Dramatic Development in *Beowulf*," *Essays in Arts and Sciences* 17 (1988): 83–95; David F. Johnson, "The Gregorian Grendel: *Beowulf* 705b–09 and the Limits of the Demonic," in *Rome and the North: The Early Reception of Gregory the Great in Germanic Europe*, ed. Rolf H. Bremmer Jr., Kees Dekker, and David F. Johnson (Paris: Peeters, 2001), 51–65. See also Joseph L. Baird, "Grendel the Exile," *Neuphilologische Mitteilungen* 67, no. 4 (1966): 375–81.

43. On the implications of these terms, see J. R. R. Tolkien, "*Beowulf*: The Monsters and the Critics," 278–80; Malmberg, "Grendel and the Devil"; Johnson, "Gregorian Grendel," 53–54.

of perpetual hostility to God. Should the contrast between Grendel and the subsequent monsters be taken to indicate that the poet wished to represent the latter as relatively sympathetic and morally justified antagonists? Some critics might answer this question in the affirmative. Indeed, several critics have perceived a progressive collapse in the moral framework that had obtained in the struggle between Beowulf and Grendel, where good was clearly pitted against evil.[44] I would argue, however, that the poet did not conceive of Grendel's mother and the dragon as sympathetic or justified figures; alternative explanations for the relaxed demonization of these two monsters are surely to be preferred.

With regard to Grendel's mother, there are several reasons why the poet might have considered it unnecessary, redundant, or even counterproductive to depict her in the same diabolical light as Grendel. In all likelihood, the poet never even entertained the possibility that members of his Christian audience could react sympathetically to the creature responsible for begetting Grendel, the fiendish enemy of God and humankind. When she is introduced, it is made clear that she too is one of the outcast and monstrous descendants of Cain (ll. 1258b–1266a). Though she generated the reprehensible Grendel, the mother is explicitly said to be less terrifying than the son:

> Wæs se gryre læssa
> efne swā micle   swā bið mægþa cræft,
> wīggryre wīfes   be wǣpnedmen,
> þonne heoru bunden,   hamere geþrūen,
> sweord swāte fāh   swīn ofer helme
> ecgum dyhttig   andweard scireð. (ll. 1282b–1287)

(The terror was less by just so much as the strength of females, the battle-intimidation of women, is in comparison to males, when a bound weapon shaped by hammers, a sword painted with battle-sweat, keen of edge, cuts against a boar on top of a helmet.)

This rather strange and gratuitous remark appears purposeful only if it is understood to reflect an intention to establish that Grendel,

44. See George Clark, "Beowulf as a Philosophical Poem," Florilegium 25 (2008): 1–27; Linda Georgianna, "King Hrethel's Sorrow and the Limits of Heroic Action in Beowulf," Speculum 62, no. 4 (1987): 829–50; Harry Berger Jr. and H. Marshall Leicester Jr., "Social Structure as Doom: The Limits of Heroism in Beowulf," in Old English Studies in Honour of John C. Pope, ed. Robert B. Burlin and Edward B. Irving Jr. (Toronto: University of Toronto Press, 1974), 37–79; T. M. Gang, "Approaches to Beowulf," Review of English Studies 3, no. 9 (1952): 1–12.

not his mother, is the main monstrous adversary around whom the first part of this bipartite poem revolves. The centrality of Grendel is suggested as well by the fact that Beowulf recovers Grendel's head, rather than the head of the mother, from the mere; it is likewise suggested by the fact that Hrothgar, in his sermon, meditates only on the suffering he endured at the hands of Grendel (ll. 1769–1781), making no mention there of the mother. All of this conspires to suggest that the poet would have considered it counterproductive to represent Grendel's mother as more diabolical and malevolent than her son. Instead, the poet makes her a fearsome adversary by suggesting that she, like the dragon, possesses a more bestial quality than her son. Though humanoid to the extent that she possesses "the likeness of a lady" ("idese onlīcnæs," l. 1351a) and is a "monstrous female" ("ides āglǣcwīf," l. 1259a), the bestial and aquatic nature of Grendel's mother is indicated when she is described as a "sea-wolf" ("brimwylf," l. 1506a), an "outcast of the deep" ("grundwyrgenne," l. 1518b), and a "mighty lake-woman" ("merewīf mihtig," l. 1519a); consistent with this animalistic characterization are adjectives such as "ravenous and gallows-minded" ("gīfre ond galgmōd," l. 1277a), "bloodthirsty" ("heorogīfre," l. 1498a), and "unyielding and greedy" ("grim ond grǣdig," l. 1499a).[45] A sense that she is more beast than human might also inhere in Beowulf's reference to her as an "abominable female" ("wīf unhȳre," l. 2120b), where the adjective *unhȳre* implies a reversal of human norms.[46]

---

45. Also relevant here is E. G. Stanley's observation that Grendel's mother is "even fiercer than [Grendel] in the fight. A mother's vengeance for her slain son might have made her so, and it is not necessarily the maternal affection of a human being. We are told of many animals that the mother goes wild when the offspring is in danger or slain." See Stanley, "'A Very Land-Fish, Languageless, a Monster': Grendel and the Like in Old English," in *Monsters and the Monstrous in Medieval Northwest Europe*, ed. K. E. Olsen and L. A. J. R. Houwen (Leuven: Peeters, 2001), 79–92, at 86. Helen Damico likewise describes Grendel's mother as "half-bestial." See Damico, *Beowulf's Wealhtheow*, 21.

46. On the characterization of Grendel's mother, see Chadwick, "Monsters and Beowulf," 172–77; Jane C. Nitzsche, "The Structural Unity of *Beowulf*: The Problem of Grendel's Mother," *Texas Studies in Literature and Language* 22, no. 3 (1980): 287–303; Gwendolyn A. Morgan, "Mothers, Monsters, Maturation: Female Evil in *Beowulf*," *Journal of the Fantastic in the Arts* 4, no. 1/13 (1991): 54–68; Christine Alfano, "The Issue of Feminine Monstrosity: A Reevaluation of Grendel's Mother," *Comitatus* 23, no. 1 (1992): 1–16; Paul Acker, "Horror and the Maternal in *Beowulf*," *PMLA* 121, no. 3 (2006): 702–16; Renée R. Trilling, "Beyond Abjection: The Problem with Grendel's Mother Again," *Parergon* 24, no. 1 (2007): 1–20; M. Wendy Hennequin, "We've Created a Monster: The Strange Case of Grendel's Mother," *English Studies* 89, no. 5 (2008): 503–23; Sara Frances Burdorff, "Re-reading Grendel's Mother: *Beowulf* and the Anglo-Saxon Metrical Charms," *Comitatus* 45, no. 1 (2014): 91–103.

The poet's emphasis on the bestial nature of both Grendel's mother and the dragon must account, in part, for the relaxed demonization of these adversaries. While Grendel's mother is ravenous and lupine, the dragon is hostile and serpentine: it is described simply as "the hostile one" ("se lāða," l. 2305a) and "the serpent" ("se wyrm," l. 2287a), and the notion that it is a ferocious beast is reiterated in epithets such as "hostile air-flier" ("lāð lyftfloga," l. 2315a), "war-flier" ("gūðflogan," l. 2528a), "bare, violent dragon" ("nacod nīðdraca," l. 2273a), and "terrible earth-dragon" ("egeslic eorðdraca," l. 2825a). The poet thus pits his protagonist—the most benevolent, considerate, and magnanimous man ever to step foot in the legendary world of the migration period—against lupine and serpentine adversaries, who possess aquatic or aerial superpowers and are implacably hostile. The poet probably never entertained the possibility that an audience witnessing such contests could sympathize with the bestial antagonists and regard them as possessing any form of moral justification for their actions. If these contests are not straightforward cases of good versus evil, they are at the very least cases wherein a virtuous hero is risking his life in a selfless struggle against daunting, elemental forces. This hero, moreover, had already been established in the conflict against Grendel as an agent of God's will, who received divine support in his vanquishing of a diabolical fiend—support that he receives again while vanquishing the fiend's mother. As the righteousness of the protagonist is progressively established, the need to demonize his adversaries is progressively reduced. With good reason, the poet considered it unnecessary to make Grendel's mother or the dragon as purely evil as Grendel. To endow them with the same satanic associations would have created a sense of redundancy opposed to the manifest fondness for variation possessed by the *Beowulf* poet and most other narrators in the West Germanic poetic tradition.[47]

Though much of the terminology applied to the dragon refers in a neutral manner to its conventional draconic activity—it is a "hoard-keeper" ("hordweard," 2293b, 2302b, 2554b), a "warden of the barrow" ("beorges weard," l. 2580b), an "old dawn-flier" ("eald ūhtfloga," l. 2760a), a "hoarder of treasures" ("frætwa hyrde," l. 3133b), and so forth—there are also terms that suggest a sinister aspect to the dragon. The application to the dragon of the term *mānsceaða* (l. 2514b), the first

---

47. On variation as a defining feature of West Germanic poetry, see R. D. Fulk, "Rhetoric, Form, and Linguistic Structure in Early Germanic Verse: Toward a Synthesis," *Interdisciplinary Journal for Germanic Linguistics and Semiotic Analysis* 1 (1996): 63–88.

element of which can mean "evil," is significant; the previous use of the same term in reference to Grendel (l. 712a, l. 737b) and his mother (l. 1339a) suggests some affinity between the three monsters.[48] Sinister connotations emanate as well from the description of the dragon as a "terrible, malicious stranger" ("atol inwitgæst," l. 2670a) and a "violent stranger" ("nīðgæst," l. 2699a). A more significant connection between the dragon and Grendel is registered in the term *ðēodsceaða*, which denotes an enemy of an entire people (*ðēod*) and is used twice in reference to the dragon (ll. 2278a, 2688a). A synonymous term, *lēodsceaða* (2093b), is applied to Grendel, who is consistently represented as an enemy of the Danish nation: his depredations are a form of "national calamity" ("þēodþrēa," l. 178a), and his death at the hands of Beowulf brings consolation and relief to all of the Danes. In the account of the dragon's devastation, the narrator emphasizes that this monster, like Grendel, is also the persecutor of an entire populace:

> Ðā se gæst ongan   glēdum spīwan,
> beorht hofu bærnan—   brynelēoma stōd
> eldum on andan;   nō ðǣr āht cwices
> lāð lyftfloga   lǣfan wolde.
> Wæs þæs wyrmes wīg   wīde gesӯne,
> nearofāges nīð   nēan ond feorran,
> hū se gūðsceaða   Gēata lēode
> hatode ond hӯnde. (ll. 2312–2319a)

(Then the stranger began to spew flames, to burn up the bright manors—firelight arose in enmity to humans; the cruel flier did not intend to leave anything there alive. The serpent's devastation was widely apparent, the hatred of the intensely hostile creature near and far, how the warlike destroyer detested and humiliated the Geatish people.)

The depiction of the dragon as an existential threat to the Geatish people provides Beowulf's fight against this monster with an element of gravity and moral justification that would not be present if the hero were fighting merely to access hoarded treasure. Like the demonic characterization of Grendel, the representation of the dragon as a national enemy is another aspect of *Beowulf* that the poet appears to have derived from hagiographical literature, where dragons bring destruction to towns and saints

---

48. See Wright, "Good and Evil," 2.

fight them in order to save populations from harm.[49] In contrast, heroes in Germanic legend usually fight dragons in order to obtain the treasures they are guarding. Kathryn Hume, in a survey of the use of monsters in Old Norse literature, identifies four functions that monsters possess as foils to heroes, one of which is that "the monster preys upon society, thus letting the hero put his strength to the service of others." She notes, however, that this function is rarely served by monsters comparable to those found in *Beowulf:* "Most Icelandic giant and dragon stories fail to make anything of this social potential. . . . We rarely see towns victimized by dragons."[50] Christine Rauer, in her survey of dragons in medieval literature, confirms that the representation of dragons as foes of entire peoples is "extremely rare in dragon-fights outside the hagiographical genre, for instance in the Scandinavian secular tradition," yet in hagiography Rauer finds no fewer than sixty-three episodes wherein a serpentine monster terrorizes a neighborhood or persecutes a populace.[51]

The poet's decision to draw on hagiography in his construction of monstrosity signals his concern with imposing a clear moral framework on his migration-period material. In native tradition, less moral ambiguity surrounded conflicts between man and monster than conflicts between kinsmen or sworn friends; though a hero's reasons for fighting a monster might be trivial or materialistic, the defeat of a monster is generally regarded as an unadulterated good. A poet concerned about the amoral nature of the antecedent legendary tradition could have satisfied his concerns by focusing his narrative on monster fights of the sort that he found in native folkloric tradition, but the *Beowulf* poet was evidently unsatisfied with this solution. To rectify the amorality of his inheritance, the poet modeled his monster fights on those he encountered in hagiographical narratives, which presented a form of moral clarity that was apparently unavailable in native tradition. The monster fights in *Beowulf* differ fundamentally from those recorded elsewhere

---

49. See Goldsmith, *Mode and Meaning,* 130–45; Lapidge, "*Beowulf,* Aldhelm," 278–82; Christine Rauer, *Beowulf and the Dragon: Parallels and Analogues* (Cambridge: D. S. Brewer, 2000), 52–86. For an incisive reading of the dragon episode overall, see Kenneth Sisam, "Beowulf's Fight with the Dragon," *Review of English Studies* 9, no. 34 (1958): 129–40.

50. Kathryn Hume, "From Saga to Romance: The Use of Monsters in Old Norse Literature," *Studies in Philology* 77, no. 1 (1980): 1–25, at 3, 5. See also Paul Sorrell, "The Approach to the Dragon-Fight in *Beowulf,* Aldhelm, and the 'traditions folkloriques' of Jacques Le Goff," *Parergon* 12, no. 1 (1994): 57–87, at 85–86; Maria Elena Ruggerini, "L'eroe germanico contro avversari mostruosi: tra testo e iconografia," in *La funzione dell'eroe germanico: storicità, metafora, paradigma; Atti del Convegno internazionale di studio Roma, 6–8 maggio 1993,* ed. Teresa Pàroli (Rome: Calamo, 1995), 201–57, at 206.

51. Rauer, *Beowulf and the Dragon,* 57.

in medieval Germanic literature. In *Beowulf*, we do not find conflicts between a vaguely good hero and a vaguely bad (and occasionally rather comical) monster of the sort that predominate elsewhere. We find, rather, an exceptionally virtuous hero risking his life on three occasions to benefit a broader community by eliminating horrific monsters that terrorize entire peoples. The evil nature of the first two monsters is established by their descent from Cain and their associations with hell, the devil, and opposition to God; the evil nature of the third monster is indicated by its willingness to inflict massive destruction in retaliation for the theft of a single treasure.[52] The poet's decision to pit such a benevolent hero against such malevolent monsters endows *Beowulf* with a sense of cosmic gravity and moral clarity that is not found in any other medieval Germanic work concerned with monsters and heroes.

The insistent monotheism of *Beowulf* works in tandem with its conception of monstrosity to establish a firm moral framework. Just as the monsters are far worse than the typical monsters of folklore, the hero is much better than the typical hero of legend. Beyond his abstention from kin-slaying and oath-breaking, Beowulf is pious and God-fearing, displaying in his words and deeds an unwavering faith in the singular deity whose existence he has intuited. He is surrounded by other characters who revere and thank this deity, most notably Hrothgar, whose frequent emphasis on the divine contributes to the religious atmosphere of the poem and keeps the role of God at the forefront of the audience's mind. The representation of Beowulf and Hrothgar as intuitive monotheists who frequently share their theological insights further differentiates *Beowulf* from other works concerned with migration-period legend. It is revealing that in the voluminous literature connected to the Nibelung cycle, there is no passage that criticism has found reason to label "Gunther's sermon": the Burgundian king does not deliver lengthy theological discourses to Siegfried, the impressive young hero who has arrived at his court. Siegfried, like Beowulf, possesses preternatural strength and a penchant for fighting monsters, but there is no sense that he is doing God's work when he kills monstrous adversaries. In *Vǫlsunga saga*, it is made clear that Sigurðr's mission to kill Fáfnir results partially from a desire to obtain the dragon's treasure and partially from the desire of Reginn, the brother of Fáfnir, to see his draconic kinsman slain. If there is a common heroic archetype behind figures such as Beowulf and Sigurðr, as the superficial similarities between

---

52. See Adrien Bonjour, "Monsters Crouching and Critics Rampant: Or the *Beowulf* Dragon Debated," *PMLA* 68, no. 1 (1953): 304–12, at 309–11; Wright, "Good and Evil," 2–4.

them might suggest, then our poet has clearly made a concerted effort to separate his protagonist from conventional manifestations of this archetype. Beowulf, on account of his courtesy, piety, and unimpeachable motives, stands out in the field of medieval Germanic monster-slaying heroes. In temperament, if not in stature, Beowulf has more in common with a dragon-fighting saint than with Sigurðr.

Monotheism and monstrosity make *Beowulf* the salient outlier that it is in the corpus of extant witnesses to migration-period legend. A strong sense of the poem's singularity can be obtained by contrasting its hero's dragon fight with the account of Frotho's dragon fight in Saxo's *Gesta Danorum*.[53] In the space of a page, Saxo narrates an episode featuring a remarkable concatenation of motifs found in the final third of *Beowulf*: as the editors of *Klaeber IV* note, similarities between the two accounts include "the description of the dragon . . . the report of a countryman . . . the use of a specially prepared shield . . . the hero's desire to engage in the contest without help from others . . . the manner of the fight itself."[54] The overlap is sufficiently striking to rule out the possibility of coincidence; the only plausible explanation is that a common tradition was known both to the *Beowulf* poet and to Saxo.[55] Yet the similarities between the two accounts render their differences all the more striking. In Saxo's episode, the dragon does not terrorize a populace; Frotho decides to seek the dragon out because his father bankrupted the treasury and he now needs money to pay for the maintenance of his retainers. The dragon fight, moreover, is a minor episode in Frotho's career, which appears at its beginning and provides the treasures that fund subsequent adventures in foreign lands. If the *Beowulf* poet knew a tradition like this and applied it to his protagonist, then he would appear to have eliminated every detail that was at odds with his moral vision while faithfully preserving every detail that he considered unproblematic. Instead of the dragon fight launching a career of amoral adventures for Frotho (and Sigurðr), it concludes a career of righteous adventures for Beowulf. The contrast suggests, in microcosm, how *Beowulf* came to be the unique work that it is, an epic poem traditional in its content yet singular in its morality.

---

53. See Friis-Jensen, *Saxo Grammaticus*, 78–81.
54. Fulk et al., *Klaeber's Beowulf*, xlv.
55. On the connections between the two accounts, see Eduard Sievers, "Béowulf und Saxo," *Berichte über die Verhandlungen der königlich sächsischen Gesellschaft der Wissenschaften zu Leipzig, philologisch-historische Klasse* 47 (1895): 175–92, at 180–88; Chambers, *Beowulf: An Introduction*, 91–97; Whitelock, *Audience of Beowulf*, 69–70; Rauer, *Beowulf and the Dragon*, 42–44.

Conclusion

In this concluding chapter, I aim to synthesize the findings of the previous chapters and address some of the objections that a reader might reasonably raise in response to their claims. Critics have long recognized that *Beowulf* is a multifaceted poem in which originally distinct heroic and folkloric traditions have been combined and in which the influence of various other social, historical, literary, and intellectual traditions can be discerned. What has less frequently and explicitly been recognized in the critical literature is the coherent plan that can be discerned in the combination and modification of these numerous sources and traditions. Disparate material was not crudely yoked together during the poem's composition. A single mind, with a singular sense of decorum, can be seen at work in the selection and alteration of source material. The same mind, with the same set of concerns, can be seen endowing *Beowulf* with what I have termed its insistent qualities, that is, those qualities that were not especially prominent in heroic or folkloric tradition yet have been made exceptionally prominent in *Beowulf*: courtliness, monotheism, and a kind of historical realism. Rather than perceive *Beowulf* as a colorful mosaic (at best) or a disorderly hodgepodge (at worst) of aspects of early medieval life and literature, it can be read as the considered result of one poet's ambition to produce a morally edifying, theologically palatable, and historically plausible epic out of material that could not independently constitute such a poem.

Chapter 1 demonstrated that moral concerns shape the *Beowulf* poet's relationship with the antecedent tradition of migration-period legend. This tradition presented an amoral vision of life in which heroes caught between conflicting ethical imperatives displayed their unwavering commitment to honor and duty by committing transgressions that were hateful to them, usually in the form of kin-slaying or oath-breaking. In other witnesses to migration-period legend, these wretched heroes are represented in a sympathetic and admiring manner, yet the *Beowulf* poet clearly felt uncomfortable with the prospect of structuring an epic poem around a hero who was driven by circumstances (or fate) to kill kinsmen or break oaths. The composition of *Beowulf* appears to have been guided by a programmatic refusal to valorize heroes who were known to have committed such transgressions. While these heroes conventionally occupied the center of attention, the *Beowulf* poet confined them to digressions, where he could use them to lend historical and literary depth to the world of his poem without endorsing their transgressive behavior. Since amoral plots involving a coerced transgression had been attached to most legendary heroes, the poet decided to focus his narrative on a hero derived from folkloric tradition, where characters with preternatural strength were known for killing monsters rather than their own kinsmen. This folkloric protagonist, who rejoices in his dying words that he abstained from kin-slaying and oath-breaking, is surrounded in the poem's foreground by other characters to whom such deeds had not been attached in antecedent tradition, such as Hrothgar, who is elsewhere known as a stay-at-home king. The poet casts an admiring light on these exemplary foregrounded characters who display courteous behavior and express monotheistic convictions.

Chapter 2 argued that the poet modified the heroic and folkloric traditions he inherited by making ideals of courtesy and courtliness central to the matter of his epic poem. Instead of focusing on the standard heroic transgressions and the circumstances leading up to them, the poet focuses his narrative not only on monster fights but also on the courteous speech and courtly behavior of the foregrounded characters. Details of court life assume central importance in *Beowulf*, where considerable emphasis is placed on the protagonist's gradual transition from courtier to king. Displaying greater interest in his courtly behavior than his martial conduct, the poet depicts Beowulf as an ideal courtier, who knows how to conduct himself in an aristocratic environment.

The hero exhibits the sophisticated self-restraint associated with court-liness, as he displays exaggerated deference toward his superiors and pronounced magnanimity toward his inferiors. He is offered a claim to the Danish throne, but he recognizes the resistance that would greet his accession and prudently refrains from pursuing it. Instead, Beowulf parlays his success in Denmark into royal status in Geatland. After a pivotal speech in which the hero stresses his aptitude for kingship and his knowledge of the customs of a superior court, he presents Hygelac with royal treasures befitting an heir to the Danish throne. Hygelac is left with little choice but to reciprocate by entering into a state of joint kingship with his nephew. *Beowulf*, in addition to its monster fights, tells the story of a lesser nobleman's rise to kingship, as it shows him advance from needing to earn an audience with the Danish king to becoming one of the king's intimates and finally a king himself. The poet, evidently dissatisfied with a folkloric inheritance where narratives possess an ahistorical and dreamlike quality, makes a concerted effort to endow his epic poem with a quality of courtly realism. His protago-nist is a human being (not a bear) whose exemplary life is situated at plausible courts of the semi-historical migration period.

Chapter 3 explored the poet's use of monotheism and monstrosity to bring greater moral clarity to the traditions he inherited. It main-tains that there is no tension in *Beowulf* between Christian and pagan elements. While the faith of characters in the background is never in-dicated, the characters in the foreground are consistently represented as pious monotheists who have apparently intuited the existence of the singular deity of Judeo-Christian tradition without the benefit of Mosaic law or Christian revelation. These intuitive monotheists are viewed by the narrator not as hopeless heathens destined to an eternity in hell but as determined adherents to natural law who can achieve salvation if they follow their better intuitions and never allow temporal circumstances to induce them to become excessively proud or resort to polytheistic practices. There is, moreover, a general doctrinal align-ment between the narrator and the foregrounded characters, who share a theological horizon that excludes explicit references to Christ and the saints while including references to providence, judgment, salvation, and damnation. Opposed to the poem's virtuous monotheists are ma-levolent monsters descended from Cain, who are embroiled in a long-standing feud with God, and a fire-breathing dragon, whose animosity threatens an entire populace. These monsters are not the vaguely bad and sometimes comical monsters of folkloric tradition. Drawing on hagiographical literature, the poet makes them far more sinister and unsympathetic, turning a troll into a satanic demon from hell, a troll's mother into a ferocious sea beast, and a dragon into a destructive enemy of an entire nation. By pitting a pious protagonist, who receives God's support and is an unwitting agent of God's will, against these sinister monsters, the poet endows his epic poem with a sense of moral clarity and cosmic gravity that is not found elsewhere in medieval Germanic literature. Neither in the extant witnesses to migration-period legend nor in the extant narratives concerning monster fights do we find any work with a moral framework quite like that of *Beowulf*.

Reading these summaries of the preceding chapters, one might object that the presence of Unferth in the poem's foreground contradicts some of the claims just articulated. I have argued that the poet, concerned about the moral ambiguity attached to heroes in the antecedent tradition, populated the foreground of his poem with an unconventional set of courtly and pious characters who were unstained by the standard heroic transgressions of kin-slaying and oath-breaking. Unferth, however, is known to have killed his kinsmen; he behaves discourteously toward Beowulf; and he is never depicted thanking God or using monotheistic language in his speech. Yet when one considers the poet's exceptionally negative treatment of Unferth, it becomes apparent that his presence offers confirmation rather than refutation of my arguments. The salient depreciation of Unferth alone among the foregrounded characters, none of whom receives similar treatment, suggests that the poet genuinely possessed the moral concerns that I have attributed to him. Handling an amoral tradition replete with characters compelled to transgress, the poet minimized the attention granted to most of them, but he decided in the case of Unferth to allow one such character to have a place in his poem's foreground in order to make didactic use of him. The poet repeatedly signals his disapproval of Unferth, who functions as a foil to the protagonist: the pettiness and cowardice of the former are highlighted to make the magnanimity and bravery of the latter all the more impressive. By representing Unferth in this deprecatory manner and not representing him as an exemplary monotheist whose transgression might have possessed a defensible justification, the poet concurs with the sentiment expressed by Alcuin, namely, that a transgressive hero from migration-period legend should not receive the admiration of a Christian audience.

In view of this counterargument, one might wonder why a poet intending to disapprove of Unferth should represent him as possessing an honored position at the Danish court, where he sits in close proximity to the royal person and receives the trust of both Hrothgar and Hrothulf. The divergence between the pejorative treatment Unferth receives from the narrator and the respectful treatment he receives from other characters has long been considered a puzzling feature of the poem in its critical literature. The solution I would propose for this puzzle is that it results from the poet's sense of literary decorum, that is, from his sense that he was free as an author to alter the moral valences associated with traditional content but not free to alter the content itself. So, if tradition held that Unferth was the most prominent nobleman at Hrothgar's court, then the poet could not deny him that status, regardless of his moral reservations. This solution gains in persuasiveness when we recognize that it also explains why the poet did not react to the amorality of antecedent legend by composing a poem like the *Jüngeres Hildebrandslied*, where the tradition is fundamentally altered and the poem ends not with the father killing the son but with reconciliation and a family reunion. The *Beowulf* poet's manifest reverence for tradition made him reluctant to alter what he likely considered tantamount to historical fact. The body of traditional knowledge pertaining to the migration period, passed down over generations to the poet and his audience, provided *Beowulf* with a historical setting that could be tactfully augmented but not essentially revised. Monster fights, decorous speeches, and theological commentary could be added, but the facts of tradition—the awe-inspiring transgressions through which empires were ended and heroes were established—could not be altered. Conjecturing a relationship to tradition along these lines would explain why the poet resorts to digression or minimization rather than outright alteration when handling the morally problematic material that lends historical depth to his poem and enhances its appeal for an aristocratic audience weaned on migration-period legend.

A theory of constrained innovation, which posits that the poet's plan for moral renovation was constrained by the facts of the traditions he inherited, accounts well for other objections that might be raised in response to the arguments of my book. For instance, critics have made much of the fact that the dragon is never made out to be a descendant of Cain, alleging that this omission disturbs the poem's unity, divests the monsters of symbolic significance, and weakens the moral framework of Beowulf's final fight.[1] Drawing on this body of criticism, a reader might object that if the poet were genuinely concerned about the moral clarity of his narrative, he would have made the dragon a descendant of Cain. The answer I would offer to this objection is that, in all likelihood, the poet was simply not at liberty to make the dragon a descendant of Cain because, in the traditions about Cain's monstrous progeny that he inherited, only humanoid monsters comparable to the *gīgantas* of the Bible were thought to descend from Cain.[2] Serpentine monsters, like the *wyrm* that kills Beowulf, could not possess an originally human progenitor. They belonged to a separate monstrous genus and were thought to dwell in different environments: tradition located dragons in caves and barrows full of treasures rather than the barren wastelands or cold streams inhabited by Cain's descendants.[3] Modern readers might imagine that a poet dealing in matters of fantasy and imagination could easily have added dragons to the list of Cain's monstrous progeny, but in this area too the poet was probably constrained by the facts of tradition. A serpentine *draca* would be out of place on a list of humanoid "abominations" ("untȳdras") that includes "ogres and elves and lumbering brutes" ("eotenas ond ylfe ond orcnēas") as well as the biblical *gīgantas* (ll. 111–114).[4] Had the poet included the dragon on this list, modern readers might not mind, but a medieval audience versed in demonological lore would probably have considered it an indecorous and implausible innovation.

1. See Gang, "Approaches to *Beowulf*"; Sisam, "Beowulf's Fight"; Howard Shilton, "The Nature of Beowulf's Dragon," *Bulletin of the John Rylands Library* 79, no. 3 (1997): 67–78; George Clark, "*Beowulf* as a Philosophical Poem."

2. For accounts of the traditions that might have been known to the poet concerning Cain's monstrous progeny, see Oliver F. Emerson, "Legends of Cain, Especially in Old and Middle English," *PMLA* 21, no. 4 (1906): 831–929; Ruth Mellinkoff, "Cain's Monstrous Progeny in *Beowulf*: Part I, Noachic Tradition," *Anglo-Saxon England* 8 (1979): 143–62; Ruth Mellinkoff, "Cain's Monstrous Progeny in *Beowulf*: Part II, Post-Diluvian Survival," *Anglo-Saxon England* 9 (1980): 183–97; David Williams, *Cain and Beowulf: A Study in Secular Allegory* (Toronto: University of Toronto Press, 1982); Orchard, *Pride and Prodigies*, 58–85.

3. See William Witherle Lawrence, "The Dragon and His Lair in *Beowulf*," *PMLA* 33, no. 4 (1918): 547–83; Whitelock, *Audience of Beowulf*, 73–74; Chadwick, "Monsters and *Beowulf*," 175; Rauer, *Beowulf and the Dragon*, 49–51. On the distinct genera of different kinds of monstrous creatures, see the text of the *Liber Monstrorum* in Orchard, *Pride and Prodigies*, 254–317.

4. The meaning of *orcneas* is uncertain. I follow here Fulk's rendering of the term as "lumbering brutes," though it might mean "animated corpses" or "hellish creatures." See Richard Jente, *Die mythologischen Ausdrücke im altenglischen Wortschatz: Eine kulturgeschichtlich-etymologische Untersuchung* (Heidelberg: Winter, 1921), 137; Stanley Marvin Wiersma, "A Linguistic Analysis of Words Referring to Monsters in *Beowulf*" (PhD diss., University of Wisconsin, 1961), 312–19; Orchard, *Pride and Prodigies*, 69.

There is, moreover, a reason why the poet might have wanted his protagonist to be killed by a monster that did not descend from Cain. The poet, cautious and censorious as he was, might have been uncomfortable with the prospect of having his virtuous protagonist killed by a monster like Grendel, that is, a determined enemy of God with satanic characteristics. Given the poet's evident concern about the morality of the antecedent legendary tradition, he might well have considered it problematic to let a diabolical monster kill his protagonist, even if that monster were also to perish in the conflict. Although there should be no theological problem with such a scenario, the poet clearly wishes to stress to his audience that God is omnipotent, that providence is eternal, and that no other supernatural entities possess any powers comparable to those of God. That message might have been undermined if one of God's enemies managed to kill God's champion. It is significant that, as noted in chapter 3, both Hrothgar and the poem's narrator continually detect God's benevolent intervention in gifts, rewards, and positive developments, while never giving voice to the logical corollary that disaster and suffering must be equally providential in a world governed by God. There would have been nothing heterodox about the articulation of this corollary, yet the poet evidently considered it indecorous. God, in *Beowulf*, is omnipotent and eternal, yet responsible only for life's comforts, for miraculous victories, and for sending saviors to distressed peoples. He must also be responsible for misery and defeat, but the poet does not consider this to be something worth mentioning. Composing for an audience that had been Christian possibly for less than a century, the poet avoids making any theological statement that could make God appear cruel, arbitrary, or less than omnipotent. The poem's theology stresses that, unlike the Norns, the true God is not sadistic, and unlike the Æsir and Vanir, this God does not share power with other deities. Furthermore, unlike Óðinn and his selected champions, this God and his chosen warrior are always victorious when they find themselves fighting against giants locked in an eternal feud with God.

Another type of objection that might be raised against this book concerns its use of sources later than *Beowulf* to illuminate the legendary tradition that existed prior to the poem's composition. Contrasts have been drawn, for instance, between *Beowulf* and *Hlǫðskviða*, a poem that possesses no textual witness prior to the fourteenth century.[5] In

---

5. See J. R. R. Tolkien, *Saga of King Heidrek*, xxix–xxxi.

view of their chronological separation, how can we be certain that the *Beowulf* poet knew and reacted to legends comparable to the one that the *Hlǫðskviða* poet told of the conflict between Hlǫðr and Angantýr? While it is entirely possible that aspects of *Hlǫðskviða* represent later developments, there are many reasons to believe that the central narrative concerning the compelled transgressions of Hlǫðr and Angantýr is representative of the type of legend that the *Beowulf* poet inherited. Perhaps the most cogent reasons to believe this emerge from *Beowulf* itself, where the digressions featuring Hengest and Ingeld unambiguously indicate that the poet knew legends about heroes who were compelled by circumstances to transgress. Also relevant is the knowledge the poet displays of Eormenric and Sigemund, two figures to whom major legends of kin-slaying and oath-breaking were attached. Furthermore, narratives similar to the one related in *Hlǫðskviða* are attested in much earlier sources: the legend of Hildebrand and Hadubrand, related in the *Hildebrandslied*, and the legend of Rosimund and Alboin, related in Paul the Deacon's *Historia Langobardorum*, are preserved in works that were probably composed within a century of *Beowulf*.[6] Other Eddic witnesses to migration-period legend, such as *Atlakviða* and *Hamðismál*, were perhaps composed during the ninth century.[7] Regardless of the date of *Hamðismál*, the account of Ermanaric's death in Jordanes's *Getica* indicates that a similar legend already existed during the sixth century.[8] Yet the chronological disposition of particular witnesses matters less than the typological alignment that these witnesses exhibit. Theodore M. Andersson, observing recurrent similarities between *Hlǫðskviða*, *Atlakviða*, *Hamðismál*, the *Hildebrandslied*, and the *Finnsburg* fragment, draws the following conclusion:

> Despite the dispersion in time (eighth to thirteenth century) and place (England, Bavaria, Iceland), these heroic survivals have so

---

6. Preserved in a manuscript from ca. 830, the *Hildebrandslied* is generally considered an eighth-century composition: see Bostock, "Lay of Hildebrand," 73–82. Some would date the *Hildebrandslied* to the seventh century: see, for instance, Frederick Norman, *Three Essays on the Hildebrandslied*, ed. A. T. Hatto (London: University of London, 1973), 48, who asserts that the poem "must have been produced well before 700." On the date and context of the *Historia Langobardorum*, which was composed toward the end of the eighth century, see Shami Ghosh, *Writing the Barbarian Past: Studies in Early Medieval Historical Narrative* (Leiden: Brill, 2016), 117–21.

7. See Bjarne Fidjestøl, *The Dating of Eddic Poetry: A Historical Survey and Methodological Investigation*, ed. Odd Einar Haugen (Copenhagen: C. A. Reitzel, 1999).

8. See Theodor Mommsen, ed., *Iordanis Romana et Getica* (Berlin: Weidmann, 1882), 91–92. On the date and context of the *Getica*, which was composed in the middle of the sixth century, see Ghosh, *Writing the Barbarian Past*, 42–46.

many common features that they are assumed to derive from a single prototypical form earlier than all the extant examples. . . . The drift of these pieces is similar enough to suggest a narrowly circumscribed genre. Typically the situation is highly charged and the issue compressed to an impossible but inescapable choice. All the poems are rich in family tensions and are peopled by men and women living under the remorseless constraints of duty, courage, honor, contempt for life, and the imperative necessity of revenge.[9]

What becomes clear from analyses of all the evidence for migration-period legend, such as those put forward by Andersson and Phillpotts, is that the witnesses are sufficiently consistent to render the elimination of one witness rather inconsequential. The reconstruction of the legendary tradition that existed prior to *Beowulf* is necessarily hypothetical, but it does not rest on the validity of a single hypothesis; it is, rather, a robust conjectural edifice that does not teeter if there is disagreement about the authenticity of a particular witness or the reconstruction of a particular legend. In the case of *Hlǫðskviða*, many elements of its plot are paralleled elsewhere: Angantýr's reluctant killing of Hlǫðr is paralleled in Hildebrand's reluctant killing of Hadubrand; Gizurr's sowing of strife between kinsmen is paralleled in Starkaðr's sowing of strife between Ingeld and his in-laws; and Hlǫðr's compulsion to avenge an insult to his parent is paralleled in Rosimund's compulsion to do the same. Thus, even if one were to believe that *Hlǫðskviða* is not valid evidence in the courtroom of *Beowulf* studies, the picture of migration-period legend painted by sources of greater proximity to *Beowulf* would still be substantially the same. Accordingly, it appears reasonable to believe that, despite its possible lateness, *Hlǫðskviða* relates a narrative that was entirely typical of the legendary tradition that existed prior to the composition of *Beowulf*.

Various objections to the arguments of my book could be leveled in connection with the grim predicament of the Geats at the end of the poem. Following the death of Beowulf, a Geatish messenger predicts that without their famous king's protection, the Geats will suffer invasion and persecution at the hands of Swedish, Frankish, and Frisian forces; he envisions a future in which Geatish men and women, deprived of treasure and weaponry, will be forced to "tread foreign ways" ("elland tredan," l. 3019b) as displaced exiles. The narrator subsequently

---

9. Andersson, *Preface to the Nibelungenlied*, 4, 6.

confirms the rectitude of the messenger's predictions (ll. 3028–3030a), and at Beowulf's funeral, an anonymous woman delivers a lament expressing fearful anticipation of "a profusion of mayhem, terror of troops, abasement and captivity" ("wælfylla worn, werudes egesan, / hȳnðo ond hæftnȳd," ll. 3154–3155a). Critics debate as to whether these passages should be taken to mean that the Geats are on the verge of permanent subjugation and annihilation, like the Burgundians following the death of Gundaharius, or merely on the verge of a temporary setback.[10] Regardless of the extent and duration of their suffering, it is clear that troubled times lie ahead for the Geats, and it seems likelier than not that the poet envisions them losing their political autonomy now that Beowulf is dead. The apparent doom of the Geats naturally raises some questions when considered in connection with my arguments. If the poet wished to impose moral clarity on his work, why would he allow his poem to end with the Geatish people anticipating invasion, displacement, and possible annihilation? Would there not seem to be more justice in a divinely ordered universe if Beowulf managed to bring a lasting form of salvation to his troubled people? What moral purpose could possibly be served by this ominous ending?

The answer I would offer to these objections is that the poet probably allowed aesthetic considerations to override moral considerations when crafting the conclusion to his epic poem. A positive outcome for the Geats, in which the treasure won by Beowulf is said to secure lasting peace and prosperity for his people, would have been easier to reconcile with the poet's moral and theological concerns, but happy endings appear to have been considered aesthetically unacceptable when rehandling migration-period legend. Happy endings appear as alien as rhyming lines in the heroic and aristocratic tradition associated with the Germanic alliterative line. Surveying a terrain that includes works such as *Atlakviða*, *Hamðismál*, *Sigurðarkviða*, *Hlǫðskviða*, the *Hildebrandslied*, and the *Nibelungenlied*, we find work after work concluding with grotesque scenes of carnage, dying heroes surrounded by piles of corpses, suicidal and filicidal heroines, halls set aflame, the destruction of nations, and

---

10. See Peter S. Baker, *Honour, Exchange and Violence in Beowulf* (Cambridge: D. S. Brewer, 2013), 232–39; Robinson, "History, Religion, Culture," 110–12; John Halverson, "The World of *Beowulf*," *ELH* 36, no. 4 (1969): 593–608, at 607; Berger and Leicester, "Social Structure as Doom," 63–64; Sisam, *Structure of Beowulf*, 54–58; R. T. Farrell, *Beowulf, Swedes and Geats* (London: Viking Society for Northern Research, 1972), 257–69; Frank, "Skaldic Verse," 157; John D. Niles, "Myth and History," in *A Beowulf Handbook*, ed. Robert E. Bjork and John D. Niles (Lincoln: University of Nebraska Press, 1997), 213–32, at 227–28.

the erasure of noble families. The only works concerned with migra-
tion-period legend to feature happy endings are those that have more
broadly abandoned the aesthetic, linguistic, and ethical norms associ-
ated with it, such as *Waltharius, Kudrun,* and the *Jüngeres Hildebrandslied*.
The *Beowulf* poet, while refusing to focus his epic on a scene of co-
erced kin-slaying or oath-breaking, also refused to abandon the com-
positional norms associated with the antecedent legendary tradition.
He would not descend into the lowest realm of the popular and the
prosaic by composing a simplistic folktale with a happy ending. Moral
concerns guided the poet's relationship with the antecedent legendary
tradition, but *Beowulf* did not consequently become a straightforward
morality tale. The poet's plan for moral renovation was constrained
not only by the facts of the traditions he inherited but also by the
aesthetic norms that were inextricably rooted in these traditions.

By positioning Beowulf as the last great king of the Geats, whose
long and prosperous reign immediately precedes the demise of his
people, the poet devised an ingenious solution to the problem of aes-
thetic conformity. In making the protagonist's death coincide with
national catastrophe on a massive scale, the poet enables the legend of
Beowulf to possess a structural resemblance to legends of Gundaha-
rius, Ermanaric, and Atilla, three historical kings of the migration pe-
riod whose deaths coincided with the demise of their nations. Legends
of Ingeld and Hlǫðr appear likewise to conclude with the death of a
hero and the demise of a nation occurring simultaneously.[11] The doom
of the Geats thus lends *Beowulf* an essential resemblance to poems that
would end with the doom of the Burgundians, the Goths, the Huns,
and the Heathobards. The ominous ending of *Beowulf* serves the crucial
function of enabling a poem with a plot largely derived from folkloric
tradition to possess a conclusion that is consistent with the generic
norms of the heroic-legendary tradition. Furthermore, the aftermath
of Beowulf's death contributes, perhaps in a more significant way than
any other detail in the poem, to its insistent historicism. In a purely
folkloric version of *Beowulf*, situated in a magical and dreamlike setting,
the poem would conclude happily and conventionally with marriage,
prosperity, and a hero's return. In *Beowulf*, however, the poem concludes
not only with the death of the hero and an elegiac mood but also with
the hero's people facing invasion from Swedes, Franks, and Frisians,

---

11. See the discussion of these legends in the introduction.

a specific set of geographically and historically plausible opponents. Given the demonstrable historicity of Hygelac's raid in Frankish territory, it appears that the poet is not merely endowing his epic with a veneer of historicity—he is actually rooting it in what he understood to be the historical facts of the period. In view of the archaeological evidence for considerable upheaval in sixth-century Scandinavia, the poet's understanding of history might well reflect the actual history of the period.[12] The doom of the Geats certainly has no folkloric basis, as it corresponds to none of the conventional functions identified by Propp. If it is not a piece of legendary history, then it would appear to be a bit of actual history used by the poet to increase the poignancy and realism of his epic creation.

The ominous conclusion of *Beowulf* has often been interpreted as one of the clearest indicators that the poem was constructed around a critical agenda and that it aims to expose something fundamentally wrong about the world it depicts, whether that be "the fatal contradiction at the core of heroic society," "the limits of all heroic action," or a flaw pertaining to the society's valorization of treasure, fame, revenge, or other institutions.[13] One objection that might be raised in response to my book is that it makes no mention of this purported critical agenda. Indeed, I have argued that the composition of *Beowulf*, in its plot and its treatment of various characters, reflects concern about the coerced kin-slaying and oath-breaking that the poet encountered in the antecedent legendary tradition, but I would not extend this concern into a fundamental critique of heroic society. If the poet is worried about heroism, he appears to be worried only about the particular kind of fanatical heroism that drives a hero to commit an outrageous yet justified transgression against a kinsman or in-law, that is, the type of heroism exhibited by figures like Starkaðr and Guðrún. This flavor of heroism,

---

12. See T. A. Shippey, "Names in *Beowulf* and Anglo-Saxon England," in *The Dating of Beowulf: A Reassessment*, ed. Leonard Neidorf (Cambridge: D. S. Brewer, 2014), 58–78, at 76–78; Lotte Hedeager, *Iron-Age Societies: From Tribe to State in Northern Europe, 500 BC to AD 700*, trans. John Hines (Oxford: Blackwell, 1992), 239–55; Martin Rundkvist, *Mead-Halls of the Eastern Geats: Elite Settlements and Political Geography AD 375–1000 in Östergötland, Sweden* (Stockholm: Kungl. Vitterhets Historie och Antikvitets Akademien, 2011), 39–46.

13. The first quotation is from John Leyerle, "Beowulf the Hero and the King," *Medium Ævum* 34, no. 2 (1965): 89–102, at 89; the second is from Georgianna, "King Hrethel's Sorrow," 848. For criticism in this vein, see Goldsmith, *Mode and Meaning*; Berger and Leicester, "Social Structure as Doom"; Stanley J. Kahrl, "Feuds in *Beowulf*: A Tragic Necessity?," *Modern Philology* 69, no. 3 (1972): 189–98; Martin Camargo, "The Finn Episode and the Tragedy of Revenge in *Beowulf*," *Studies in Philology* 78, no. 5 (1981): 120–34; Fajardo-Acosta, *Condemnation of Heroism*; North, "Gold and the Heathen Polity."

depicted at length in the other early Germanic works mentioned above, is not so much critiqued in *Beowulf* as it is omitted and obscured. It is more or less present in some digressions, especially those on Hengest and Ingeld, but it never receives sustained narration in the poem's foreground. The poet appears, accordingly, to have been a fairly cautious and censorious author with a paternalistic tendency to remove from his audience's sight the morally objectionable subject matter he found in his sources. In this respect, the poet is not unlike Wulfila or Ælfric, who felt obligated as translators of the Bible to omit or alter material that they did not trust their audiences to interpret correctly.[14] With this kind of literary sensibility, the *Beowulf* poet seems rather unlikely to present before his audience a heroic world that he considered fundamentally flawed, a world lovingly and carefully evoked merely to pronounce on it an oblique form of disapproval. Lines 175–188 suggest that if the poet wished to condemn a certain practice, such as idol worship, he would condemn it without equivocation.

The notion that *Beowulf* is a poem of critique appears to stem from a widespread tendency to conflate elegy with critique or to assume that elegy implies critique. There are several problems with this tendency. First, if *Beowulf* is a critique of heroism because it ends with elegy, doom, and disaster, then nearly every medieval Germanic heroic poem must be a critique of heroism. The *Nibelungenlied* ends with the extermination of the Burgundians; *Hamðismál* and *Atlakviða* end with the devastation of the Goths and the Huns, respectively; doom and gloom pervade *Sigurðarkviða*; aspects of elegy are present in *Hlǫðskviða* and the *Hildebrandslied*, among numerous other poems.[15] The improbability

---

14. On Wulfila's omission, see Peter Heather and John Matthews, *The Goths in the Fourth Century* (Liverpool: Liverpool University Press, 1991), 134–35, for Philostorgius's remark that Wulfila "translated all the Scriptures into their language—with the exception, that is, of Kings. This was because these books contain the history of wars, while the Gothic people, being lovers of war, were in need of something to restrain their passion for fighting rather than to incite them to it—which those books have the power to do, for all that they are held in the highest honour, and are well fitted to lead believers to the worship of God." See also Carla Falluomini, *The Gothic Version of the Gospels and Pauline Epistles: Cultural Background, Transmission and Character* (Berlin: De Gruyter, 2015), 4. On Ælfric's omissions and alterations, see Magennis, "No Sex Please"; E. Gordon Whatley, "Lost in Translation: Omission of Episodes in Some Old English Prose Saints' Legends," *Anglo-Saxon England* 26 (1997): 187–208; Mary Swan, "Identity and Ideology in Ælfric's Prefaces," in *A Companion to Ælfric*, ed. Hugh Magennis and Mary Swan (Leiden: Brill, 2009), 247–69.

15. On the pervasiveness of elegy and its connection to heroic legend, see Harris, "Elegy in Old English." On the presence of the elegiac in the *Hildebrandslied*, see Harris, "Hadubrand's Lament."

that all of these works should mount critiques of heroism reduces the likelihood that *Beowulf* mounts such a critique. Accordingly, the notion that *Beowulf* is a poem of critique appears sustainable only when the poem is read in isolation from other works that relate migration-period legend. Rather than perceive elegy as a form of critique, I would argue that elegy should be perceived as a decidedly aristocratic form, which the poet uses to establish that *Beowulf*, though possessing a folkloric plot, belongs to an aristocratic poetic tradition. It is worth recalling that when the protagonist recounts to Hygelac the noble customs of the Danish court, he mentions that Hrothgar himself recited "true and tragic" ("sōð ond sārlic," l. 2109a) poetry to the court, then engaged in moving recollections of his lost youth as "the breast welled up inside him" ("hreðer inne wēoll," l. 2113b). The Vandalic king Gelimer (480–553) is likewise reported to have personally performed elegiac poetry.[16] Such accounts suggest that elegy was marked as a high literary form, which conveyed the refined sensibility and capacity for wise reflection that a leisured aristocrat had time to cultivate. Instead of relating the elegiac features of *Beowulf* to a covert project of critique, I would relate them to the poem's insistent courtliness, its pervasive fascination with courtly etiquette, material splendor, and the royal aspirations of early medieval aristocrats.

The present book has differed from many books on *Beowulf* in that it has thus far made no ultimate statement as to what the poem is *about*. Most monographs on *Beowulf*, along with the many articles on the poem's structure, contain a statement somewhere within them about the poem possessing a particular theme or idea around which its content was selected and shaped. In my own account of the considerations shaping the poem's composition, I have not mentioned any particular theme that would explain, for instance, how one digression is connected to another and how the totality of digressions is connected in turn to the three monster fights. I have, however, argued that concerns about the amorality of the antecedent legendary tradition explain why the *Beowulf* poet focused his poem on the monster fights of a folkloric hero, and that these concerns are likewise evident in the placement of

---

16. See Fulk et al., *Klaeber's Beowulf*, 234: "The practice of the art of minstrelsy by nobles and kings in the heroic age is attested by Scandinavian (also Middle High German) and, indeed, Homeric parallels; a celebrated historic example is that of Gelimer, the last king of the Vandals (Procopius, *Histories: Vandal War* II, 6, 33)." For additional discussion of Gelimer's elegy, see Klinck, *Old English Elegies*, 230–31; Joaquín Martínez Pizarro, "Kings in Adversity: A Note on Alfred and the Cakes," *Neophilologus* 80, no. 2 (1996): 319–26.

material into the poem's background and foreground, with the background featuring the kin-slaying and oath-breaking heroes of tradition and the foreground featuring a sanitized set of courteous and pious characters. I have also argued that the poem is genuinely concerned with the courtly and spiritual life of these characters, and that their courtliness and spirituality is fundamental rather than incidental, central rather than peripheral, being showcased and developed in the various speeches that make up so much of the poem.[17] If forced to provide an answer to the question of what *Beowulf* is about, then, I would suggest that an answer might be reflected in the semantics of Old English *gedēfe*, an adjective glossed by the editors of *Klaeber's Beowulf* as "fitting, seemly, proper, just."[18] The poem is unified not by a particular theme but by a poet's particular sense of normativity and his ambition to situate examples of behavior that he considered *gedēfe* in the familiar migration-period world of the venerable legendary tradition.

As the glosses of the word indicate, *gedēfe* is the kind of word that could be used in a courtly context to describe the behavior expected of one aristocrat toward another. The word is used by Wealhtheow in the speech that frustrates Hrothgar's plan to make Beowulf an heir to the Danish throne. Addressing Beowulf, she instructs him:

Bēo þū suna mīnum
dǣdum gedēfe,   drēamhealdende. (ll. 1226b–1227)

(Be just in your actions toward my sons, you who are key to our contentment.)

We might translate *gedēfe* here with a single Modern English adjective, such as "just" or even "courteous," but it seems to point toward an ethical system that was self-evident at the time yet has become rather obscure with the passage of more than a millennium. The broad scope of this ethical system is suggested by the fact that the same word is used twice by Beowulf with regard to his killing of monsters. It is used first in reference to the sea monsters that harassed him during his youthful swimming contest and second in reference to Grendel and his mother:

Swā mec gelōme   lāðgetēonan
þrēatedon þearle.   Ic him þēnode

---

17. As Orchard, *Critical Companion to Beowulf*, observes: "For a poem in which action is often held to play a major role, there is an inordinate amount of talk in *Beowulf*; over 1200 lines (some 38%) of the poem are taken up with around forty separate speeches" (203).

18. Fulk et al., *Klaeber's Beowulf*, 363.

deoran sweorde,   swā hit gedēfe wæs. (ll. 559–561)

(Thus, ugly villains continually pressed me hard. I served them with a costly sword, as was fitting.)

Ic þæt hilt þanan
fēondum ætferede,   fyrendǣda wræc,
dēaðcwealm Denigea,   swā hit gedēfe wæs. (ll. 1668b–1670)

(I brought the hilt from the enemies there, avenged their criminal doings, the murder of Danes, as was only right.)

The logic of the passages appears to be that the killing of these monsters was *gedēfe* because it possessed ample justification; it was not a form of immoderate or unprovoked violence, but a form of socially sanctioned and essentially righteous violence. By killing monsters and avenging their misdeeds, Beowulf restores order to the world. His heroic action, like his considerate behavior at court, has a stabilizing function: the two facets of the hero are *gedēfe* because they put things in order and prevent the kind of turmoil that heroes had traditionally created through immoderate regard for personal or familial honor. In the fourth and final occurrence of *gedēfe*, the word is used in an approving comment on the Geatish retainers who praise Beowulf at his funeral:

swā hit gedē(fe) bið
þæt mon his winedryhten   wordum herge,
ferhðum frēoge,   þonne hē forð scile
of l(ī)chaman   (lǣ)ded weorðan. (ll. 3174b–3177)

(just as it is proper for a man to commend his friend and lord in speech, cherish him in his soul when he must be led forth from the flesh.)

This passage indicates that the ethical system implied in the approbatory term *gedēfe* includes not only courteous behavior and heroic action but also the profound piety and affection required in the sacrosanct relationship between lord and retainer. The mourning of the Geats for their beloved lord is *gedēfe* because it attempts to redress a grievous loss and restore a sense of order to a chaotic world. By publicly fulfilling their obligation to mourn, moreover, the retainers demonstrate that Beowulf fulfilled his obligation to lead and protect them well. In the use of the term *gedēfe*, then, we find the poet commending a system of understood norms that embraces courtliness, bellicosity, reciprocity, piety, and probably most of the other categories that are often assumed to coexist in a state of tension in the long critical tradition of discerning profound moral ambivalence at the heart of *Beowulf*.

The poet's ambivalence played an important role in the composition of *Beowulf*, but it affected what was left out of the poem rather than what remains within it. Such care was taken to omit the immoderate and the transgressive from the character of the protagonist—that is, to differentiate him from figures like Sigurðr or Starkaðr—that the sanitized form of heroism embodied in the figure of Beowulf must represent an ethical ideal presented with complete authorial approval. Beowulf is still, in many respects, a conventional hero who boasts of his martial prowess, reveres the lord-retainer relationship, and valorizes the pursuit of fame, vengeance, and treasure. At the same time, he is the kindest and gentlest hero, and he behaves courteously, expresses monotheistic convictions, and abstains from the standard transgressions. What would appear to explain the coexistence of the conventional and the unconventional within the figure of Beowulf is a poet seeking to morally renovate but not completely obliterate the tradition he inherited. The poet is censorious, but he is guided by a precise sense of what required censoring. Thus, with regard to the much-discussed topic of heroism, the poet has no evident desire to censor (or censure) heroism as such; he is concerned only about the particular form of immoderate heroism that had been valorized in traditional accounts of kin-slaying and oath-breaking heroes.[19] Likewise, with regard to the much-discussed topic of paganism, the poet appears to have abhorred and condemned anything he considered pagan, but he considered paganism equivalent to polytheism. Paganism, for the *Beowulf* poet, was not a category that embraced every aspect of the life of the Germanic peoples during the centuries in which they were historically pagan. He condemns idol worship, since it is explicitly polytheistic, while apparently regarding funerary customs and totemic animals as inoffensive details about life in the past that can lend verisimilitude to his poem. What remains of Germanic paganism in *Beowulf* remains there because the poet considers it innocuous, not because he considers it pagan and wishes to express an ambivalent perspective on paganism.[20]

---

19. This form of immoderate heroism appears better encapsulated in the Old Norse term *ofrkapp* rather than in one of the conventional terms for pride (such as *oferhygd* or *ofermōd*). On the meaning of *ofrkapp*, see Thomas D. Hill, "Confession of Beowulf," 166–69.

20. See C. E. Fell, "Paganism in *Beowulf*: A Semantic Fairy-Tale," in *Pagans and Christians: The Interplay between Christian Latin and Traditional Germanic Cultures in Early Medieval Europe*, ed. T. Hofstra, L. A. J. R. Houwen, and A. A. MacDonald (Groningen: Egbert Forsten, 1995), 9–34.

Beowulf, in my reading, does not possess thematic unity, insofar as its content is not organized around one particular theme or message, but it possesses compositional unity, in that it consistently reflects one author's unique sense of decorum. *Beowulf* is the work of a clear-sighted and conscientious artist, who can be seen wrestling with a set of moral and aesthetic problems that emerged from the traditional materials he inherited and combined. Concern about the amoral and extreme character of the antecedent legendary tradition prompted the poet to focus on a plot from folkloric tradition, while concern about the ahistorical and nonaristocratic character of the folkloric tradition prompted the poet to infuse his narrative with a quality of courtly realism. Concern about the inadequate moral clarity of both the heroic and the folkloric tradition, meanwhile, prompted the poet to emphasize the monotheism of his foregrounded characters and to draw on hagiographical tradition in his construction of monstrous adversaries. Behind all of these concerns lies an ambition to compose a serious and poignant epic poem, which presents exemplary behavior and expresses belief in God's eternal providence yet still appeals to an aristocratic audience accustomed to the recitation of amoral legends from the migration period. The resulting epic possesses the tragic grandeur and the elegiac sensibility that this audience expected from a refined work of literary art, but it attaches these qualities to a morally clearer narrative about the noble conduct and righteous adventures of a pristine protagonist. Through the deployment of considerable art and thought, the *Beowulf* poet managed to take the amoral poetry of Ingeld and make it have something to do with Christ. In the process, he produced a masterpiece of world literature that transcends its voluminous analogues, a work built on demonstrably traditional content yet infused with qualities that are unmatched elsewhere in the extant corpus of medieval Germanic literature or in the annals of recorded human folklore.

BIBLIOGRAPHY

Aarne, Antti, and Stith Thompson. *The Types of the Folktale: A Classification and Bibliography*. Helsinki: Academia Scientiarum Fennica, 1961.

Acker, Paul. "Horror and the Maternal in *Beowulf*." *PMLA* 121, no. 3 (2006): 702–16.

Alfano, Christine. "The Issue of Feminine Monstrosity: A Reevaluation of Grendel's Mother." *Comitatus* 23, no. 1 (1992): 1–16.

Allen, Judson Boyce. "God's Society and Grendel's Shoulder Joint: Gregory and the Poet of the *Beowulf*." *Neuphilologische Mitteilungen* 78, no. 3 (1977): 239–40.

Altmann, Barbara K., and Carleton W. Carroll, ed. *The Court Reconvenes: Courtly Literature across the Disciplines*. Cambridge: D. S. Brewer, 2003.

Andersson, Theodore M. *The Legend of Brynhild*. Ithaca, NY: Cornell University Press, 1980.

——. *A Preface to the Nibelungenlied*. Stanford, CA: Stanford University Press, 1987.

Andrew, Malcolm. "Grendel in Hell." *English Studies* 62, no. 5 (1981): 401–10.

Arnovick, Leslie Katherine. "Sounding and Flyting the English Agonistic Insult: Writing Pragmatic History in a Cross-Cultural Context." In *The Twenty-First LACUS Forum 1994*, edited by Mava Jo Powell, 600–619. Chapel Hill, NC: Linguistic Association of Canada and the United States, 1995.

Augustyn, Prisca S. "The Semiotics of *Fate*, *Death*, and the *Soul* in Germanic Culture: The Christianization of Old Saxon." PhD diss., University of California, Berkeley, 2000.

Babcock, Michael A. *The Stories of Attila the Hun's Death: Narrative, Myth, and Meaning*. Lewiston, ME: Edwin Mellen Press, 2001.

Baird, Joseph L. "Grendel the Exile." *Neuphilologische Mitteilungen* 67, no. 4 (1966): 375–81.

——. "Unferth the *Þyle*." *Medium Ævum* 39, no. 1 (1970): 1–12.

——. "The Uses of Ignorance: *Beowulf* 435, 2330." *Notes and Queries* 14, no. 1 (1967): 6–8.

Baker, Peter S. "Beowulf the Orator." *Journal of English Linguistics* 21, no. 1 (1988): 3–23.

——. *Honour, Exchange and Violence in Beowulf*. Cambridge: D. S. Brewer, 2013.

Bammesberger, Alfred. "The Meaning of Old English *Folcscaru* and the Compound's Function in *Beowulf*." *NOWELE* 72, no. 1 (2019): 1–10.

Bandy, Stephen C. "Cain, Grendel, and the Giants of *Beowulf*." *Papers on Language and Literature* 9, no. 3 (1973): 235–49.

Barnes, Daniel R. "Folktale Morphology and the Structure of *Beowulf*." *Speculum* 45, no. 3 (1970): 416–34.

Barthélemy, Dominique. *La chevalerie: De la Germanie antique à la France du XIIe siècle*. Paris: Fayard, 2007.

Bartsch, Karl, ed. *Kudrun*. 5th ed. Revised by Karl Stackmann. Tübingen: Max Niemeyer, 2000.Bately, Janet. "Bravery and the Vocabulary of Bravery in *Beowulf* and the *Battle of Maldon*." In *Unlocking the Wordhord: Anglo-Saxon Studies in Memory of Edward B. Irving, Jr.*, edited by Mark C. Amodio and Katherine O'Brien O'Keeffe, 274–301. Toronto: University of Toronto Press, 2003.

——. "Linguistic Evidence as a Guide to the Authorship of Old English Verse: A Reappraisal, with Special Reference to *Beowulf*." In *Learning and Literature in Anglo-Saxon England: Studies Presented to Peter Clemoes on the Occasion of His Sixty-Fifth Birthday*, edited by Michael Lapidge and Helmut Gneuss, 409–31. Cambridge: Cambridge University Press, 1985.

Battles, Paul. "Dying for a Drink: 'Sleeping after the Feast' Scenes in *Beowulf*, *Andreas*, and the Old English Poetic Tradition." *Modern Philology* 112, no. 3 (2015): 435–57.

Bauschatz, Paul C. *The Well and the Tree: World and Time in Early Germanic Culture*. Amherst: University of Massachusetts Press, 1982.

Bazelmans, Jos. *By Weapons Made Worthy: Lords, Retainers and Their Relationship in Beowulf*. Amsterdam: Amsterdam University Press, 1999.

Benediktsson, Jakob. "Icelandic Traditions of the Scyldings." *Saga-Book* 15 (1957–59): 48–66.

Benson, Larry D. "The Originality of *Beowulf*." In *The Interpretation of Narrative: Theory and Practice*, edited by Morton W. Bloomfield, 1–43. Cambridge, MA: Harvard University Press, 1970.

——. "The Pagan Coloring of *Beowulf*." In *Old English Poetry: Fifteen Essays*, edited by Robert P. Creed, 193–213. Providence, RI: Brown University Press, 1967.

Berger, Harry, Jr., and H. Marshall Leicester Jr. "Social Structure as Doom: The Limits of Heroism in *Beowulf*." In *Old English Studies in Honour of John C. Pope*, edited by Robert B. Burlin and Edward B. Irving Jr., 37–79. Toronto: University of Toronto Press, 1974.

Bethmann, Ludwig, and Georg Waitz, ed. *Pauli Historia Langobardorum*. Hannover: Hahnsche Buchhandlung, 1878.

Biggs, Frederick M. "*Beowulf* and Some Fictions of the Geatish Succession." *Anglo-Saxon England* 32 (2003): 55–77.

——. "The Politics of Succession in *Beowulf* and Anglo-Saxon England." *Speculum* 80, no. 3 (2005): 709–41.

Bintley, Michael. "*Hrinde Bearwas*: The Trees at the Mere and the Root of All Evil in *Beowulf*." *Journal of English and Germanic Philology* 119, no. 3 (2020): 309–26.

Bjork, Robert E. "Speech as Gift in *Beowulf*." *Speculum* 69, no. 4 (1994): 993–1022.

Blackburn, F. A. "The Christian Coloring in the *Beowulf*." *PMLA* 12, no. 2 (1897): 205–25.

Bliss, A. J. "*Beowulf*, Lines 3074–3075." In *J. R. R. Tolkien, Scholar and Storyteller: Essays in Memoriam*, edited by Mary Salu and Robert T. Farrell, 41–63. Ithaca, NY: Cornell University Press, 1979.

Bloomfield, Morton W. "Patristics and Old English Literature: Notes on Some Poems." *Comparative Literature* 14, no. 1 (1962): 36–43.

Bolton, W. F. *Alcuin and Beowulf: An Eighth-Century View*. New Brunswick, NJ: Rutgers University Press, 1978.

Bonjour, Adrien. *The Digressions in Beowulf*. Oxford: Basil Blackwell, 1950.

——. "Monsters Crouching and Critics Rampant: Or the *Beowulf* Dragon Debated." *PMLA* 68, no. 1 (1953): 304–12.

——. "Young Beowulf's Inglorious Period." *Anglia* 70 (1951): 339–44.

Bostock, J. Knight. "The Lay of Hildebrand." In *A Handbook on Old High German Literature*, revised by K. C. King and D. R. McLintock, 2nd ed., 43–82. Oxford: Clarendon Press, 1976.

Braccini, Giovanna Princi. "Perché Hroðgar *Stod on Stapole* (*Beowulf* 926a)." In *Echi di Memoria: Scritti di varia filologia, critica e linguistica in recordo di Giorgio Chiarini*, edited by Gaetano Chiappini, 139–57. Florence: Alinea, 1998.

Brady, Caroline. *The Legends of Ermanaric*. Berkeley: University of California Press, 1943.

Braeger, Peter C. "Connotations of (Earm) Sceapen: *Beowulf* II. 2228–2229 and the Shape-Shifting Dragon." *Essays in Literature* 13, no. 2 (1986): 327–28.

Braune, Wilhelm, ed. *Althochdeutsches Lesebuch*. Revised by Ernst A. Ebbinghaus, 17th ed. Tübingen: Max Niemeyer, 1994.

Bremmer, Rolf H., Jr. "The Importance of Kinship: Uncle and Nephew in *Beowulf*." *Amsterdamer Beiträge zur älteren Germanistik* 15, no. 1 (1980): 21–38.

Brodeur, Arthur Gilchrist. *The Art of Beowulf*. Berkeley: University of California Press, 1959.

Brown, Katherine DeVane. "Courtly Rivalry, Loyalty Conflict, and the Figure of Hagen in the *Nibelungenlied*." *Monatshefte* 107, no. 3 (2015): 355–81.

Bruce-Mitford, R. L. S. *The Sutton Hoo Ship Burial: A Handbook*. 3rd ed. London: British Museum, 1979.

Buchholz, Peter. "Death Traditions as an Oral Nucleus of Scandinavian Heroic Literature." *Mankind Quarterly* 28, no. 2 (1987): 151–60.

Bugge, Sophus. *Studien über die Entstehung der nordischen Götter- und Heldensagen*. Munich: Christian Kaiser, 1889.

Bullough, Donald A. "What Has Ingeld to Do with Lindisfarne?" *Anglo-Saxon England* 22 (1993): 93–125.

Bumke, Joachim. *Höfische Kultur: Literatur und Gesellschaft im hohen Mittelalter*. Munich: Deutscher Taschenbuch Verlag, 1986.

Burdorff, Sara Frances. "Re-reading Grendel's Mother: *Beowulf* and the Anglo-Saxon Metrical Charms." *Comitatus* 45, no. 1 (2014): 91–103.

Burnley, David. *Courtliness and Literature in Medieval England*. London: Longman, 1998.

Busby, Keith, and Erik Kooper, ed. *Courtly Literature: Culture and Context*. Amsterdam: John Benjamins, 1990.

Byock, Jesse L. *The Saga of King Hrolf Kraki*. London: Penguin, 1998.

Cahill, James. "Reconsidering Robinson's *Beowulf*." *English Studies* 89, no. 3 (2008): 251–62.

Camargo, Martin. "The Finn Episode and the Tragedy of Revenge in *Beowulf*." *Studies in Philology* 78, no. 5 (1981): 120–34.

Campbell, James. "Anglo-Saxon Courts." In *Court Culture in the Early Middle Ages: The Proceedings of the First Alcuin Conference*, edited by Catherine Cubitt, 155–69. Turnhout, Belgium: Brepols, 2003.

Carston, Robyn. *Thoughts and Utterances: The Pragmatics of Explicit Communication*. Malden, MA: Blackwell, 2002.

Cavell, Megan. "Constructing the Monstrous Body in *Beowulf*." *Anglo-Saxon England* 43 (2014): 151–81.

Cavill, Paul. "Christianity and Theology in *Beowulf*." In *The Christian Tradition in Anglo-Saxon England: Approaches to Current Scholarship and Teaching*, edited by Paul Cavill, 15–40. Woodbridge, UK: D. S. Brewer, 2004.

Chadwick, Nora K., ed. and trans. *Anglo-Saxon and Norse Poems*. Cambridge: Cambridge University Press, 1922.

——. "The Monsters and Beowulf." In *The Anglo-Saxons: Studies in Some Aspects of Their History and Culture Presented to Bruce Dickins*, edited by Peter Clemoes, 171–203. London: Bowes & Bowes, 1959.

——. "Norse Ghosts (A Study in the *Draugr* and the *Haugbúi*)." *Folklore* 57, no. 2 (1946): 50–65.

——. "Norse Ghosts II." *Folklore* 57, no. 3 (1946): 106–27.

Chambers, R. W. *Beowulf: An Introduction to the Study of the Poem with a Discussion of the Stories of Offa and Finn*. Revised by C. L. Wrenn, 3rd ed. Cambridge: Cambridge University Press, 1959.

——. "*Beowulf* and the 'Heroic Age' in England." In *Man's Unconquerable Mind: Studies of English Writers, from Bede to A. E. Housman and W. P. Ker*, 53–59. London: Jonathan Cape, 1939.

——, ed. *Widsith: A Study in Old English Heroic Legend*. Cambridge: Cambridge University Press, 1912.

Cherniss, Michael D. *Ingeld and Christ: Heroic Concepts and Values in Old English Christian Poetry*. The Hague: Mouton, 1972.

Ciklamini, Marlene. "The Problem of Starkaðr." *Scandinavian Studies* 43, no. 2 (1971): 169–88.

Clark, David, ed. *Beowulf in Contemporary Culture*. Newcastle upon Tyne: Cambridge Scholars, 2020.

——. "Kin-Slaying in the *Poetic Edda*: The End of the World?" *Viking and Medieval Scandinavia* 3 (2007): 21–41.

Clark, George. *Beowulf*. Boston: Twayne, 1990.

——. "*Beowulf*: The Last Word." In *Old English and New: Studies in Language and Linguistics in Honor of Frederic G. Cassidy*, edited by Joan H. Hall, Nick Doane, and Dick Ringler, 15–30. New York: Garland, 1992.

——. "*Beowulf* as a Philosophical Poem." *Florilegium* 25 (2008): 1–27.

Clarke, M. G. *Sidelights on Teutonic History during the Migration Period, Being Studies from Beowulf and Other Old English Poems*. Cambridge: Cambridge University Press, 1911.

Classen, Albrecht, ed. *Violence in Medieval Courtly Literature: A Casebook.* New York: Routledge, 2004.

Clemoes, Peter. *Interactions of Thought and Language in Old English Poetry.* Cambridge: Cambridge University Press, 1995.

Clover, Carol J. "The Germanic Context of the Unferþ Episode." *Speculum* 55, no. 3 (1980): 444–68.

Colgrave, Bertram, ed. and trans. *The Life of Bishop Wilfrid by Eddius Stephanus.* Cambridge: Cambridge University Press, 1927.

Colgrave, Bertram, and R. A. B. Mynors, ed. and trans. *Bede's Ecclesiastical History of the English People.* Rev. ed. Oxford: Clarendon Press, 1991.

Cooke, William. "Hrothulf: A Richard III, or an Alfred the Great?" *Studies in Philology* 104, no. 2 (2007): 175–98.

Coulson, Seana. *Semantic Leaps: Frame-Shifting and Conceptual Blending in Meaning Construction.* Cambridge: Cambridge University Press, 2001.

Cox, Betty S. *Cruces of Beowulf.* The Hague: Mouton, 1971.

Crane, John Kenny. "To Thwack or Be Thwacked: An Evaluation of Available Translations and Editions of *Beowulf.*" *College English* 32, no. 3 (1970): 321–40.

Cronan, Dennis. "*Beowulf*, the Gaels, and the Recovery of the Pre-Conversion Past." *Anglo-Saxon* 1 (2007): 137–80.

——. "Hroðgar and the *Gylden Hilt* in *Beowulf.*" *Traditio* 72 (2017): 109–32.

——. "'*Lofgeorn*': Generosity and Praise." *Neuphilologische Mitteilungen* 92, no. 2 (1991): 187–94.

——. "Poetic Meanings in the Old English Poetic Vocabulary." *English Studies* 84, no. 5 (2003): 397–425.

Crouch, David. *The Birth of Nobility: Constructing Aristocracy in England and France, 900–1300.* London: Routledge, 2005.

Currie, Edward. "Political Ideals, Monstrous Counsel, and the Literary Imagination in *Beowulf.*" In *Imagination and Fantasy in the Middle Ages and Early Modern Time: Projections, Dreams, Monsters, and Illusions*, edited by Albrecht Classen, vol. 24, 275–302. Berlin: De Gruyter, 2020.

Damico, Helen. *Beowulf's Wealhtheow and the Valkyrie Tradition.* Madison: University of Wisconsin Press, 1984.

Davidson, Donald. *Truth, Language, and History.* Oxford: Oxford University Press, 2005.

Davidson, H. R. Ellis. *Gods and Myths of Northern Europe.* Harmondsworth, UK: Penguin, 1964.

Deskis, Susan E. "An Addendum to Beowulf's Last Words." *Medium Ævum* 63, no. 2 (1994): 301–5.

——. *Beowulf and the Medieval Proverb Tradition.* Tempe, AZ: ACMRS, 1996.

de Vries, Jan. *Altgermanische Religionsgeschichte.* 2nd ed. 2 vols. Berlin: De Gruyter, 1956.

——. "Die Starkadsage." *Germanisch-Romanisch Monatsschrift* 36 (1955): 281–97.

Doane, A. N., ed. *Genesis A: A New Edition, Revised.* Tempe, AZ: ACMRS, 2013.

Donahue, Charles. "*Beowulf* and Christian Tradition: A Reconsideration from a Celtic Stance." *Traditio* 21 (1965): 55–116.

——. "*Beowulf*, Ireland and the Natural Good." *Traditio* 7 (1951): 263–77.

Donoghue, Daniel. "On the Non-Integrity of *Beowulf*." *SELIM* 1 (1991): 29–44.

Donovan, Leslie A. "Þyle as Fool: Revisiting *Beowulf*'s Hunferth." In *Poetry, Place, and Gender: Studies in Medieval Culture in Honor of Helen Damico*, edited by Catherine E. Karkov, 75–97. Kalamazoo: Medieval Institute Publications, 2009.

Dronke, Ursula. "*Beowulf* and Ragnarǫk." *Saga-Book* 17 (1969): 302–25.

——, ed. and trans. *The Poetic Edda:* vol. 2, *Mythological Poems*. Oxford: Clarendon Press, 1997.

Drout, Michael D. C. "'*Beowulf:* The Monsters and the Critics' Seventy-Five Years Later." *Mythlore* 30, no. 1 (2011): 5–22.

——. "Blood and Deeds: The Inheritance Systems in *Beowulf*." *Studies in Philology* 104, no. 2 (2007): 199–226.

Drout, Michael D. C., and Nelson Goering. "The Emendation *Eorle* (Heruli) in *Beowulf*, Line 6a: Setting the Poem in 'The Named Lands of the North.'" *Modern Philology* 117, no. 3 (2020): 285–300.

Dumézil, Georges. "The Three Sins of Starcatherus." In *The Destiny of the Warrior*, translated by Alf Hiltebeitel, 82–95. Chicago: University of Chicago Press, 1970.

Dümmler, Ernst, ed. *Epistolae Karolini Aevi II*. Monumenta Germaniae Historica, Epistolae 4. Berlin: Weidmann, 1895.

Dumville, David N. "The Anglian Collection of Royal Genealogies and Regnal Lists." *Anglo-Saxon England* 5 (1976): 23–50.

Earl, James W. "The Forbidden *Beowulf:* Haunted by Incest." *PMLA* 125, no. 2 (2010): 289–305.

Ecay, Aaron, and Susan Pintzuk. "The Syntax of Old English Poetry and the Dating of *Beowulf*." In *Old English Philology: Studies in Honour of R. D. Fulk*, edited by Leonard Neidorf, Rafael J. Pascual, and Tom Shippey, 144–71. Cambridge: D. S. Brewer, 2016.

Edwards, Cyril, trans. *The Nibelungenlied: The Lay of the Nibelungs*. Oxford: Oxford University Press, 2010.

Elias, Norbert. *Die höfische Gesellschaft: Untersuchungen zur Soziologie des Königtums und der höfischen Aristokratie*. Neuwied: Luchterhand, 1969.

——. *Über den Prozess der Zivilisation: Soziogenetische und psychogenetische Untersuchungen*. Basel: Haus zum Falken, 1939.

Eliason, Norman E. "Beowulf's Inglorious Youth." *Studies in Philology* 76, no. 2 (1979): 101–8.

——. "The Þyle and Scop in *Beowulf*." *Speculum* 38, no. 2 (1963): 267–84.

Emerson, Oliver F. "Legends of Cain, Especially in Old and Middle English." *PMLA* 21, no. 4 (1906): 831–929.

Engelhardt, George J. "On the Sequence of Beowulf's *Geogoð*." *Modern Language Notes* 68, no. 2 (1953): 91–95.

Enright, Michael J. "The Warband Context of the Unferth Episode." *Speculum* 73, no. 2 (1998): 297–337.

Fajardo-Acosta, Fidel. *The Condemnation of Heroism in the Tragedy of Beowulf: A Study in the Characterization of the Epic*. Lewiston, ME: Edwin Mellen Press, 1989.

Falluomini, Carla. *The Gothic Version of the Gospels and Pauline Epistles: Cultural Background, Transmission and Character*. Berlin: De Gruyter, 2015.

Farrell, John. *The Varieties of Authorial Intention: Literary Theory beyond the intentional Fallacy*. Cham, Switzerland: Palgrave Macmillan, 2017.

Farrell, R. T. *Beowulf, Swedes and Geats*. London: Viking Society for Northern Research, 1972.

Fast, Lawrence. "Hygelac: A Centripetal Force in *Beowulf*." *Annuale Mediaevale* 12 (1971): 90–98.

Fell, C. E. "Paganism in *Beowulf*: A Semantic Fairy-Tale." In *Pagans and Christians: The Interplay between Christian Latin and Traditional Germanic Cultures in Early Medieval Europe*, edited by T. Hofstra, L. A. J. R. Houwen, and A. A. MacDonald, 9–34. Groningen: Egbert Forsten, 1995.

Fidjestøl, Bjarne. *The Dating of Eddic Poetry: A Historical Survey and Methodological Investigation*, edited by Odd Einar Haugen. Copenhagen: C. A. Reitzel, 1999.

Finch, R. G., ed. and trans. *The Saga of the Volsungs*. London: Nelson, 1965.

Fjalldal, Magnús. "*Beowulf* and the Old Norse Two-Troll Analogues." *Neophilologus* 97, no. 3 (2013): 541–53.

Florey, Kenneth. "Grendel, Evil, 'Allegory,' and Dramatic Development in *Beowulf*." *Essays in Arts and Sciences* 17 (1988): 83–95.

Foley, John Miles. *Immanent Art: From Structure to Meaning in Traditional Oral Epic*. Bloomington: Indiana University Press, 1991.

——. *Traditional Oral Epic: The Odyssey, Beowulf, and the Serbo-Croatian Return Song*. Berkeley: University of California Press, 1990.

Forni, Kathleen. *Beowulf's Popular Afterlife in Literature, Comic Books, and Film*. New York: Routledge, 2018.

Frank, Roberta. "F-Words in *Beowulf*." In *Making Sense: Constructing Meaning in Early English*, edited by Antonette diPaolo Healey and Kevin Kiernan, 1–22. Toronto: Pontifical Institute of Mediaeval Studies, 2007.

——. "Skaldic Verse and the Date of *Beowulf*." In *The Dating of Beowulf*, edited by Colin Chase, 123–40. Toronto: University of Toronto Press, 1981.

Friis-Jensen, Karsten, ed. *Saxo Grammaticus: Gesta Danorum: The History of the Danes*. Translated by Peter Fisher. 2 vols. Oxford: Clarendon Press, 2015.

Fulk, R. D. "Archaisms and Neologisms in the Language of *Beowulf*." In *Studies in the History of the English Language III: Managing Chaos; Strategies for Identifying Change in English*, edited by Christopher M. Cain and Geoffrey Russom, 267–87. Berlin: Mouton de Gruyter, 2007.

——, ed. and trans. *The Beowulf Manuscript: Complete Texts and The Fight at Finnsburg*. Cambridge, MA: Harvard University Press, 2010.

——, ed. *Interpretations of Beowulf: A Critical Anthology*. Bloomington: Indiana University Press, 1991.

——. "Old English *Þa* 'Now That' and the Integrity of *Beowulf*." *English Studies* 88, no. 6 (2007): 623–31.

——. "On Argumentation in Old English Philology, with Particular Reference to the Editing and Dating of *Beowulf*." *Anglo-Saxon England* 32 (2003): 1–26.

——. "Rhetoric, Form, and Linguistic Structure in Early Germanic Verse: Toward a Synthesis." *Interdisciplinary Journal for Germanic Linguistics and Semiotic Analysis* 1 (1996): 63–88.

Fulk, R. D., Robert E. Bjork, and John D. Niles, ed. *Klaeber's Beowulf and The Fight at Finnsburg.* 4th ed. Toronto: University of Toronto Press, 2008.

Gang, T. M. "Approaches to *Beowulf.*" *Review of English Studies* 3, no. 9 (1952): 1–12.

Garmonsway, G. N., and Jacqueline Simpson, ed. and trans. *Beowulf and its Analogues.* New York: Dutton, 1971.

Garrison, Mary. "'Quid Hinieldus cum Christo?'" In *Latin Learning and English Lore: Studies in Anglo-Saxon Literature for Michael Lapidge,* edited by Katherine O'Brien O'Keeffe and Andy Orchard, 2 vols., 1:237–59. Toronto: University of Toronto Press, 2005.

Gehl, Walter. *Der Germanische Schicksalsglaube.* Berlin: Junker & Dünnhaupt, 1939.

Gentry, Francis G., and James K. Walter, ed. and trans. *German Epic Poetry: The Nibelungenlied, the Older Lay of Hildebrand, and Other Works.* New York: Continuum, 1995.

Georgianna, Linda. "King Hrethel's Sorrow and the Limits of Heroic Action in *Beowulf.*" *Speculum* 62, no. 4 (1987): 829–50.

Ghosh, Shami. *Writing the Barbarian Past: Studies in Early Medieval Historical Narrative.* Leiden: Brill, 2016.

Gillespie, George T. "Heroic Lays: Survival and Transformation in Ballad." *Oxford German Studies* 9, no. 1 (1978): 1–18.

Girvan, Ritchie. *Beowulf and the Seventh Century: Language and Content.* 2nd ed. London: Methuen, 1971.

Goldsmith, Margaret E. *The Mode and Meaning of Beowulf.* London: Athlone Press, 1970.

Gould, Kent. "*Beowulf* and Folktale Morphology: God as Magical Donor." *Folklore* 96, no. 1 (1985): 98–103.

Greenfield, Stanley B. "Of Words and Deeds: The Coastguard's Maxim Once More." In *The Wisdom of Poetry: Essays in Early English Literature in Honor of Morton W. Bloomfield,* edited by Larry D. Benson and Siegfried Wenzel, 45–51. Kalamazoo: Medieval Institute Publications, 1982.

Griffith, M. S. "Some Difficulties in *Beowulf,* Lines 874–902: Sigemund Reconsidered." *Anglo-Saxon England* 24 (1995): 11–41.

Grinda, Klaus R. "Pigeonholing Old English Poetry: Some Criteria of Metrical Style." *Anglia* 102, nos. 3–4 (1984): 305–22.

Gschwantler, Otto. "Die Heldensage von Alboin und Rosimund." In *Festgabe für Otto Höfler zum 75. Geburtstage,* edited by Helmut Birkhan, 214–54. Vienna: W. Braunmüller, 1976.

Gutenbrunner, Siegfried. *Von Hildebrand und Hadubrand: Lied, Sage, Mythos.* Heidelberg: Winter, 1976.

Gwara, Scott. *Heroic Identity in the World of Beowulf.* Leiden: Brill, 2008.

——. "Paradigmatic Wisdom and the Native Genre *Giedd* in Old English." *Studi Medievali* 53, no. 2 (2012): 783–852.

Hall, Alaric. "Hygelac's Only Daughter: A Present, a Potentate and a Peaceweaver in *Beowulf.*" *Studia Neophilologica* 78, no. 1 (2006): 81–87.

Halverson, John. "The World of *Beowulf.*" *ELH* 36, no. 4 (1969): 593–608.

Hardy, Adelaide. "The Christian Hero Beowulf and Unferð Þyle." *Neophilologus* 53, no. 1 (1969): 55–69.

Harris, Joseph. "Beowulf's Last Words." *Speculum* 67, no. 1 (1992): 1–32.

——. "Elegy in Old English and Old Norse: A Problem in Literary History." In *The Old English Elegies: New Essays in Criticism and Research*, edited by Martin Green, 46–56. Rutherford, NJ: Fairleigh Dickinson University Press, 1983.

——. "Hadubrand's Lament: On the Origin and Age of Elegy in Germanic." In *Heldensage und Heldendichtung im Germanischen*, edited by Heinrich Beck, 81–114. Berlin: De Gruyter, 1988.

——. "Heroic Poetry and Elegy: *Beowulf*'s Lay of the Last Survivor." In *Heldenzeiten—Heldenräume: Wann und wo spielen Heldendichtung und Heldensage?*, edited by Johannes Keller and Florian Kragl, 27–41. Wien: Fassbaender, 2007.

——. "A Nativist Approach to *Beowulf*: The Case of Germanic Elegy." In *Companion to Old English Poetry*, edited by Henk Aertsen and Rolf H. Bremmer Jr., 45–62. Amsterdam: VU University Press, 1994.

——. "The *Senna*: From Description to Literary Theory." *Michigan Germanic Studies* 5, no. 1 (1979): 65–74.

Haydock, Nickolas, and E. L. Risden. *Beowulf on Film: Adaptations and Variations.* Jefferson, NC: McFarland, 2013.

Haymes, Edward, and Susann T. Samples. *Heroic Legends of the North: An Introduction to the Nibelung and Dietrich Cycles.* New York: Garland, 1996.

Heather, Peter, and John Matthews. *The Goths in the Fourth Century.* Liverpool: Liverpool University Press, 1991.

Hedeager, Lotte. *Iron-Age Societies: From Tribe to State in Northern Europe, 500 BC to AD 700.* Translated by John Hines. Oxford: Blackwell, 1992.

Hennequin, M. Wendy. "We've Created a Monster: The Strange Case of Grendel's Mother." *English Studies* 89, no. 5 (2008): 503–23.

Heusler, Andreas, and William Ranisch, ed. *Eddica minora: Dichtungen eddischer Art aus den Fornaldarsögur und anderen Prosawerken.* Dortmund: W. Ruhfus, 1903.

Higley, Sarah Lynn. "*Aldor on Ofre*, or the Reluctant Hart: A Study of Liminality in *Beowulf*." *Neuphilologische Mitteilungen* 87, no. 3 (1986): 342–53.

Hill, John M. *The Anglo-Saxon Warrior Ethic: Reconstructing Lordship in Early English Literature.* Gainesville: University Press of Florida, 2000.

——. "Beowulf and the Danish Succession: Gift Giving as an Occasion for Complex Gesture." *Medievalia et Humanistica*, n.s., 11 (1982): 177–97.

——. *The Cultural World in Beowulf.* Toronto: University of Toronto Press, 1995.

——. *The Narrative Pulse of Beowulf: Arrivals and Departures.* Toronto: University of Toronto Press, 2008.

Hill, Joyce. "'Þæt Wæs Geomuru Ides!': A Female Stereotype Examined." In *New Readings on Women in Old English Literature*, edited by Helen Damico and Alexandra Hennessey Olsen, 235–47. Bloomington: Indiana University Press, 1990.

Hill, Thomas D. "*Beowulf* and Conversion History." In *The Dating of Beowulf: A Reassessment*, edited by Leonard Neidorf, 191–201. Cambridge: D. S. Brewer, 2014.

——. "Beowulf as Seldguma: *Beowulf,* Lines 247–51." *Neophilologus* 74, no. 4 (1990): 637–39.

——. "The Christian Language and Theme of *Beowulf.*" In *Companion to Old English Poetry,* edited by Henk Aertsen and Rolf H. Bremmer Jr., 63–77. Amsterdam: VU University Press, 1994.

——. "The Confession of Beowulf and the Structure of *Volsunga Saga.*" In *The Vikings: Papers from the Cornell Lecture Series Held to Coincide with the Viking Exhibition 1980–1981,* edited by Robert T. Farrell, 165–79. London: Phillimore, 1982.

——. "Hrothgar's Speech of Adoption: A Danish-Latin Analog." *Notes and Queries* 66, no. 2 (2019): 163–66.

——. "The 'Variegated Obit' as an Historiographic Motif in Old English Poetry and Anglo-Latin Historical Literature." *Traditio* 44 (1988): 101–24.

Hirsch, E. D., Jr. "The Politics of Theories of Interpretation." *Critical Inquiry* 9, no. 1 (1982): 235–47.

——. *Validity in Interpretation.* New Haven, CT: Yale University Press, 1967.

Hollander, Lee M., ed. and trans. *Old Norse Poems: The Most Important Non-Skaldic Verse not Included in the Poetic Edda.* New York: Columbia University Press, 1936.

Hollis, Stephanie. "Beowulf and the Succession." *Parergon* 1, no. 1 (1983): 39–54.

Hollowell, Ida Masters. "Unferð the Þyle in *Beowulf.*" *Studies in Philology* 73, no. 3 (1976): 239–65.

Hope-Taylor, Brian. *Yeavering: An Anglo-British Centre of Early Northumbria.* London: Her Majesty's Stationery Office, 1977.

Horgan, A. D. "Religious Attitudes in *Beowulf.*" In *Essays and Poems Presented to Lord David Cecil,* edited by W. W. Robson, 9–17. London: Constable, 1970.

Howlett, David R. "Form and Genre in *Beowulf.*" *Studia Neophilologica* 46, no. 2 (1974): 309–25.

Hughes, Geoffrey. "Beowulf, Unferth and Hrunting: An Interpretation." *English Studies* 58, no. 5 (1977): 385–95.

Hume, Kathryn. "The Concept of the Hall in Old English Poetry." *Anglo-Saxon England* 3 (1974): 63–74.

——. "From Saga to Romance: The Use of Monsters in Old Norse Literature." *Studies in Philology* 77, no. 1 (1980): 1–25.

Irving, Edward B., Jr. "Beowulf Comes Home." In *Acts of Interpretation: The Text in Its Contexts, 700–1600: Essays on Medieval and Renaissance Literature in Honor of E. Talbot Donaldson,* edited by Mary J. Carruthers and Elizabeth D. Kirk, 129–43. Norman, OK: Pilgrim Books, 1982.

——. "Christian and Pagan Elements." In *A Beowulf Handbook,* edited by Robert E. Bjork and John D. Niles, 175–92. Lincoln: University of Nebraska Press, 1997.

——. "Heroic Role-Models: Beowulf and Others." In *Heroic Poetry in the Anglo-Saxon Period: Studies in Honor of Jess B. Bessinger, Jr.,* edited by Helen Damico and John Leyerle, 347–72. Kalamazoo: Western Michigan University Press, 1993.

——. *Rereading Beowulf.* Philadelphia: University of Pennsylvania Press, 1989.

Jaeger, C. Stephen. *The Origins of Courtliness: Civilizing Trends and the Formation of Courtly Ideals, 939–1210.* Philadelphia: University of Pennsylvania Press, 1985.

——. "Origins of Courtliness after 25 Years." *Haskins Society Journal* 21 (2010): 187–216.

Jambeck, Thomas J. "The Syntax of Petition in *Beowulf* and *Sir Gawain and the Green Knight.*" *Style* 7, no. 1 (1973): 21–29.

Jente, Richard. *Die mythologischen Ausdrücke im altenglischen Wortschatz: Eine kulturgeschichtlich-etymologische Untersuchung.* Heidelberg: Winter, 1921.

Jochens, Jenny. *Old Norse Images of Women.* Philadelphia: University of Pennsylvania Press, 1996.

John, Eric. "*Beowulf* and the Margins of Literacy." *Bulletin of the John Rylands Library* 56, no. 2 (1974): 388–422.

Johnson, David F. "The Gregorian Grendel: *Beowulf* 705b-09 and the Limits of the Demonic." In *Rome and the North: The Early Reception of Gregory the Great in Germanic Europe*, edited by Rolf H. Bremmer Jr., Kees Dekker, and David F. Johnson, 51–65. Paris: Peeters, 2001.

Jorgensen, Peter A. "Additional Icelandic Analogues to *Beowulf.*" In *Sagnaskemmtun: Studies in Honour of Hermann Pálsson on His 65th Birthday, 26th May 1986*, edited by Rudolf Simek, Jónas Kristjánsson, and Hans Bekker-Nielsen, 201–8. Vienna: Hermann Böhlaus, 1986.

——. "The Two-Troll Variant of the Bear's Son Folktale in *Hálfdanar saga Brönufóstra* and *Gríms saga loðinkinna.*" *Arv: Journal of Scandinavian Folklore* 31 (1975): 35–43.

Juhl, P. D. *Interpretation: An Essay in the Philosophy of Literary Criticism.* Princeton, NJ: Princeton University Press, 1980.

Jurasinski, Stefan. *Ancient Privileges: Beowulf, Law and the Making of Germanic Antiquity.* Morgantown: West Virginia University Press, 2006.

Kahrl, Stanley J. "Feuds in *Beowulf*: A Tragic Necessity?" *Modern Philology* 69, no. 3 (1972): 189–98.

Kasik, Jon C. "The Use of the Term *Wyrd* in *Beowulf* and the Conversion of the Anglo-Saxons." *Neophilologus* 63, no. 1 (1979): 128–35.

Kaske, R. E. "Hygelac and Hygd." In *Studies in Old English Literature in Honor of Arthur G. Brodeur*, edited by Stanley B. Greenfield, 200–206. Eugene: University of Oregon Press, 1963.

——. "*Sapientia et Fortitudo* as the Controlling Theme of *Beowulf.*" *Studies in Philology* 55, no. 3 (1958): 423–56.

——. "The Sigemund-Heremod and Hama-Hygelac Passages in *Beowulf.*" *PMLA* 74, no. 5 (1959): 489–94.

Kelly, A. Keith. "Teaching Good Manners: Civil Discourse Patterns in *Beowulf* and *Sir Gawain and the Green Knight.*" In *Literary Speech Acts of the Medieval North: Essays Inspired by the Works of Thomas A. Shippey*, edited by Eric Shane Bryan and Alexander Vaughan Ames, 223–42. Tempe, AZ: ACMRS, 2020.

Ker, W. P. *The Dark Ages.* Edinburgh: William Blackwood & Sons, 1904.

——. *Epic and Romance: Essays on Medieval Literature.* London: Macmillan, 1897.

Kiernan, Kevin S. *Beowulf and the Beowulf Manuscript*. New Brunswick, NJ: Rutgers University Press, 1981.

Kightley, Michael R. "Reinterpreting Threats to Face: The Use of Politeness in *Beowulf*, ll. 407–472." *Neophilologus* 93, no. 3 (2009): 511–20.

——. "Repetition, Class, and the Nameless Speakers of *Beowulf*." In *Literary Speech Acts of the Medieval North: Essays Inspired by the Works of Thomas A. Shippey*, edited by Eric Shane Bryan and Alexander Vaughan Ames, 141–56. Tempe, AZ: ACMRS, 2020.

Klaeber, Fr., ed. *Beowulf and The Fight at Finnsburg*. 3rd ed. Boston: Heath, 1950.

Klinck, Anne L. *The Old English Elegies: A Critical Edition and Genre Study*. Montreal: McGill–Queen's University Press, 1992.

Kluge, Friedrich. "Der Beowulf und die Hrolfs saga kraka." *Englische Studien* 22 (1896): 144–45.

Knapp, Steven, and Walter Benn Michaels. "Against Theory." *Critical Inquiry* 8, no. 4 (1982): 723–42.

Kohnen, Thomas. "Understanding Anglo-Saxon 'Politeness': Directive Constructions with *Ic Wille / Ic Wolde*." *Journal of Historical Pragmatics* 12, nos. 1–2 (2011): 230–54.

Kratz, Dennis M., ed. and trans. *Waltharius and Ruodlieb*. New York: Garland, 1984.

Laing, Gregory L. "Bound by Words: Oath-taking and Oath-breaking in Medieval Iceland and Anglo-Saxon England." PhD diss., Western Michigan University, 2014.

Langeslag, Paul S. "Monstrous Landscape in *Beowulf*." *English Studies* 96, no. 2 (2015): 119–38.

Lapidge, Michael. "The Archetype of *Beowulf*." *Anglo-Saxon England* 29 (2000): 5–41.

——. "*Beowulf*, Aldhelm, the *Liber Monstrorum* and Wessex." *Studi Medievali* 23, no. 1 (1982): 151–92.

Larrington, Carolyne. "Eddic Poetry and Heroic Legend." In *A Handbook to Eddic Poetry: Myths and Legends of Early Scandinavia*, edited by Carolyne Larrington, Judy Quinn, and Brittany Schorn, 147–72. Cambridge: Cambridge University Press, 2016.

——, trans. *The Poetic Edda*. 2nd ed. Oxford: Oxford University Press, 2014.

Larson, Laurence Marcellus. "The King's Household in England before the Norman Conquest." PhD diss., University of Wisconsin, 1904.

Lawrence, William Witherle. *Beowulf and Epic Tradition*. Cambridge, MA: Harvard University Press, 1928.

——. "The Dragon and His Lair in *Beowulf*." *PMLA* 33, no. 4 (1918): 547–83.

Layher, William. "Starkaðr's Teeth." *Journal of English and Germanic Philology* 108, no. 1 (2009): 1–26.

Leneghan, Francis. *The Dynastic Drama of Beowulf*. Cambridge: D. S. Brewer, 2020.

Leyerle, John. "Beowulf the Hero and the King." *Medium Ævum* 34, no. 2 (1965): 89–102.

Lindow, John. *Handbook of Norse Mythology*. Oxford: ABC-CLIO, 2001.

Liuzza, Roy Michael. "On the Dating of *Beowulf*." In *Beowulf: Basic Readings*, edited by Peter S. Baker. New York: Garland, 1995.

Lönnroth, Lars. "Hjálmar's Death-Song and the Delivery of Eddic Poetry." *Speculum* 46, no. 1 (1971): 1–20.

Louviot, Elise. *Direct Speech in Beowulf and Other Old English Narrative Poems.* Cambridge: D. S. Brewer, 2016.

Lühr, Rosemarie. *Studien zur Sprache des Hildebrandliedes.* Frankfurt am Main: Peter Lang, 1982.

Magennis, Hugh. *Images of Community in Old English Poetry.* Cambridge: Cambridge University Press, 1996.

———. "'No Sex Please, We're Anglo-Saxons'? Attitudes to Sexuality in Old English Prose and Poetry." *Leeds Studies in English* 26 (1995): 1–27.

Magoun, Francis P., Jr. "*Béowulf A*: A Folk-Variant." *Arv: Journal of Scandinavian Folklore* 14 (1958): 95–101.

———. "*Béowulf B*: A Folk-Poem on Beowulf's Death." In *Early English and Norse Studies Presented to Hugh Smith in Honour of His Sixtieth Birthday*, edited by Arthur Brown and Peter Foote, 127–40. London: Methuen, 1963.

———. "Oral-Formulaic Character of Anglo-Saxon Narrative Poetry." *Speculum* 28, no. 3 (1953): 446–67.

Malmberg, Lars. "Grendel and the Devil." *Neuphilologische Mitteilungen* 78, no. 3 (1977): 241–43.

Malone, Kemp. "Grendel and His Abode." In *Studia Philologica et Litteraria in Honorem L. Spitzer*, edited by Anna G. Hatcher and K. L. Selig, 297–308. Bern: Francke, 1958.

———. "Hrethric." *PMLA* 42, no. 2 (1927): 268–313.

———. "Primitivism in Saxo Grammaticus." *Journal of the History of Ideas* 19, no. 1 (1958): 94–104.

———. "The Tale of Ingeld." In *Studies in Heroic Legend and Current Speech*, edited by Stefán Einarsson and Norman E. Eliason, 1–62. Copenhagen: Rosenkilde & Bagger, 1959.

———, ed. *Widsith.* 2nd ed. Copenhagen: Rosenkilde & Bagger, 1962.

———. "*Widsith* and the *Hervararsaga*." *PMLA* 40, no. 4 (1925): 769–813.

———. "Young Beowulf." *Journal of English and Germanic Philology* 36, no. 1 (1937): 21–23.

Martin Clarke, D. E. "The Office of Thyle in *Beowulf*." *Review of English Studies* 12, no. 45 (1936): 61–66.

Martínez Pizarro, Joaquín. "Kings in Adversity: A Note on Alfred and the Cakes." *Neophilologus* 80, no. 2 (1996): 319–26.

Meier, John, ed. *Deutsche Volkslied: Balladen I.* Berlin: Reclam, 1935.

Mellinkoff, Ruth. "Cain's Monstrous Progeny in *Beowulf*: Part I, Noachic Tradition." *Anglo-Saxon England* 8 (1979): 143–62.

———. "Cain's Monstrous Progeny in *Beowulf*: Part II, Post-Diluvian Survival." *Anglo-Saxon England* 9 (1980): 183–97.

Mitchell, Bruce. "Literary Lapses: Six Notes on *Beowulf* and Its Critics." *Review of English Studies* 43, no. 169 (1992): 1–17.

Momma, Haruko. "The Education of Beowulf and the Affair of the Leisure Class." In *Verbal Encounters: Anglo-Saxon and Old Norse Studies for Roberta Frank*, edited by Antonina Harbus and Russell Poole, 163–82. Toronto: University of Toronto Press, 2005.

Mommsen, Theodor, ed. *Iordanis Romana et Getica.* Berlin: Weidmann, 1882.

Morgan, Gerald. "The Treachery of Hrothulf." *English Studies* 53, no. 1 (1972): 23–39.

Morgan, Gwendolyn A. "Mothers, Monsters, Maturation: Female Evil in *Beowulf.*" *Journal of the Fantastic in the Arts* 4, no. 1/13 (1991): 54–68.

Müllenhoff, Karl. "Die innere Geschichte des *Beovulfs.*" *Zeitschrift für deutsches Altertum* 14 (1869): 193–244.

Müller-Oberhäuser, Gabriele. "*Cynna Gemyndig*: Sitte und Etikette in der altenglischen Literatur." *Frühmittelalterliche Studien* 30, no. 1 (1996): 19–59.

Murdoch, Brian. "Heroic Verse." In *German Literature of the Early Middle Ages*, edited by Brian Murdoch, 121–38. Woodbridge, UK: Camden House, 2004.

——, trans. *Kudrun*. London: Dent, 1987.

Naumann, Hans. *Germanischer Schicksalsglaube*. Jena: Eugen Diederichs, 1934.

Neckel, Gustav, ed. *Edda: Die Lieder des Codex Regius nebst verwandten Denkmälern*. Vol. 1, *Text*, revised by Hans Kuhn, 5th ed. Heidelberg: Winter, 1983.

Neidorf, Leonard. "The Archetype of *Beowulf.*" *English Studies* 99, no. 3 (2018): 229–42.

——. "Beowulf before *Beowulf*: Anglo-Saxon Anthroponymy and Heroic Legend." *Review of English Studies* 64, no. 266 (2013): 553–73.

——. "The Dating of *Widsið* and the Study of Germanic Antiquity." *Neophilologus* 97, no. 1 (2013): 165–83.

——. "The Gepids in *Beowulf.*" *ANQ* 34, no. 1 (2021): 3–6.

——. "Hildeburh's Mourning and *The Wife's Lament.*" *Studia Neophilologica* 89, no. 2 (2017): 197–204.

——. "On *Beowulf* and the *Nibelungenlied*: Counselors, Queens, and Characterization." *Neohelicon* 47, no. 2 (2020): 655–72.

——. *The Transmission of Beowulf: Language, Culture, and Scribal Behavior*. Ithaca, NY: Cornell University Press, 2017.

——. "Unferth's Ambiguity and the Trivialization of Germanic Legend." *Neophilologus* 101, no. 3 (2017): 439–54.

Neidorf, Leonard, Madison S. Krieger, Michelle Yakubek, Pramit Chaudhuri, and Joseph P. Dexter. "Large-Scale Quantitative Profiling of the Old English Verse Tradition." *Nature Human Behaviour* 3, no. 6 (2019): 560–67.

Nelson, Janet L. "Ninth-Century Knighthood: The Evidence of Nithard." In *Studies in Medieval History Presented to R. Allen Brown*, edited by Christopher Harper-Bill, Christopher J. Holdsworth, and Janet L. Nelson, 255–66. Woodbridge, UK: Boydell, 1989.

——. "Was Charlemagne's Court a Courtly Society?" In *Court Culture in the Early Middle Ages: The Proceedings of the First Alcuin Conference*, edited by Catherine Cubitt, 39–57. Turnhout, Belgium: Brepols, 2003.

Nelson-Campbell, Deborah, and Rouben Cholakian, ed. *The Legacy of Courtly Literature: From Medieval to Contemporary Culture*. Cham, Switzerland: Palgrave Macmillan, 2017.

Newton, Sam. *The Origins of Beowulf and the Pre-Viking Kingdom of East Anglia*. Cambridge: D. S. Brewer, 1993.

Niles, John D. *Beowulf: The Poem and Its Tradition*. Cambridge, MA: Harvard University Press, 1983.

——. "Myth and History." In *A Beowulf Handbook*, edited by Robert E. Bjork and John D. Niles, 213–32. Lincoln: University of Nebraska Press, 1997.

Nitzsche, Jane C. "The Structural Unity of *Beowulf*: The Problem of Grendel's Mother." *Texas Studies in Literature and Language* 22, no. 3 (1980): 287–303.

Norman, Frederick. *Three Essays on the Hildebrandslied*, edited by A. T. Hatto. London: University of London, 1973.

North, Richard. "Gold and the Heathen Polity in *Beowulf*." In *Gold in der Europäischen Heldensage*, edited by Wilhelm Heizmann, 72–114. Berlin: De Gruyter, 2019.

——. "Hrothulf's Childhood and Beowulf's: A Comparison." In *Childhood and Adolescence in Anglo-Saxon Literary Culture*, edited by Susan Irvine and Winfried Rudolf, 222–43. Toronto: University of Toronto Press, 2018.

——. *The Origins of Beowulf: From Vergil to Wiglaf*. Oxford: Oxford University Press, 2006.

——. *Pagan Words and Christian Meanings*. Amsterdam: Rodopi, 1991.

O'Donoghue, Heather. "What Has Baldr to Do with Lamech? The Lethal Shot of a Blind Man in Old Norse Myth and Jewish Exegetical Traditions." *Medium Ævum* 72, no. 1 (2003): 82–107.

Ogilvy, J. D. A. "Unferth: Foil to Beowulf?" *PMLA* 79, no. 4 (1964): 370–75.

Olsen, Alexandra Hennessey. "Gender Roles." In *A Beowulf Handbook*, edited by Robert E. Bjork and John D. Niles, 300–324. Lincoln: University of Nebraska Press, 1997.

Olson, Oscar Ludvig. "The Relation of the *Hrólfs Saga Kraka* and the *Bjarkarímur* to *Beowulf*." *Publications of the Society for the Advancement of Scandinavian Study* 3, no. 1 (1916): 1–104.

Orchard, Andy. *A Critical Companion to Beowulf*. Cambridge: D. S. Brewer, 2003.

——. *Pride and Prodigies: Studies in the Monsters of the Beowulf-Manuscript*. Cambridge: D. S. Brewer, 1995.

Osborn, Marijane. "The Alleged Murder of Hrethric in *Beowulf*." *Traditio* 74 (2019): 153–77.

——. "The Great Feud: Scriptural History and Strife in *Beowulf*." *PMLA* 93, no. 5 (1978): 973–81.

Owen-Crocker, Gale R. *The Four Funerals in Beowulf and the Structure of the Poem*. Manchester: Manchester University Press, 2000.

Panzer, Friedrich. *Studien zur germanischen Sagengeschichte*, I: *Beowulf*. Munich: C. H. Beck, 1910.

Paravicini, Werner. *Die ritterlich-höfische Kultur des Mittelalters*. Munich: Oldenbourg Verlag, 2011.

Parker, Roscoe E. "*Gyd, Leoð*, and *Sang* in Old English Poetry." *University of Tennessee Studies in the Humanities* 1 (1956): 59–63.

Parks, Ward. *Verbal Dueling in Heroic Narrative: The Homeric and Old English Traditions*. Princeton, NJ: Princeton University Press, 1990.

Pascual, Rafael J. "Material Monsters and Semantic Shifts." In *The Dating of Beowulf: A Reassessment*, edited by Leonard Neidorf, 202–18. Cambridge: D. S. Brewer, 2014.

——. "Old English Metrical History and the Composition of *Widsið*." *Neophilologus* 100, no. 2 (2016): 289–302.

Payne, F. Anne. "Three Aspects of Wyrd in *Beowulf*." In *Old English Studies in Honour of John C. Pope*, edited by Robert B. Burlin and Edward B. Irving Jr., 15–35. Toronto: University of Toronto Press, 1974.

Pedersen, David. "*Wyrd ðe Warnung* . . . or God: The Question of Absolute Sovereignty in *Solomon and Saturn II*." *Studies in Philology* 113, no. 4 (2016): 713–38.

Pepperdene, Margaret W. "Beowulf and the Coast-Guard." *English Studies* 47, nos. 1-6 (1966): 409–19.

Phillpotts, Bertha S. "Wyrd and Providence in Anglo-Saxon Thought." *Essays and Studies* 13 (1928): 7–27.

Pigg, Daniel F. "Cultural Markers in *Beowulf*: A Re-Evaluation of the Relationship between Beowulf and Christ." *Neophilologus* 74, no. 4 (1990): 601–7.

Pollington, Stephen. *The Mead Hall: The Feasting Tradition in Anglo-Saxon England*. Norfolk, UK: Anglo-Saxon Books, 2003.

Poole, Russell. "Some Southern Perspectives on Starcatherus." *Viking and Medieval Scandinavia* 2 (1996): 141–66.

Pope, John C. "*Beowulf* 505, 'Gehedde', and the Pretensions of Unferth." In *Modes of Interpretation in Old English Literature: Essays in Honour of Stanley B. Greenfield*, edited by Phyllis Rugg Brown, Georgia Ronan Crampton, and Fred C. Robinson, 173–87. Toronto: University of Toronto Press, 1986.

——. "Beowulf's Old Age." In *Philological Essays: Studies in Old and Middle English Language and Literature in Honour of Herbert Dean Meritt*, edited by James L. Rosier, 55–64. The Hague: Mouton, 1970.

Porck, Thijs. *Old Age in Early Medieval England: A Cultural History*. Woodbridge, UK: Boydell, 2019.

Propp, V. *Morphology of the Folktale*. Translated by Laurence Scott and revised by Louis A. Wagner. Austin: University of Texas Press, 1968.

Rauer, Christine. *Beowulf and the Dragon: Parallels and Analogues*. Cambridge: D. S. Brewer, 2000.

Reichert, Hermann. *Das Nibelungenlied: Text und Einführung*. Berlin: De Gruyter, 2017.

Renoir, Alain. *A Key to Old Poems: The Oral-Formulaic Approach to the Interpretation of West-Germanic Verse*. University Park: Pennsylvania State University Press, 1988.

Richards, M. P. "A Reexamination of *Beowulf* ll. 3180–3182." *English Language Notes* 10 (1973): 163–67.

Riisoy, Anne Irene. "Performing Oaths in Eddic Poetry: Viking Age Fact or Medieval Fiction?" *Journal of the North Atlantic* 8 (2015): 141–56.

Roberts, Jane. "The Old English Vocabulary of Nobility." In *Nobles and Nobility in Medieval Europe: Concepts, Origins, Transformations*, edited by Anne J. Duggan, 69–84. Woodbridge, UK: Boydell, 2000.

Robinson, Fred C. *Beowulf and the Appositive Style*. Knoxville: University of Tennessee Press, 1985.

——. "*Beowulf* in the Twentieth Century." *Proceedings of the British Academy* 94 (1997): 45–62.

——. "Elements of the Marvellous in the Characterization of *Beowulf*: A Reconsideration of the Textual Evidence." In *Old English Studies in Honour of John C. Pope*, edited by Robert B. Burlin and Edward B. Irving Jr., 119–37. Toronto: University of Toronto Press, 1974.

——. "History, Religion, Culture: The Background Necessary for Teaching *Beowulf*." In *Approaches to Teaching Masterpieces of World Literature*, edited by

Jess B. Bessinger Jr. and Robert F. Yeager, 107–22. New York: Modern Language Association of America, 1984.

——. "The Significance of Names in Old English Literature." *Anglia* 86 (1968): 14–58.

Rosenberg, Bruce A. "Folktale Morphology and the Structure of *Beowulf*: A Counterproposal." *Journal of the Folklore Institute* 11, no. 3 (1975): 199–209.

Ruggerini, Maria Elena. "L'eroe germanico contro avversari mostruosi: tra testo e iconografia." In *La funzione dell'eroe germanico: storicità, metafora, paradigma; Atti del Convegno internazionale di studio Roma, 6–8 maggio 1993*, edited by Teresa Pàroli, 201–57. Rome: Calamo, 1995.

Rundkvist, Martin. *Mead-Halls of the Eastern Geats: Elite Settlements and Political Geography AD 375–1000 in Östergötland, Sweden.* Stockholm: Kungl. Vitterhets Historie och Antikvitets Akademien, 2011.

Russom, Geoffrey. "At the Center of *Beowulf*." In *Myth in Early Northwest Europe*, edited by Stephen O. Glosecki, 225–40. Tempe, AZ: ACMRS, 2007.

——. "Historicity and Anachronism in *Beowulf*." In *Epic and History*, edited by David Konstan and Kurt A. Raaflaub, 243–61. Malden, MA: Wiley-Blackwell, 2010.

Ryan, J. S. "Othin in England: Evidence from the Poetry for a Cult of Woden in Anglo-Saxon England." *Folklore* 74, no. 3 (1963): 460–80.

Salkeld, Duncan. "Shakespeare and 'the I-word.'" *Style* 44, no. 3 (2010): 328–41.

Scaglione, Aldo. *Knights at Court: Courtliness, Chivalry, and Courtesy from Ottonian Germany to the Italian Renaissance.* Berkeley: University of California Press, 1991.

Schabram, Hans. *Superbia: Studien zum altenglischen Wortschatz.* Munich: Wilhelm Fink, 1965.

Schoenfeldt, Michael. "The Sonnets." In *The Cambridge Companion to Shakespeare's Poetry*, edited by Patrick Cheney, 125–43. Cambridge: Cambridge University Press, 2007.

Schücking, Levin Ludwig. *Beowulfs Rückkehr: Eine kritische Studie.* Halle: Max Niemeyer, 1905.

Schultz, James A. *Courtly Love, the Love of Courtliness, and the History of Sexuality.* Chicago: University of Chicago Press, 2006.Schwetman, John W. "Beowulf's Return: The Hero's Account of His Adventures among the Danes." *Medieval Perspectives* 13 (1998): 136–48.

Scowcroft, R. Mark. "The Irish Analogues to *Beowulf*." *Speculum* 74, no. 1 (1999): 22–64.

Searle, John R. "Literary Theory and Its Discontents." *New Literary History* 25, no. 3 (1994): 637–67.

——. "Reiterating the Differences: A Reply to Derrida." *Glyph* 1 (1977): 198–208.

Shilton, Howard. "The Nature of Beowulf's Dragon." *Bulletin of the John Rylands Library* 79, no. 3 (1997): 67–78.

Shippey, T. A. *Beowulf.* London: Edward Arnold, 1978.

——. "The Fairy-Tale Structure of *Beowulf*." *Notes and Queries* 16, no. 1 (1969): 2–11.

——. "*Hrólfs saga kraka* and the Legend of Lejre." In *Making History: Essays on the Fornaldarsögur*, edited by Martin Arnold and Alison Finlay, 17–32. London: Viking Society for Northern Research, 2010.

——. *Laughing Shall I Die: Lives and Deaths of the Great Vikings*. London: Reaktion Books, 2018.

——. "Maxims in Old English Narrative: Literary Art or Traditional Wisdom?" In *Oral Tradition, Literary Tradition: A Symposium*, edited by Hans Bekker-Nielsen, Peter Foote, Andreas Haarder, and Hans Frede Nielsen, 28–46. Odense: Odense University Press, 1977.

——. "Names in *Beowulf* and Anglo-Saxon England." In *The Dating of Beowulf: A Reassessment*, edited by Leonard Neidorf, 58–78. Cambridge: D. S. Brewer, 2014.

——. "Old English Poetry: The Prospects for Literary History." In *Proceedings of the Second International Conference of SELIM (Spanish Society for English Medieval Language and Literature)*, edited by A. León Sendra, 164–79. Córdoba: SELIM, 1993.

——. *Old English Verse*. London: Hutchison, 1972.

——. "Principles of Conversation in Beowulfian Speech." In *Techniques of Description: Spoken and Written Discourse: A Festschrift for Malcolm Coulthard*, edited by John M. Sinclair, Michael Hoey, and Gwyneth Fox, 109–26. London: Routledge, 1993.

——. "Structure and Unity." In *A Beowulf Handbook*, edited by Robert E. Bjork and John D. Niles, 149–74. Lincoln: University of Nebraska Press, 1997.

Shippey, T. A., and Andreas Haarder, eds. *Beowulf: The Critical Heritage*. London: Routledge, 1998.

Sievers, Eduard. "Béowulf und Saxo." *Berichte über die Verhandlungen der königlich sächsischen Gesellschaft der Wissenschaften zu Leipzig, philologisch-historische Klasse* 47 (1895): 175–92.

Sisam, Kenneth. "Anglo-Saxon Royal Genealogies." *Proceedings of the British Academy* 39 (1953): 287–348.

——. "Beowulf's Fight with the Dragon." *Review of English Studies* 9, no. 34 (1958): 129–40.

——. *The Structure of Beowulf*. Oxford: Clarendon Press, 1965.

Smithers, G. V. "Destiny and the Heroic Warrior in *Beowulf*." In *Philological Essays: Studies in Old and Middle English Literature in Honour of Herbert Dean Meritt*, edited by J. L. Rosier, 65–68. The Hague: Mouton, 1970.

——. *The Making of Beowulf: Inaugural Lecture of the Professor of English Language Delivered in the Appleby Theatre on 18 May, 1961*. Durham: University of Durham, 1961.

Smyser, H. M., and Francis P. Magoun Jr., ed. and trans. *Walther of Aquitaine: Materials for the Study of His Legend*. New London: Connecticut College, 1950.

Sorrell, Paul. "The Approach to the Dragon-Fight in *Beowulf*, Aldhelm, and the 'traditions folkloriques' of Jacques Le Goff." *Parergon* 12, no. 1 (1994): 57–87.

Sperber, Dan, and Deirdre Wilson. *Relevance: Communication and Cognition*. 2nd ed. Oxford: Blackwell, 1995.

Stanley, E. G. "Courtliness and Courtesy in *Beowulf* and Elsewhere in English Medieval Literature." In *Words and Works: Studies in Medieval English Language and Literature in Honour of Fred C. Robinson*, edited by Peter S. Baker and Nicholas Howe, 67–104. Toronto: University of Toronto Press, 1998.

——. "Did Beowulf Commit 'Feaxfeng' against Grendel's Mother?" *Notes and Queries* 23, no. 8 (1976): 339–40.

——. "*Hæþenra Hyht* in *Beowulf*." In *Studies in Old English Literature in Honor of Arthur G. Brodeur*, edited by Stanley B. Greenfield, 136–51. Eugene: University of Oregon Press, 1963.

——. *Imagining the Anglo-Saxon Past: The Search for Anglo-Saxon Paganism and Trial by Jury*. Cambridge: D. S. Brewer, 2000.

——. "'A Very Land-Fish, Languageless, a Monster': Grendel and the Like in Old English." In *Monsters and the Monstrous in Medieval Northwest Europe*, edited by K. E. Olsen and L. A. J. R. Houwen, 79–92. Leuven, Belgium: Peeters, 2001.

Stevick, Robert D. "Christian Elements and the Genesis of *Beowulf*." *Modern Philology* 61, no. 2 (1963): 79–89.

Stitt, J. Michael. *Beowulf and the Bear's Son: Epic, Saga, and Fairytale in Northern Germanic Tradition*. New York: Garland, 1992.

Sundquist, John D. "Relative Clause Variation and the Unity of *Beowulf*." *Journal of Germanic Linguistics* 14, no. 3 (2002): 243–69.

Swan, Mary. "Identity and Ideology in Ælfric's Prefaces." In *A Companion to Ælfric*, edited by Hugh Magennis and Mary Swan, 247–69. Leiden: Brill, 2009.

ten Brink, Bernhard. *Beowulf: Untersuchungen*. Strassburg: K. J. Trübner, 1888.

Timmer, B. J. "*Wyrd* in Anglo-Saxon Prose and Poetry." *Neophilologus* 26, nos. 1 and 3 (1941): 24–33, 213–28.

Tolkien, Christopher. "The Battle of the Goths and the Huns." *Saga-Book* 14 (1955–56): 141–63.

——, ed. and trans. *The Saga of King Heidrek the Wise*. London: Thomas Nelson & Sons, 1960.

Tolkien, J. R. R. *Beowulf: A Translation and Commentary; Together with Sellic Spell*. Edited by Christopher Tolkien. London: HarperCollins, 2014.

——. "*Beowulf*: The Monsters and the Critics." *Proceedings of the British Academy* 22 (1936): 245–95.

——. *Finn and Hengest: The Fragment and the Episode*. Edited by A. J. Bliss. London: George Allen & Unwin, 1982.

Trilling, Renée R. "Beyond Abjection: The Problem with Grendel's Mother Again." *Parergon* 24, no. 1 (2007): 1–20.

Tripp, Raymond P., Jr. "Did *Beowulf* Have an 'Inglorious Youth'?" *Studia Neophilologica* 61, no. 2 (1989): 129–43.

——. *More about the Fight with the Dragon: Beowulf, 2208b–3182: Commentary, Edition, and Translation*. Lanham, MD: University Press of America, 1983.

Turville-Petre, E. O. G. *Myth and Religion of the North: The Religion of Ancient Scandinavia*. New York: Holt, Rinehart & Winston, 1964.

Waugh, Robin. "Competitive Narrators in the Homecoming Scene of *Beowulf*." *Journal of Narrative Technique* 25, no. 2 (1995): 202–22.

Weber, Gerd Wolfgang. *Wyrd: Studien zum Schicksalsbegriff der altenglischen und altnordischen Literatur*. Bad Homburg: Gehlen, 1969.

Weil, Susanne. "Grace under Pressure: 'Hand Words,' 'Wyrd,' and Free Will in *Beowulf*." *Pacific Coast Philology* 24 (1989): 94–104.

Welch, Martin. "The Kingdom of the South Saxons: The Origins." In *The Origins of Anglo-Saxon Kingdoms*, edited by Steven Bassett, 75–83. London: Leicester University Press, 1989.

Wentersdorf, Karl P. "*Beowulf*: The Paganism of Hrothgar's Danes." *Studies in Philology* 78, no. 5 (1981): 91–119.

Whatley, E. Gordon. "Lost in Translation: Omission of Episodes in Some Old English Prose Saints' Legends." *Anglo-Saxon England* 26 (1997): 187–208.

Whitelock, Dorothy. *The Audience of Beowulf*. Oxford: Clarendon Press, 1951.

Wieland, Gernot R. "The Unferth Enigma: The *Þyle* between the Hero and the Poet." In *Fact and Fiction from the Middle Ages to Modern Times: Essays Presented to Hans Sauer on the Occasion of His 65th Birthday—Part II*, edited by Renate Bauer and Ulrike Krischke, 35–46. Frankfurt am Main: Peter Lang, 2011.

Wiersma, Stanley Marvin. "A Linguistic Analysis of Words Referring to Monsters in *Beowulf*." PhD diss., University of Wisconsin, 1961.

Williams, David. *Cain and Beowulf: A Study in Secular Allegory*. Toronto: University of Toronto Press, 1982.

Williams, Graham. "*Wine Min Unferð*: Courtly Speech and a Reconsideration of (Supposed) Sarcasm in *Beowulf*." *Journal of Historical Pragmatics* 18, no. 2 (2017): 175–94.

Wilson, Deirdre, and Dan Sperber. *Meaning and Relevance*. Cambridge: Cambridge University Press, 2012.

Wilson, R. M. *The Lost Literature of Medieval England*. London: Methuen, 1952.

Wright, Herbert G. "Good and Evil; Light and Darkness; Joy and Sorrow in *Beowulf*." *Review of English Studies* 8, no. 29 (1957): 1–11.

Zachrisson, R. E. "Grendel in *Beowulf* and in Local Names." In *A Grammatical Miscellany Offered to Otto Jespersen on His Seventieth Birthday*, edited by N. Bøgholm, Aage Brusendorff, and C. A. Bodelsen, 39–44. Copenhagen: Levin & Munksgaard, 1930.

INDEX